GOD

OTHER BOOKS BY J. CARL LANEY

The Divorce Myth

1 and 2 Samuel

Ezra–Nehemiah

Marching Orders

Zechariah

Your Guide to Church Discipline

Balancing Your Act without Losing It

Concise Bible Atlas

Divorce and Remarriage: Four Christian Views

New Bible Companion

Commentary on the Gospel of John

Everything I Know about Success I Learned from the Bible

Answers to Tough Questions from Every Book of the Bible

Messiah's Coming Temple

SWINDOLL
LEADERSHIP
LIBRARY

who he is

WHAT HE DOES

HOW to know Him better

GOD

J. CARL LANEY

CHARLES R. SWINDOLL, GENERAL EDITOR
ROY B. ZUCK, MANAGING EDITOR

WORD PUBLISHING
NASHVILLE
A Thomas Nelson Company

GOD
J. Carl Laney
Swindoll Leadership Library

Published in association with Dallas Theological Seminary (DTS):

General Editor: Charles Swindoll
Managing Editor: Roy B. Zuck

The theological opinions expressed by the author are not necessarily the official
position of Dallas Theological Seminary.

Library of Congress Cataloging-in-Publication Data

Laney, J. Carl.
God / by J. Carl Laney
p. cm.—(Swindoll leadership library)
Includes index.

ISBN 0-8499-1368-3

1. God.   I. Title.   II. Series

BT765.H56   1999   98-26780
234'.8—dc21   CIP

Printed in the United States of America
99 00 01 02 03 04 05 06 BVG 9 8 7 6 5 4 3 2 1

Contents

FOREWORD

THE WORLD HAS RECENTLY WITNESSED a shocking number of human tragedies. The culprits have been volcanic eruptions, earthquakes of seven points and higher on the Richter Scale, floods, tornadoes, hurricanes, and tidal waves in the South Pacific responsible for the complete destruction of several villages and entire people groups. We have also watched in horror as satellite television broadcasts the bloody fallout of ethnic cleansing, ruthless terrorist attacks, and massacres in our public schools, horrifyingly, at the hands of children who have not yet reached puberty! Atrocious. Unspeakable.

These events leave the thinking person asking why. If there is a God and if He is indeed a good God, then how can such evil prevail? Will it ever end? Is there any purpose in human suffering? These are deep questions that deserve thoughtful answers rooted in an understanding of the nature and person of God.

J. Carl Laney has written a helpful survey of what the Bible teaches on who God is and what He does. Laney provides a thorough theology of God, full of enormous practical value. Carefully researched and unswervingly committed to the truths of the Scriptures, the chapters of this book build on each other, working toward the author's noble desire to draw his readers into a closer relationship with their Creator and Friend. But in doing so, Laney does not leave the former questions unanswered. He writes with his rose-colored glasses still on the shelf, as he faithfully sets out to respond to some of life's most difficult questions. In fact, he devotes an entire chapter to this often-overlooked but critical need.

Laney asserts what I have believed and taught for over thirty years in pastoral ministry. If we are to serve God, we must know Him. If we are to know Him, we must understand Him. If we are to understand Him, we must study Him. This book gives us a marvelous course on learning and discovering the grand truths of an infinite God, who ultimately wants to be discovered by all.

Pastors, Sunday school teachers, missionaries, small-group leaders, and lay people alike will be grateful for this book. He has rendered an enormous service to all of us who humbly desire to "rightly divide the word of truth." Like carefully measured doses of salt before a long day's journey, Laney's chapters will cause you to drink deeply from the thirst-quenching water of God's Word and to know Him better. I invite you to embark on this exciting quest with the words of the writer of the ancient Book of Proverbs: "The fear of the LORD is the beginning of wisdom, and the knowledge of the Holy One is understanding" (Prov. 9:10).

—CHARLES R. SWINDOLL
General Editor

Acknowledgments

I have written a number of books during my career as a Bible teacher, but never has one affected my spiritual life as this project has. My goal in writing this book has been to get to know God better myself and then to share insights with my readers. Through this refreshing and engaging study I have come to know God better, and I pray that this will be your experience also as you read and study this book. My goal has been to touch the heart, as well as the mind, in exploring the greatness of our God.

I want to thank Dr. Charles R. Swindoll and Dr. Roy B. Zuck for trusting me with this project and for editing this volume. I have also appreciated the helpfulness of the editors and staff at Word Publishing. This book is dedicated to the glory of God. I pray that God's character and attributes will be magnified in the lives of those who read and study this book. "To him who sits on the throne, and to the Lamb, be blessing and honor and glory and dominion forever and ever" (Rev. 5:13).

Introduction

*But grow in the grace and knowledge of our
Lord and Savior Jesus Christ.*
—2 Peter 3:18

My wife, Nancy, and I recently celebrated our twenty-fifth wedding anniversary. I had just returned from leading a group of forty students on a trip to Israel, and there were piles of mail to clear from my desk at the office. But a twenty-fifth wedding anniversary comes only once in a lifetime. So I made reservations for Nancy and me to spend a night at a resort nestled in the forest overlooking the Columbia River Gorge.

We enjoyed a wonderful anniversary together, walking in the forest, looking at wildflowers, enjoying the view, and soaking in the outdoor spa. We talked about the years we have spent together and all that God has accomplished during that time. We also talked about the next decade of our lives together and what our family might be like when we celebrate our thirty-fifth anniversary.

One of the things I told Nancy is that I would like to get to know her better in the years ahead. "You already know everything about me," she replied. "How can you know me any better than you do?" It is true that spending twenty-five years together has provided ample opportunity for me to get to know Nancy. I know what kind of music she enjoys, what she likes to read, and what she would do with a day off. I know that she is an enthusiastic, friendly, cheerful person. I know that she loves chocolate, pansies, and little babies. One could say that I know my wife very well.

But I'm not satisfied with what I know of Nancy. I want to know her better. I want to know her deepest longings, her hidden fears, the driving force behind her vivacious personality. I want to know her more personally, more intimately, and more intelligently than I have in the past. It will take time and effort to do so, but I am willing to make that investment because I love her.

This book is about knowing God *better*. Most of you who are reading this book have already come to know God. By trusting Jesus Christ as your personal Savior, you have entered into the family of God. And through Jesus Christ you have come to know God the Father. You know that He is loving, compassionate, and just. You know that He seeks the lost and invites them to Himself. You know that God is holy, righteous, and sovereign. You know that He is the Good Shepherd, the Almighty, the King of kings.

You know God and He knows you in an intimate and personal way. But are you content with the level of your intimacy with God? Or would you like to know Him better? Do you think it is possible to know God better? If you could know God better, what would you like to know about Him? In what ways might your life be different if you knew God better? How do you think that knowing God better might affect you?

In my study of the Bible I have found that the great leaders among God's people have had a longing to know God more intimately. Take Moses, for example. He had met God at the burning bush. He had witnessed the power of God in the plagues on Egypt. He had spent forty days on Mount Sinai in the presence of God. According to Exodus 33:11, "The LORD would speak to Moses face to face, as a man speaks with his friend." Certainly Moses knew God! Yet he desired to know Him *better*. Israel's great leader said to God, "If I have found favor in Thy sight, let me know Thy ways, that I may know Thee" (33:13, NASB).

When Moses said he wanted to know God's "ways," he was referring to God's moral character and behavior. In Psalm 18:30 David declared, "As for God, His way is perfect." His character and behavior are above reproach. Moses knew God well, but from his experience on Mount Sinai, he wanted to know Him *better*.

Moses was not simply interested in knowing God *better* as an academic exercise. The Hebrew word translated *know* in Exodus 33:13 refers to an intimate, personal knowledge. This word is used to describe how Adam *knew* Eve (Gen. 4:1, NASB). It speaks of personal experience. I thought

I knew my wife when we got married, but what I knew was primarily factual. I knew about Nancy and her family, but I did not know her then as I know her now after twenty-five years of marriage. Moses wanted to know God more deeply, more personally, more intimately as a result of spending time with Him.

Moses isn't the only one in the Bible who wanted to know God better. I am reminded of the apostle Paul. On the road to Damascus, when Paul first met the Lord, he was blinded and confused. He cried out, "Who are you, Lord"? The answer he received was, "I am Jesus, whom you are persecuting" (Acts 9:5). That was quite an introduction! Saul was quick to repent and believe. Then he began growing in his knowledge of God.

Three missionary journeys later, Paul was in Rome waiting the outcome of his appeal to Caesar (25:11). While biding his time, Paul wrote several letters to the churches he had ministered to on his journeys. In his letter to the Philippians, Paul shared his heart with friends in Philippi. The most important thing in the world to Paul was knowing Christ. He wrote, "I consider everything a loss compared to the surpassing greatness of knowing Christ Jesus my Lord" (Phil. 3:8). Then he expressed his desire to know Him *better*: "I want to know Christ and the power of his resurrection and the fellowship of sharing in his sufferings, becoming like him in his death" (3:10). The Greek word translated "know" (*ginōskō*), like the Hebrew word used by Moses, refers to an intimate, personal, experiential knowledge. Paul was not looking for a list of divine attributes for further study. He desired to experience God more deeply, more powerfully, and more personally than he ever had before.

All committed Christians share the desire of Moses and Paul to have a deeper acquaintance with God. I desire this myself. But *how* can we know God better? Some people think that some remarkable experience with God will enable them to know Him better. Often, however, these people are susceptible to Satan's deception and false teaching. In their search for some unusual experience with God they get involved with spiritual activities that appear exciting and life-changing but that are contrary to sound biblical teaching.

The one sure way to know God better is through His own self-revelation recorded in the Bible. Through careful study of the Bible, under the illuminating ministry of the Holy Spirit, we can "grow in respect to salvation" (1 Pet. 2:2, NASB) and come to know God better. To get to know my wife better, I will need to listen to her. Studying God's Word enables us to listen to Him.

But study by itself is not enough. Knowing *about* God is not the same as knowing *God*. In addition to study, there must be a love for Christ and a willingness to obey His teachings. Jesus addressed this in the Upper Room on the night before His death. "Whoever has my commands and obeys them, he is the one who loves me. He who loves me will be loved by my Father, and I too will love him and show myself to him" (John 14:21).

Judas (not Judas Iscariot) was a bit confused by this remark. Like his Jewish countrymen Judas expected the Messiah to appear in glory before the whole world, judge the Gentiles, and restore the kingdom to the Jews. Jesus Himself had announced that "all the nations" would see "the Son of Man coming" (Matt. 24:30). Now Judas wondered why this previously announced plan had changed.

Jesus answered that concern by linking His self-disclosure with love and obedience. Jesus explained that love issuing in obedience is the necessary prerequisite for His disclosing Himself to His disciples (John 14:23). Those who are characterized by loving obedience will be loved by the Father and will enjoy fellowship with the Father and Son. Jesus promised, "And we will come to him and make our home with him."

Obedience, motivated by love, is the essential prerequisite for knowing God better. Jesus promised that the Father and the Son would make their united home in the lives of His obedient disciples. God is not interested in providing more theology to those who are unwilling to respond to the truth. But He takes pleasure in making Himself known to those who love and obey Him.

Why, then, should a Christian be concerned about knowing God better? What difference will it make whether we simply know God or know Him well?

Think of these many benefits: (a) Knowing God better will enhance our understanding of His plan and purposes. (b) Increased knowledge of God will provide a stimulus to obedience and Christian service. (c) It will enable us to communicate with God through prayer more effectively. (d)

Knowing God better will also help us deal with our doubts and understand how He guides believers according to His will. (e) Believers who are growing in their knowledge of God will be better prepared to cope with unexpected circumstances or tragedies in life. (f) Knowing God better will provide increased wisdom for making life's decisions in a manner consistent with God's character and will. It is definitely worthwhile getting to know God better!

1

Does God Exist?

And without faith it is impossible to please God, because anyone who comes to him must believe that he exists and that he rewards those who earnestly seek him.

—Hebrews 11:6

As a young teenager, I was struggling with the question, Does God exist or doesn't He? Since I wanted to know for sure, I devised a simple test. I took a coin out of my pocket and then prayed this short prayer, "God, if you exist, make this coin come up heads."

I flipped the coin and, amazingly, the coin landed heads up. That seemed like a pretty clear indication that God exists! But I still had some doubts. I wondered if it were just by *chance* that the coin came up heads. I decided to toss the coin again. This time it came up tails. Well, did God exist or didn't He? With some hesitation, I decided on one final test. I flipped the coin a third time. It came up heads! I decided not to try the test again. I wanted to quit my little experiment with the weight of evidence on the side of God's existence!

Does God exist? This is the most fundamental and important question in the universe. If God does not exist, then people populate this planet by chance. There is no design, no purpose, and no accountability for this life. But if He does exist, then a host of other questions arise. What is He like? How can we know Him? Why did He create this world? What does He expect of us? Should we worship Him? What will He do if we ignore or disobey Him?

This chapter presents arguments for the existence of God. If you don't believe in God, I hope this chapter will open your mind to the fact of His existence. My prayer is that you will respond to His self-revelation and join the ranks of those who believe. If you already believe in God, I trust that these arguments will both strengthen your faith and provide you with convincing evidence you might share with others.

GENERAL REVELATION

Theologians generally recognize two broad categories of God's revelation—general and special. General revelation is that disclosure which is available to all people throughout the world. General revelation is not sufficient to lead people to salvation in Christ, but it serves to make them accountable before God. Because of general revelation, no one can say, "I never knew there was a God." Paul wrote to the Romans, "What may be known about God is plain to them, because God has made it plain to them. For since the creation of the world God's invisible qualities—His eternal power and divine nature—have been clearly seen, being understood from what has been made, so that men are without excuse" (Rom. 1:19–20). It is evident from the second century B.C. that Judaism recognized the significance of general revelation. A Jewish writing called the Wisdom of Solomon, one of the books of the Apocrypha, says, "The greatness and beauty of created things gives us a corresponding idea of their Creator" (Wisd. of Sol. 13:5). General revelation proclaims the existence of God as the majestic, all-powerful, wise, and benevolent Creator.

The Witness of Creation

The first proof for the existence of God is the witness of His creation. In Psalm 19:1 David wrote, "The heavens declare the glory of God; the skies proclaim the work of his hands." David added, "Day after day they pour forth speech" and "night after night they display knowledge" (19:2). Although "day" and "night" have no literal words or voice (19:3), their silent but significant message has gone out "to the ends of the world" (19:4). Paul quoted Psalm 19:4 in Romans 10:18 to show that no one could ever say, "But we never heard about God." The message of nature is loud and clear: God exists!

Have you listened to the voice of nature testifying to God's existence? Our family's favorite recreational activity is camping. I love to settle in at a campsite near a mountain lake and spend a week enjoying the beauty of God's creation. I have many wonderful memories of swimming, hiking, canoeing, and catching crawdads with my kids. But a special time comes at night when the campfire has died out and we lie down on a big tarp and snuggle under blankets to look at the stars.

Lying on our backs in the darkness of a wilderness meadow, we are able to see a few thousand of the estimated one hundred billion stars in our Milky Way galaxy. I remind my children that it has taken four years for light traveling from Alpha Centauri, the nearest star beyond our solar system, to reach our eyes. Some of those stars have a temperature 160,000 times that of the sun. The immensity of our universe overwhelms us and calls out for us to believe in God.

Our human bodies also testify to the existence of the Creator. Think of the wonder of the human body. Consider, for example, the body's camera, the eye. The retina within the eye functions like film, receiving the inverted image and sending it through the optic nerve to the brain. The brain corrects the image so that things don't appear upside down. The muscles of the eye continually adjust the shape of the eye to enable us to see things close up or at a distance. Tear ducts continually bathe this organ with salty fluid, keeping it moist so it can respond to the muscles that move the eye. This complex organ is part of God's general revelation pointing to the existence of a marvelous Creator.

The apostle Paul appealed to God's revelation in nature when he was preaching with Barnabas at Lystra. Paul challenged his listeners to turn from their vain idols to "the living God, who made heaven and earth and sea and everything in them" (Acts 14:15). Although God permitted the nations to go their own ways, "yet he has not left himself without testimony: He has shown kindness by giving you rain from heaven and crops in their seasons; he provides you with plenty of food and fills your heart with joy" (14:17). Paul was saying that God's provision of rain and food points to the existence of a caring Creator. Everywhere in creation there is evidence of harmony, intelligence, and design. None of this has happened by accident. What we witness in creation is the work of a wise and loving God.

The Witness of Conscience

Another aspect of God's general revelation is His disclosure of Himself within our own human conscience. Paul pointed out in Romans 2:14–15 that God has placed a sense of moral law in every human being. "Indeed, when Gentiles, who do not have the law, do by nature things required by the law, they are a law for themselves, even though they do not have the law, since they show that the requirements of the law are written on their hearts, their consciences also bearing witness, and their thoughts now accusing, now even defending them." Elsewhere Paul wrote that even those unbelievers who hate God "know God's righteous decree" (1:32). The word for "righteous decree" (*dikaiōma*) refers to a concrete expression of righteousness—knowing what God has declared "right."

According to Paul the moral law of God is present in the hearts of all people, whether educated or not, whether civilized or not. The human conscience is the sense of moral obligation which confronts people with the recognition of the difference between right and wrong.

My wife, Nancy, is a substitute schoolteacher. She interacts with children on a regular basis on the subject of right and wrong. Most children, she reports, know that it is wrong to take someone else's things, to lie to the teacher, or to hit someone. This doesn't mean, of course, that all her students are perfect little angels. They often act contrary to their own consciences! But when confronted, they will usually admit that what they did was wrong.

This is not to suggest that everyone's conscience is exactly the same. The human conscience can become perverted or calloused as the result of continual abuse. A person usually feels badly about lying to a friend. But if the person does not repent of the sin, the next lie is not quite so difficult. Little by little, if a person continues to reject the voice of conscience, lying becomes easier. A continually violated conscience offers little help in distinguishing right from wrong.

Within the heart of each one of us, God has written a sense of moral obligation. We know it is wrong to steal, to kill, and to commit adultery. The commonly held values of the human conscience point to the existence of one God who has given each person a sense of right and wrong.

The Witness from Cause and Effect

My brother-in-law just finished having a new home built for his family. Soon after they moved in, they had an open house to welcome friends and neighbors into their home. It is a lovely home with lots of room and a view of Oregon's snow-capped Mount Hood. I have never met the builder, but I've seen the home. And I am quite confident that those two-by-fours, siding, and shingles didn't come together on their own. It took a lot of planning, gathering materials, and hard work to build that home. The existence of the home testifies to the activity of a builder. The writer of Hebrews drew some implications from this principle when he wrote, "For every house is built by someone, but God is the builder of everything" (Heb. 3:4).

A watch testifies to the existence of a watchmaker. A book testifies to the existence of an author and a publisher. A painting testifies to the existence of an artist. Nothing comes into existence by itself. For every effect, there must be a corresponding cause. Since the world exists, there must be a cause for its existence—a Creator who brought it into being.

Without the Creator, how could there be butterflies, rainbow trout, and songbirds? Not only did God create the world; He created it with beauty! The colors of wildflowers in the mountain meadows remind me that God takes pleasure in creating things of beauty. Snorkeling in a lagoon off the shores of Guam introduced me to the beauty of God's underwater world. Tropical fish have such brilliant, florescent colors. But God planned each one and created them with their varied shapes and colors. Their existence testifies to His existence as Creator. Theologians call this the cosmological argument for God's existence. *Cosmological* comes from the Greek word *kosmos*, meaning "world." Everything that exists in the world has a cause, and that cause is ultimately God.

The Witness of Human Intuition

All people have an inner witness that God exists. There is virtually no people group, ancient or modern, that does not acknowledge the existence of some supreme deity. The Canaanites worshiped Baal. The Babylonians revered Marduk. The Greeks recognized Zeus. The Romans believed in Jupiter.

In Athens Paul appealed to the Greeks' common knowledge of God's existence. As evidence, he quoted two Greek poets. "'For in him we live and move and have our being.' As some of your own poets have said, 'We are his offspring'" (Acts 17:28). Epimenides praised Zeus saying, "But You are not dead; You live and abide forever, for in You we live and move and have our being."[1] Paul took the liberty of substituting "Him" for "You," but the substance of the quote is unchanged. He also quoted Aratus of Cilicia, who wrote of Zeus, "It is with Zeus that everyone of us in every way has to do, for we are also his offspring."[2] Paul then pointed out that there were some things the Athenians, "God's offspring" (17:29), should recognize. Although these ancient poets were confused as to the identity of God, they had no doubt as to His existence.

The Witness of Logic

The ontological argument for the existence of God attempts to prove through logic that to conceive of the existence of God demands the objective reality of an infinite, supreme being. The term *ontological* comes from the Greek *ontos* (from the verb *eimi*) and means "being" or "existence." This is not an easy argument to understand and it fails to persuade most people. But it has appealed to some great minds, usually people who are inclined toward mathematics and philosophy, like René Descartes and Baruch Spinoza. Anselm (1033–1109), archbishop of Canterbury, was the first proponent of this view.

The ontological argument for the existence of God rests on the fact that all people have an awareness of the existence of an infinite, supreme being. It is argued that because an infinite, perfect God can be conceived of, He must have placed this idea within the minds of humans. If the most perfect being exists only in thought and not in reality, then it would not really be the most perfect being, for the one that existed in reality would be more perfect. Anselm concluded that no one who understands what God is can conceive that God does not exist. Therefore God exists!

Did you follow that logic? Here is another way the ontological argument has been expressed: "If man could conceive of a Perfect God who does not exists, then he could conceive of someone greater than God himself—which is impossible. Therefore, God must exist."[3]

The Witness of Personal Experience

Personal experience is highly subjective and may not serve as convincing proof for the existence of God. People have "experienced" some incredible things, including being kidnapped by aliens. Our minds are capable of fantastic imagination, much of which may be light-years from reality.

On the other hand, personal experience can serve to validate other more objective proofs for the existence of God. My belief in God is founded on many things, including the witness of creation, the influence of God's Spirit on my conscience, and the evidence of the Word of God. But fundamentally I have experienced God in my life, and therefore I believe. God has answered my prayers, quieted my fears, provided for my needs, delivered me from temptation, strengthened my resolve, granted me peace, and demonstrated His reality in my life again and again. No argument, no matter how logical or factual, could convince me that God is not real. My personal relationship with God on a daily basis refutes any and every suggestion that God does not exist.

SPECIAL REVELATION

General revelation is available to all people, enabling them to recognize God's existence. But general revelation is not sufficient to bring people into a saving relationship with God. For that purpose, special revelation is necessary. Special revelation is that divine disclosure that comes through Christ (John 1:18), the Bible (1 John 5:9–12), and God's mighty works (John 10:25).

The Witness of Christ

Jesus came to this earth, taking on humanity, in order to reveal God to mankind. John the apostle declared, "No one has ever seen God, but God the One and Only, who is at the Father's side, has made him known" (John 1:18). Sharing the deepest intimacy with God the Father, Jesus is in a position to reveal deep truths about God. The words "made known" literally mean "to show the way." Through His incarnation, Jesus showed lost sinners the way to God.

In Colossians 1:15 Paul declared that Jesus is "the image [*eikōn*] of the invisible God." Although God does not have a physical body, and therefore is not visible, His image can be seen in Christ. The word *eikōn* refers to the impression or mark on a coin. Just as a coin reflects exactly the die from which it is made, so Christ reflects God the Father exactly. God's invisible person is made visible through Christ. Jesus Himself declared, "I and the Father are one" (John 10:30). And later, "Anyone who has seen me has seen the Father" (14:9).

The Witness of Scripture

When I asked my teenage daughter why she believes God exists, her answer surprised me. She said, "Because the Bible says so." Although people have undoubtedly benefited from rational and philosophical arguments for the existence of God, the most powerful witness to His existence is found in Scripture (1 John 5:9–10).

It is rather significant, I believe, that the Bible doesn't begin by defending God's existence. Moses did not begin the Book of Genesis by presenting six reasons why people should believe in God. Rather, Moses assumed God's existence and proceeded to chronicle His work. God's special revelation, the Bible, is launched with the words, "In the beginning God created the heavens and the earth" (Gen. 1:1). This statement builds on the fact that everyone, based on general revelation, is aware of God's existence. Every verse in Scripture that begins with the words "God said," or "God did" testifies to the existence of God.

The Witness of God's Wondrous Works

Throughout Bible history God revealed Himself to His people through His wondrous works (Pss. 77:11–14; 81:10). This aspect of God's special revelation was especially important before the incarnation of Christ and the completion of the canon of Scripture. God revealed Himself to Moses through the miracle of the burning bush (Exod. 3:1–6). God revealed Himself to the Israelites through the plagues on Egypt (9:16; 10:2) and the miracles of the Exodus (15:1–3). He revealed Himself to those gathered on Mount Carmel with Elijah when he called down fire from heaven (1 Kings 18:36–39).

A classic study of the impact of God's mighty works is found in the account of David's slaying of the giant Goliath (1 Samuel 17). The Israelites and Philistines were gathered in the Elah Valley west of Bethlehem. Every day Goliath, the champion of Gath, intimidated the Israelites with his threatenings. One day David, taking food to his brothers, who were serving in Saul's army, heard Goliath's threats and asked, "Who is this uncircumcised Philistine that he should defy the armies of the living God?" (17:26). David then took his sling and stones into the battlefield to face the giant.

As the giant sneered and cursed his youthful foe, David announced that a theology lesson was at hand. "This day the Lord will hand you over to me, and I'll strike you down and cut off your head. Today I will give the carcasses of the Philistine army to the birds of the air and the beasts of the earth, and the whole world will know that there is a God in Israel" (17:46). God's existence was mightily proclaimed through David's victory over Goliath.

The revelation of God through His mighty acts is not limited to the Old Testament. The miracles of Jesus and the apostles are also a powerful testimony to God's existence (see, for example, John 10:25; 20:30–31; Acts 3:12–16). The most significant of the New Testament miracles that testify to God's existence is the resurrection of Jesus. The apostles held up the resurrection as the ultimate vindication of Jesus' claims and the truth of His message (1 Cor. 15:3–4).

The psalmist declared that God's wondrous works must be proclaimed to future generations so that they might know God and keep His commandments (Ps. 78:4–7). After the Exodus, Moses instructed Israelite fathers to teach their children that "the LORD sent miraculous signs and wonders—great and terrible—upon Egypt and Pharaoh and his whole household" (Deut. 6:22). God's wondrous works testify to His existence and call forth a response of faith and obedience. This is evident in the Ten Commandments which follow the words, "I am the LORD your God, who brought you out of Egypt, out of the land of slavery" (Exod. 20:2).

RESPONDING TO REVELATION

Believing in God's existence is the first step in knowing God. The writer of Hebrews made this clear when he wrote, "And without faith it is impossible to please God, because anyone who comes to him must believe that he exists, and that he rewards those who earnestly seek him" (Heb. 11:6). This indicates that as people respond by faith to God's general revelation, acknowledging His existence, He provides special revelation which enables them to know Christ and experience personal salvation. It is by faith that people understand spiritual truth and come to know God.

But how do people take that first step of believing in God's existence? How does an atheist come to believe in the existence of God? How do lost and sinful people come to treat the unseen spiritual world as reality? Paul pointed out to the Corinthians that "the world through its wisdom did not come to know him" (1 Cor. 1:21). If it took brilliant thinking to know God, most of us would never be able to know Him. But God works in mysterious ways.

Instead of demanding academic brilliance or worldly wisdom, God reached down from heaven and jump-started our spiritual lives through the gift of faith. Paul wrote, "For it is by grace you have been saved, through faith—and this not from yourselves, it is the gift of God" (Eph. 2:8). Faith is not something people conjure up as a result of intellectual or philosophical arguments for the existence of God. Faith is something God grants as a gift. He stirs the hearts of the unregenerate with faith, which enables them to respond to His general revelation. God then provides "seekers" with the special revelation necessary for their salvation in Christ.

For Further Study

Erickson, Millard J. *Does It Matter If God Exists?* Grand Rapids: Baker Books, 1996.

Kreeft, Peter, and Ronald K. Tacelli. *Handbook of Christian Apologetics.* Downers Grove, Ill.: InterVarsity Press, 1994.

Miethe, Terry L., and Antony G. N. Flew. *Does God Exist? A Believer and an Atheist Debate.* New York: HarperSan Francisco, 1991.

Miethe, Terry L., and Gary R. Habermas. *Why Believe? God Exists!* Joplin, Mo.: College Press Publishing Co., 1993.

Moreland, J. P., and Kai Nielsen. *Does God Exist? The Great Debate.* Nashville: Thomas Nelson Publishers, 1990.

Zacharias, Ravi. *Can Man Live without God?* Dallas: Word Books, 1994.

2
FAULTY VIEWS OF GOD

For although they knew God, they neither glorified him as God nor gave thanks to him, but their thinking became futile and their foolish hearts were darkened.

—Romans 1:21

THE GODDESS IS ALIVE, and there's magic in the air." So reads a bumper sticker that has appeared on cars recently. Pre-Christian, earth-centered goddess cults are blossoming throughout America. It is reported that religious groups of this variety can be found at leading educational institutions in America, including Harvard Divinity School, the University of Pennsylvania, and the University of Santa Cruz.[1] The goddess cult is another dimension of New Age spirituality, which is making its inroads into the religious life and thought of Americans. Significantly, this is nothing new. In ancient Babylon, she was known as Ishtar; in Greece, Artemis; and in Rome, Diana.

The goddess cult is nature oriented and female dominated. The "seekers" in this religious movement are heirs of the feminist revolution who have thrown off "male-dominated" Christianity. Diana Hayes, professor of theology at Georgetown University, regards this with favor. "Within Christianity, theology and spirituality have been male-oriented, male-dominated, because they are the ones articulating it. . . . Women do not think or act the way men do. Therefore our spirituality will not be the same as men's."[2]

On a spring day in May, a few years ago, about two hundred people clustered in a rolling meadow near Goldendale, Washington, to help create a four-hundred-foot-long, two-hundred-foot-wide dancing "earth goddess." Dried sage leaves were burned in abalone shells to create a perfumed smoke to enable participants to "cleanse their energy" in preparation for the event. Mirrors strategically aimed toward the sun created a blaze of light around the goddess. "I was lying back on the earth and feeling the hum," responded one volunteer, "just marveling at the power."

This is one of many false ideas people have about God, views far afield from how the Bible describes God.

ATHEISM

The word *atheist* describes one who believes there is no God. It is derived from the Greek word *theos* and the negative prefix *a* (Greek alpha). The word appears once in the New Testament (Eph. 2:12), where it refers to unsaved Gentiles—those who are "without God." The ancient Greeks used the term to refer to people who did not believe in any god, including the Greek concept of God. Both Jews and Christians who denied the existence of the Greek gods were regarded as "atheists."

Not all atheists are the same. The *dogmatic* atheist repudiates God and absolutely denies His existence. David wrote of this person in Psalm 14:1: "The fool says in his heart, 'There is no God.'" This viewpoint is very evident in modern science, which operates on the premise that there is no God and then seeks to explain life apart from God's involvement. To them, the material world, not the spiritual world, is the ultimate reality. The evolutionary hypothesis affirms that human beings are chance products of lifeless chemicals in the sea, acted on by sunlight. Eventually these chemicals came to life and have since developed by natural selection and favorable mutations into all living plants and animals, including humans. God is not included in this view because those advocating it do not believe He exists.

The *practical* atheist does not actually deny the existence of God, but he lives as if there is no God. This may be the person David had in mind when he wrote of the wicked, "There is no fear of God before his eyes" (36:1). If there is no God, then there is no need to honor His commands in Scripture. If there is no God, then there is no morality or accountability. The practical atheist assumes that the good things in life are available through human achievement rather than as a result of God's benevolence and grace.

AGNOSTICISM

The term *agnostic* stems from the Greek word *gnōsis*, meaning "knowledge" and the *a* prefix. An agnostic, then, is one who is literally "without knowledge." While the theists affirm God's existence, the atheists deny it, and agnostics profess ignorance about it. Thomas Huxley first used this term in 1869 at a meeting of what later became the Metaphysical Society. As a religious skeptic, the agnostics reject the idea that people can have knowledge of spiritual things.

Like the term *atheist*, the word *agnostic* can be used in different ways. In its most positive context this term may describe a person who does not know anything about God. He or she may be open to spiritual things but have no personal opinion on matters relating to God, the Bible, or immortality. The term can also be used to describe a person with a secular and skeptical attitude. So agnostics think belief in God is impractical and irrelevant. An *agnostic* may also refer to someone who believes we *cannot* know whether God exists. Such a person is usually quite antireligious and very much anti-Christian.

Why are some people agnostics? First, being an agnostic is more socially acceptable than being an atheist. It sounds less abrasive to say "I don't know" than "I don't believe." Second, unlike atheists, agnostics avoid having to provide the burden of proof. One does not need proofs when merely pleading ignorance.[3]

While agnosticism enjoys a certain measure of respect in the intellectual community, it is dangerous to avoid making decisions on matters that count for eternity. If God exists, then it is blasphemy to say His existence is unprovable! Such blasphemy may have eternal consequences. Blaise Pascal in his *Pensées* ("Thoughts") proposed that we "wager" on the possibility of God's existence.[4] If our gamble for God is right, we will win everything—happiness and eternal life. But nothing is lost if we turn out to be wrong. In other words it is better to live as if God exists and discover that He doesn't, than to live as if He doesn't exist and discover that He does!

POLYTHEISM

Polytheism comes from the Greek words *poly*, "many," and *theos*, "God." A *polytheist* believes in many gods. This view was prevalent in the biblical period. Among their many deities the Egyptians worshiped Re, the sun-disk god; Osiris, the ruler of the netherworld; Seth, the god of nature; and Hathor, queen of all gods and goddesses. The Canaanites gave their allegiance to the fertility god, Baal, and his sister-consort, Anath. The Greeks honored Zeus as king of the gods, but they also revered eleven others, including Ares, god of war; Aphrodite, goddess of love and beauty; and Apollo, god of music and light.

Polytheism is not limited to the ancient world. It exists today in Hinduism, in which worshipers seek a particular benefit from any of a multitude of deities. Yet each god in the crowded Hindu pantheon is considered but one aspect of Brahman, the "Supreme Being." Polytheism is also found in Buddhism, Confucianism, Taoism, and Shintoism in the East, and in the tribal religions of Africa. While polytheism may not seem to be a problem in America, D. B. Fletcher has pointed out that "as the West becomes infiltrated with Eastern religions and their derivative movements, Western Christians will need directly to confront polytheism."[5]

God addressed the issue of polytheism in the very first of His Ten Commandments. This first commandment focuses on the exclusive nature of true worship: God said, "You shall have no other gods before me" (Exod. 20:3). The Israelites were to give their devotion and allegiance exclusively to the Lord, to obligate themselves to none but the true God.

The first commandment takes aim at both atheism and polytheism. To atheists, the commandment says, "God exists. Recognize Him!" To polytheists, the commandment says, "The Lord is the only true God. He also refuses to share His worship with any other so-called gods." The gods and goddesses of polytheistic religions are nothing but the result of depraved imaginations. After witnessing the miracle of Israel's deliverance through the Red Sea and the destruction of the Egyptians, Moses sang,

"Who among the gods is like you, O LORD?" (15:11). The question is answered by David: "Among the gods, there is no one like you, O Lord; no deeds can compare with yours" (Ps. 86:8). In a prayer of thanksgiving, David declared the exclusive nature of true worship, "How great you are, O Sovereign LORD! There is none like you, and there is no God but you" (2 Sam. 7:22).

PANTHEISM

The word *pantheism* stems from the Greek words *pan*, "all," and *theos*, "God." According to pantheism, God is everything, and everything is God. This word was first used by John Toland in 1705 to refer to philosophical and religious systems that tend to identify God with the physical world or nature. Pantheism was common in ancient religions that identified the material universe with deity.

According to the Greek poet Hesiod, of the eighth century B.C., from the dark void of Chaos emerged *Gaea*, "Mother Earth," benevolent, broad-breasted, with nourishing soil. This goddess, remembered in the word "geography," gave birth to the starlit sky, Uranus, "Father Heaven." As he covered Gaea with rain, there sprouted flowers, grass, and trees. Rivers flowed and lakes and seas were filled. The concept of "Mother Earth" is again prevalent today among environmentalists who have come under the influence of New Age theology or Eastern religions.

Pantheism comes in a number of forms. Materialistic pantheism affirms the eternality of matter and says that matter is the cause of all life. Hylozoistic pantheism holds that the divine is the basic element of the world, but that the universe remains a plurality of separate elements. Acosmic pantheism proposes that God is absolute and makes up the totality of reality. The world we live in and experience only *appears* to be real. Scientific pantheism fuses religion and science, providing an ethical basis for environmental concerns. In this view people should reverence and protect forests, air, oceans, and other aspects of the earth's environment because the universe and nature are divine. New Age pantheism holds that all things are divine, including people. New Age guru Shirley MacLaine says that her spirit guide, supposedly her "Higher Self," told her, "Each soul is its own God. You must never worship anyone or anything other than self. For *you* are God. To love self is to love God."[6] New Age pantheism deifies self and recognizes no higher moral absolute.

Pantheism is clearly incompatible with the teaching of Scripture that God is distinct from His creation. God has existed from eternity, but the universe was created in time. God is eternal, but creation is finite.

The major problem with pantheism is that it overemphasizes God's immanence (presence) and denies His transcendence (supremacy and separateness). The Bible teaches that God is active in His creation, but He is not to be identified with it. God is holy, lofty, and separate from all that is fallen and sinful. But He ministers to humans in need. Jesus illustrates this perfect balance. In Christ, God manifested His immanence by taking on a human nature. But God's transcendence was maintained in the fact that Christ is the sinless God-Man. While pantheists worship God's creation as divine, Christians believe that we should worship only God, yet we should be good stewards of His creation and those resources entrusted to us.

PANENTHEISM

Panentheism is a term used by Karl C. F. Krause (1781–1832) to describe his view of God. The term literally means "all [is] in God." While panentheism differs from the similar sounding "pantheism," both reflect attempts to explain the relationship of God and the world.

According to panentheism, God is in everything, and everything is God. Among the problems with panentheism is the existence of evil in the world. If God is in everything, how do we account for evil? Is God equally in a lovely tree and an X-rated videotape? Obviously, there is a conflict here.

Like pantheism, panentheism recognizes the presence of God everywhere in the world. But while pantheism says that "God *is* the tree," panentheism says, "the tree is *in* God." The difference may seem slight, but it is significant. Pantheism affirms that God and the world are one. All is God—the rocks, trees, birds, and fish. Panentheism affirms that all is "in" God, somewhat as fish are in the ocean.

Think of two eggs—one hard-boiled and one scrambled. Pantheism may be likened to the scrambled egg in which the egg and yoke are blended into one. God and the world are one. Panentheism, on the other hand, may be likened to the hard-boiled egg, in which the yellow yoke is separate. Panentheism says there is a divine egg (God) and within it is the yoke (the world).

Panentheism is an attempt to combine the strengths of classical theism with pantheism. According to panentheism, God exists, and the world—which is in God—shares in divinity. The major problem with this view is that the world changes, and as it changes, so must God change. As the world grows, God grows in knowledge and understanding of His creation. Panentheism leaves us with a God who changes and who has limited knowledge. This view of God contradicts clear biblical statements concerning God's immutability (Mal. 3:6; James 1:17) and omniscience (Ps. 139:3–4; John 21:17; 1 John 3:20).

DEISM

The word *deism* is derived from the Latin term *deus*, "God." Deism is a religious view expressed among a group of English writers beginning with Lord Herbert of Cherbury in the first half of the seventeenth century. Deists believe that God created the world and then left it subject to natural law. For deists, God is beyond the world and not active in it in a supernatural way. According to deistic thinking, God wound up the clock of the world at creation, and now things proceed according to the principles of natural law without His intervention or involvement.

Deists come to their views through the testimony of human reason rather than through divine revelation. For this reason they reject the authority of Scripture. In denying the supernatural, they reject the possibility of miracles. They adhere to a Unitarian concept of God, denying the doctrines of the Trinity, the deity of Christ, and the redemption provided at the Cross.

Deism is the opposite of pantheism. Pantheism stresses God's immanence (involvement in our world), but deism stresses God's transcendence (exaltation above the universe). The Bible teaches both God's immanence and His transcendence. God is highly exalted over His creation (Exod. 15:1;

Ps. 99:2), but He graciously comes down to assist and deliver the needy and afflicted (Exod. 3:8; Phil. 2:5–8).

A major problem with deism is its rejection of the supernatural and God's continued involvement in His creation. According to the Bible the God who created the earth sustains it by His power (Col. 1:16–17). The psalmist Asaph praised "the God who performs miracles" (Ps. 77:14). His miraculous interventions in the affairs of humankind are recorded throughout the Old and New Testaments. Deists base their views on human reason, an approach to truth that Paul said is flawed and inadequate (1 Cor. 1:21). The Christian faith rests not on "men's wisdom, but on God's power" (2:5).

Deism spread from England to Germany, France, and America. By the end of the eighteenth century, deism had become a dominant religious attitude among intellectual and upper-class Americans. Among great Americans who considered themselves deists were Benjamin Franklin, George Washington, and Thomas Jefferson. M. H. Macdonald has pointed out that although deism is not widely held today, its significance historically has been great, and it still exerts influence on religious thought in our time.[7]

IDOLATRY

Idolatry misrepresents God in that it depicts Him as having a material body which can be represented by a physical image. In Bible times idolatry was very prevalent in the ancient Near East. The Babylonians paraded their image of Marduk through the streets of their city during their annual enthronement festival in His honor. Idols of the Egyptian deities Osiris, Isis, and Seth have been found in the tombs of the pharaohs. The Canaanite gods and goddesses were represented by idols. The presence of these idols in the land of Canaan presented a serious temptation for the Israelites. I'll never forget viewing a glass-enclosed case in the Rockefeller Museum in Jerusalem and realizing that the idols before me were in Israelite cities centuries ago! But idolatry is not simply an error of the past. You can see idolatry practiced today as worshipers present a basket of fruit before an image of Buddha, or flower petals to a Hindu idol, or burn incense before pictures of their ancestors.

Idolatry gives devotees a sense of physical closeness to the deity they worship. It also enables them to have some control over the deity. An idol can be moved around, put away in a closet, and brought out at a time of emergency. Gods and goddesses were often depicted as animals, objects people were familiar with. For example, Baal, the fertility god of the Canaanites, was represented by a strong, virile bull. In idolatry worshipers visualize their gods and fashion their deities after their own imaginations.

Worshiping idols has three serious problems. First, God has no physical body. When speaking with the Samaritan woman, Jesus said, "God is spirit" (John 4:24). Since God's essential nature is spirit, He does not have a physical body. Therefore it is wrong to depict God as if He had material substance.

Second, God is invisible. Paul wrote that Jesus is "the image of the invisible God" (Col. 1:15). In a great statement of praise to God, Paul wrote that He is "eternal, immortal, invisible" (1 Tim. 1:17). And he described God as One "whom no one has seen or can see" (6:16).

Third, to attempt to represent God by human or animal form would be to contain and limit Him. God is infinite and omnipresent. After building a magnificent temple to the Lord, Solomon said to God, "The highest heaven cannot contain you. How much less this temple which I have built!" (1 Kings 8:27).

The first two commandments in the Decalogue (Exod. 20:3–17) are directed toward the danger of idolatry. As already noted, the first commandment focuses on the exclusive nature of true worship. "You shall have no other gods before me" (20:3). God's people are to obligate themselves to no deity other than the one true God. Obedience to this command would enable the Israelites to avoid the idolatrous forms of worship practiced by neighboring nations.

The second commandment addresses the issue of how God is represented in worship. "You shall not make for yourself an idol in the form of anything in heaven above or on the earth beneath or in the waters below. You shall not bow down to them or worship them" (20:4–5). This command forbids worshiping God in the form of an idol or image. The reason for prohibiting idol worship is found in the words of verse 5, "For I, the

LORD your God, am a jealous God." The Lord is "jealous" in the sense that He is unwilling to share His worship with a false god or an idol. He alone is to be worshiped. The consequences of idolatry are recorded in 20:5–6. While God honors loyalty and faithfulness, the offspring of idolaters will inherit the consequences of their parents' sinful actions.[8]

Although there are many "so-called gods" (1 Cor. 8:5), there is just "one God, the Father, from whom all things came" (8:6). Idols are the vain imaginations of fallen humanity in their attempt to conceptualize God and are a sign of human folly (Isa. 40:18–20; Rom. 1:22–23). As Christians, we are not tempted to worship idols, but we may be in danger of limiting Him by our thoughts and actions. We may also be in danger of allowing people and things to take God's place. Anything that takes God's place in a person's life is idolatry. John's warning is still appropriate today: "Dear children, keep yourselves from idols" (1 John 5:21).

POST EVANGELICALISM

Theologian Millard Erickson has commented that the doctrine of God has come under more intense scrutiny in recent years than virtually any other doctrine.[9] Many Christian scholars are suggesting that the traditional or "classical" view of God is no longer adequate. This is particularly troubling when we discover that some of these Christians have or have had a close association with evangelicalism. Erickson's book, *The Evangelical Left*, discusses these divergences from the traditional (orthodox) view of God. A brief summary is offered here.

The so-called "process" view of God seems to have been strongly influenced by a revised view of reality, as presented by twentieth-century physics. Newtonian physics had understood reality as composed of substances and fixed entities possessing definite, permanent qualities. But twentieth-century Einsteinian physics says reality is more dynamic and relative. Applying this underlying philosophy of dynamic change, the process view of God suggests that God is ever changing. While the method of process theology is more philosophically than biblically based, many of its proponents have sought to relate biblical themes to process concepts.

In contrast with the traditional view of God as perfect, complete, and unchanging, process theology views Him as "contingent, dependent, temporal, relative, and constantly changing."[10] And if God is constantly changing, then so are His expectations for people. According to process theologians, God is not a divine Lawgiver and Judge who expects people to conform to His rules. Instead, He is more interested in fostering moral attitudes which may be applied differently in different situations.[11] The view that God is constantly changing and adjusting to decisions and actions of people is contradicted by many clear statements of Scripture. In spite of the fact that Israel had broken God's covenant and deserved His wrath, God said, "I the LORD do not change. So you, O descendants of Jacob, are not destroyed" (Mal. 3:6). James wrote that with God "does not change like shifting shadows" (James 1:17).

Most contemporary evangelical theologians have sought to distance themselves from process theology. Clark Pinnock, however, holds to a so-called "open" view of God and identifies his position somewhere between classical theism and process theology.[12] The central thesis of his view of God is that God's experience of the world is open, rather than closed. Pinnock says God does not know all of time—past, present, and future. He becomes aware of developments in the world and responds to them, changing His mind and His course of actions as necessary. According to Pinnock, "God experiences temporal passage, learns new facts when they occur and changes plans in response to what humans do."[13] Pinnock believes that God is "voluntarily self-limited," "delighting in a universe which he does not totally control."[14] He has argued that "God does not foreknow every future choice or the outcome of every human decision."[15] According to Pinnock, "The popular belief in God's total omniscience is not so much a biblical idea as an old tradition."[16]

Most readers will immediately recognize that the views of Pinnock and those who hold to an "open" view of God are inconsistent with the classic understanding of God as set forth in the Scriptures. This will be evident as we examine the attributes of God in chapter 7, "The Greatness of God." The major problems with Pinnock's view are that it overemphasizes (a) God's immanence at the expense of His transcendence, (b) His interaction with His creation at the expense of His sovereign control over it, and (c) human freedom at the expense of God's power and knowledge.[17] While

Pinnock criticizes process theology, Erickson has pointed out that the open view of God has a number of points of similarity to it.[18]

In evaluating such divergences from the traditional orthodox view of God, it is helpful to keep in mind the warning given by the apostle John, "Dear friends, do not believe every spirit, but test the spirits to see whether they are from God, because many false prophets have gone out into the world" (1 John 4:1).

FATALLY FLAWED DIRECTIONS

A woman with a baby was traveling west on a train through a heavy snowstorm. The steam engine was pulling hard to move through the snow that had drifted across the tracks. It was late at night and she did not want to miss her stop at the station where her husband was to meet her. So she asked the brakeman to be sure to let her know as they approached her stop.

The train slowed to a stop, and a fellow traveler said, "Here is your station." She quickly gathered her things and hopped off the train into the blinding storm. Moments later, the train moved on.

Forty-five minutes later the brakeman came to the place where the woman had been seated. "Where's the woman with the baby?" he asked.

"She got off at the last stop," a traveler replied.

Alarmed, the brakeman exclaimed, "We stopped only because of something blocking the tracks. We were not at a station!"

They called for volunteers to go back and search for the woman and child. When they found her hours later, not far from where they had stopped, she was covered with ice and snow. Her little child was found protected under her coat. The woman had followed directions, but the directions were fatally flawed. The wrong directions resulted in her death.

Many sincere people are following wrong directions in seeking to know God. A "Peanuts" cartoon depicted Charlie Brown returning from a disastrous baseball game. The caption read, "One-hundred and fifteen to nothing! How could we lose when we were so sincere." Well, sincerity is not enough to win a game of baseball. Nor is it sufficient to win in life. The Bible teaches that there is only one way to God, and that is through

Jesus Christ. Jesus said, "I am the way and the truth and the life; no one comes to the Father, except through me" (John 14:6).

For Further Study

Erickson, Millard J. *The Evangelical Left*. Grand Rapids: Baker Book House, 1997.

Geisler, Norman L. *Christian Apologetics*. Grand Rapids: Baker Book House, 1979.

3

THE NAME OF GOD

I am the LORD [Yahweh]; that is my name!
—Isaiah 42:8

W HAT IS THE FIRST QUESTION you usually ask a person whom
you meet for the first time? If you are like most people, you want to know
that person's name.

A person's name sets him or her apart from the crowd as a distinct
individual. Most people are rather fond of their names and appreciate
being called by their names. In his classic book, *How to Win Friends and
Influence People,* Dale Carnegie wrote that a person's name is "the sweetest and most important sound in any language."[1] If someone's name is
the sweetest sound, we might guess that the worst sound is the mispro-
nunciation of that person's name! I can always identify someone who is
soliciting by phone. They invariably mispronounce my last name! It is
even worse to have your name mispronounced by someone whom you
consider a friend. Perhaps you have suffered the embarrassment of knowing someone for some time only to discover that you have been
mispronouncing his or her name.

Sometimes we forget someone's name. A student I had not seen in
ten years came to my office door. I recognized him immediately, but his
name was locked in an inaccessible "file" somewhere in the recesses of my
mind. I finally had to stop him and say, "I know who you are, but for
some reason your name escapes me. Could you remind me?"

Names are important not only to people; they are also important to God. In the Bible, names are not simply an identity tag. They usually say something about the character of the person. They are "a revelation of one's true being."[2] People in the Bible are sometimes named or renamed on the basis of a particular character trait. The name of Jesus, for example, means "Yahweh saves." When Joseph was told that this was to be the name of Mary's son (Matt. 1:21), the angel explained, "because he will save his people from their sins." The importance of a person's name is also evidenced by the Good Shepherd who "calls his own sheep by name" (John 10:3).

A MEETING AT THE BURNING BUSH (EXOD. 3:4–12)

The miracle of the burning bush took place near Mount Horeb (Exod. 3:1), another name for Mount Sinai (19:1–2; Deut. 4:10). Moses was there in the Sinai desert tending the flocks of his father-in-law, Jethro, when he observed an amazing thing. Moses saw a bush blazing with fire, and yet the bush was not consumed! As he turned to examine this unusual phenomenon more closely, he heard his name spoken, "Moses, Moses." Then he heard a voice command him, "Do not come any closer. . . . Take off your sandals, for the place where you are standing is holy ground" (Exod. 3:5).

The Speaker identified Himself in relationship to the patriarchs. "I am the God of your father, the God of Abraham, the God of Isaac and the God of Jacob" (3:6). The reference to Abraham, Isaac, and Jacob would have brought to Moses' mind the promise made to these patriarchs—the promise of a land, a nation, and a blessing (Gen. 12:1–3; 26:2–4; 28:13–15). Moses was being confronted by the God who had committed Himself unconditionally to the descendants of Abraham, Isaac, and Jacob.

The sufferings of Abraham's descendants had not gone unnoticed by the God of the patriarchs. God had seen their afflictions and He promised to "rescue them from the hand of the Egyptians and to bring them up out of that land into a good and spacious land, a land flowing with milk and honey" (Exod. 3:8). When God said, "I have come down" (3:8),[3] He was identifying Himself as a personal God who acts in history on behalf of His own.

But while God promised to intervene on behalf of His people, He was not going to act alone. He needed a helper, someone to speak as His representative. God did not give Moses a chance to volunteer or decline. He simply declared, "I am sending you to Pharaoh to bring my people the Israelites out of Egypt" (3:10).

Moses may have lacked self-confidence. So while he liked God's plan, he wasn't so sure he ought to be the one to execute it. "Who am I," he asked, "that I should go to Pharaoh and bring the Israelites out of Egypt?" (3:11). Moses questioned his own ability to accomplish the task. To comfort and assure Moses, God promised him His personal presence, "I will be with you" (3:12). God would encourage and support him in his assigned task. How encouraging to know that, as with Moses, God will never give us a ministry that He will not also empower us to fulfill!

A QUESTION ABOUT GOD'S NAME (EXOD. 3:13–15)

Moses had a problem. He was certain the people would ask, "Who sent you? If you have been sent by God, as you say, tell us His name." Many gods were worshiped in Egypt, and they all had names. Moses wanted to be able to validate his call by naming the One in whom his authority rested. And so Moses asked God what he should tell them (Exod. 3:13).

God graciously answered Moses' request. He first revealed the meaning of His name (3:14) and then the name itself (3:15). "God said to Moses, 'I AM WHO I AM.' This is what you are to say to the Israelites: 'I AM has sent me to you'" (3:14). Most Bible versions rightly put in capital letters the words "I AM," to show that something special is being asserted about God, namely, His absolute being. The words "I AM," translate the first-person form of the verb *hāyâ*, "to be." The meaning is that God is the self-existent One. As Ronald Allen states, "He exists dependent upon nothing or no one excepting his own will."[4]

The words "I AM" refer not to God's static being but to His active existence. He is actively involved with humanity, responding to their needs and revealing His person. He exists not only for His own sake, but also for the sake of His people. God's active involvement is made evident by the very context of the passage. "So I have come down to rescue them from the hand of the Egyptians and to bring them up out of that land" (3:8). When God said "I AM," He was referring to His active, life-giving existence. As Walther Eichrodt commented, the words "I AM" mean that God is "really and truly present, ready to help and to act."[5]

The words "I AM" express the meaning of God's name but they are not the name itself. God's name is revealed in verse 15. God spoke further to Moses, instructing him to say to the people of Israel, "The LORD, the God of your fathers—the God of Abraham, the God of Isaac and the God of Jacob—has sent me to you" (3:15). The word "LORD" is probably from the third-person form of the Hebrew verb "to be." Thus many scholars rightly believe this name of God speaks of His existence. In the Hebrew the word of "LORD" is written with the four consonants *yhwh*, and thus can be rendered Yahweh.

YAHWEH

Sometimes this name is shortened to *Yah* (Exod. 15:2; 17:16; Ps. 118:14). This occurs numerous times in the so-called Hallel psalms (Pss. 113–118; 146–150), which are marked by the exhortation, *hallelujah*. The word *hallelujah* consists of two elements. The first is the imperative "praise" represented by the *hallelu*, and the second part is the shortened form of the name of God, *Yah*. Thus the word *hallelujah* means "Give a shout of joyful praise to Yahweh."

Sometimes God's name Yahweh is strengthened by the addition of the words "of hosts," as in "Yahweh of hosts." Whereas the New American Standard Bible has the translation "LORD of hosts," the New International Version renders the words "LORD Almighty." This variation of God's name is sometimes used in military contexts and refers to Him as the One who commands the angelic armies of heaven (1 Kings 18:15; see also Luke 2:13; Rev. 19:14) and the armies of Israel (1 Sam. 17:45; see also Josh. 5:13–15). The term emphasizes the sovereignty of God in His rule over both heaven and earth. Isaiah saw a vision of God in which angelic beings called seraphs spoke of "the LORD Almighty [literally, 'Yahweh of hosts']" as holy (Isa. 6:3). This One who is "Yahweh of [angelic] hosts" is with His people (Ps. 46:7, 11; Hag. 2:4).

Sometimes God's name Yahweh is combined with another word to recall the name of a place or event.

Yahweh-Yērāʾê ("The LORD Will Provide," Gen. 22:14)

Yahweh-Rōpʾekā ("The LORD, who heals you," Exod. 15:26)

Yahweh-Nissî ("The LORD is my Banner," Exod. 17:15)

Yahweh-Šālôm ("The LORD is Peace," Judg. 6:24)

Yahweh-Ṣidēnû ("The LORD Our Righteousness," Jer. 23:6)

Yahweh-Šāmmâ ("THE LORD IS THERE," Ezek. 48:35)

THE IRREVERENT USE OF GOD'S NAME (EXOD. 20:7)

Many Christians are unaware that God's name is Yahweh. This may have come about as a result of a zealous concern to avoid a *misuse* of God's name. In Exodus 20:7 the third commandment states, "You shall not misuse the name of the LORD [Yahweh] your God, for the LORD [Yahweh] will not hold anyone guiltless who misuses his name." Most people take this commandment to apply to swearing and profanity (perhaps because of the KJV and NASB rendering of "misuse" as "take . . . in vain"). While these are appropriate applications of the commandment, it applies most directly to misusing God's personal name *Yahweh*. God's people are not to use His name in a foolish, empty, or unworthy way.

THE NAME IN JEWISH TRADITION

A sincere concern to avoid blasphemy and the dire consequences of misusing God's name resulted in a rather minimal use of God's name. The Israelites apparently thought, "It is better to avoid the use of God's name than to chance misusing it." In time, the Jewish people stopped using the name Yahweh. Whenever they came to this name of God in Scripture, they substituted the designation *ʾĂdōnāy*, meaning "Lord" or "Master."

The ritual on the Day of Atonement called for the high priest to speak the name of God ten times. Each time he did so, the priests and entire congregation would fall to the ground and say, "Blessed be the Name, the glory of His kingdom is forever and ever."[6] In ancient times the name was pronounced distinctly. Then, because some attempted to make use of it for magical purposes, it was spoken in a whisper, the name being lost among the sounds of the priests' instruments and levitical choirs. Eventually the Jews did not speak the name Yahweh at all.

The custom of using the designation 'Ădōnāy ("Lord") as a substitute for the name of God continues among Jewish people to this day. If you visit a Shabbat service in a Jewish synagogue on a Friday evening, you will hear the word 'Ădōnāy pronounced in place of Yahweh in the Hebrew Scriptures. Most observant Jews consider it extremely disrespectful and irreligious to pronounce the name Yahweh.

THE HYBRID NAME "JEHOVAH"

If God's name should probably be pronounced "Yahweh," how did the name "Jehovah" come into being? This is an interesting story. Along with a concern for reformation of the church in the 1500s there was a renewed interest in biblical studies. The Jewish tradition that had resulted in a neglect of the name Yahweh was overcome by a renewed realization of the significance of the name.

The words in the original Hebrew text of the Old Testament had only consonants and no vowels. This is true of modern Hebrew literature as well. Those who are familiar with the Hebrew language simply read the consonants and add the vowels when pronouncing the text. Over the years a traditional reading of the Hebrew text became established. Jewish scribes known as Masoretes preserved and handed down a fixed textual tradition (*masorah*). Around A.D. 1000 they added the vowels to the Hebrew text in order to preserve the accepted reading. When they added the vowels to the text, the four consonants in Yahweh (yhwh) were preserved, but the vowels of 'Ădōnāy were added as a reminder to pronounce the designation "Lord" rather than "Yahweh."

What happened next is something that happens frequently in the world of fruit, flowers, and animals. Someone crosses two species and introduces a hybrid. Sometime during the sixteenth century scholars began mixing the consonants of the name Yahweh with the vowels of 'Ădōnāy and introduced the hybrid "Jehovah." This name was introduced to the public through translations and popularized by some editions of the King

James Version and through Christian hymns. But "Jehovah" is a composite, hybrid name and does not represent the original pronunciation of the divine name.

THE RELATIONSHIP OF YAHWEH TO JESUS

Before Jesus' birth an angel appeared to Joseph in a dream announcing that Mary had conceived a child by the Holy Spirit and would bear a son. Then the angel instructed Joseph about the naming of the son. "You are to give him the name Jesus, because he will save his people from their sins" (Matt. 1:21). The name "Jesus" is the Greek form of the Hebrew name *yᵉšûaʿ*. This is a compound name made from an abbreviation of God's name *Yahweh* and the Hebrew verb "to save." So Jesus' name literally means "Yahweh saves" and is explained by the clause, "He will save his people from their sins." In the person of Jesus we have the ultimate demonstration of what God promised Moses in Exodus 3:8, "I have come down to rescue them." In Jesus, Yahweh's saving and delivering work is fully realized.

On many occasions in His earthly ministry Jesus was challenged by His listeners. One of the most dramatic of those confrontations was when His enemies accused Him of being demon-possessed (John 8:52). The basic question in the minds of His accusers was, "Who is Jesus?" They asked Him to explain Himself. Jesus answered their question by saying He is the prophetic hope of Abraham. "Your father Abraham rejoiced at the thought of seeing my day; he saw it and was glad" (8:56). The Jews implied from this remark that Christ meant He must have seen Abraham, and to them, that was impossible. Jesus backed up His words with a stupendous claim, "Before Abraham was born, I AM!" (8:58). This clearly refers to Yahweh's statement in Exodus 3:14, "I am who I am."

Commenting on Jesus' words, "I am," Leon Morris wrote, "It is the style of deity, and it points to the eternity of God according to the strictest understanding of the continuous nature of the present [tense of the Greek] *eimi*. He continually IS."[7] The Jewish listeners recognized that Jesus was identifying Himself by the same words God used to describe Himself in Exodus 3:14. Taking His words as blasphemy, they picked up stones to put Him to death for using the divine name for Himself.

Yet His words were a clear affirmation of His preexistence and deity. When the New Testament quotes the Old Testament verses that have the Hebrew *Yahweh*, the New Testament uses the Greek *kyrios* ("Lord"). This too confirms Jesus' deity. As *kyrios*, He is identical with Yahweh.[8]

The marvelous name Yahweh reminds us that God exists, that He is the self-existent One who is always willing to reach down and help His people.

For Further Reading

Motyer, J. A. *The Revelation of the Divine Name.* London: Tyndale Publishing House, 1959.

4

DESIGNATIONS OF DEITY

I will be glad and rejoice in you; I will sing praise to your name, O Most High.

—Psalm 9:2

ALTHOUGH MY NAME IS CARL LANEY, I am sometimes referred to in other ways. Because I earned my doctor's degree at Dallas Seminary, some students refer to me as "Doctor," a term derived from a Latin root meaning "teacher." Because I was ordained to the ministry in 1975, some people have referred to me as "Reverend." This is my least preferred designation because God is the only one truly worthy of our reverence. Because I am a seminary professor, some students have referred to me as "Prof." When I was teaching in the Philippines at the Asian Theological Seminary, my Filipino students addressed me as "Sir." When I was pastoring the Chinese Faith Baptist Church, the people there affectionately called me Pastor. My kids call me Dad, and my wife calls me Honey.

There are many *titles* by which I have been addressed. But I have just one *name*—Carl. Similarly while God has just one name, Yahweh, many designations of deity are found in the Bible. As the titles by which I am called tell something about me, so the designations used for God tell us something about Him. This chapter focuses on the meaning and significance of the biblical designations for deity. This study will enable us to know God better as we become acquainted with various ways He is identified.

OLD TESTAMENT DESIGNATIONS

In the Old Testament God is called a Warrior (Exod. 15:3), a Rock (Ps. 18:2), Redeemer (19:14), King (10:16), Shepherd (23:1), and Husband (Hos. 2:16). These poetic terms communicate powerful images which we will discuss later. But here we focus on the more common Old Testament designations for deity.

ʾĔlōhîm

ʾĔlōhîm is a plural form which is used more than twenty-five hundred times in the Hebrew Bible. It is a general term for God and can also be used to apply to false gods as well as to judges and kings. ʾĔlōhîm is usually translated "God" in our English translations.

ʾĔlōhîm is often used with a descriptive phrase which served as something of a title by which God's people came to know Him. For example, He is called "the God of heaven, who made the sea and the land" (Jon. 1:9). This description calls attention to His work as Creator. The expression "the God of all the earth" (Isa. 54:5) emphasizes His sovereignty. The words "God who judges the earth" (Ps. 58:11) remind us of His justice and our accountability before Him.

Some descriptive phrases focus on a particular attribute of God, like the expressions "everlasting God" (Isa. 40:28), "living God" (Jer. 10:10), or "holy God" (1 Sam. 6:20). The phrase "the God of . . . Abraham" (Gen. 26:24) calls to mind His promise to Abraham (12:1–3) and His faithfulness to him. Often this is heightened, as in the expression "the God of Abraham, the God of Isaac and the God of Jacob" (Exod. 3:6). His work as Redeemer is emphasized in the phrase "God my Savior" (Ps. 18:46). His work as Defender is seen in the expression "God of the armies of Israel" (1 Sam. 17:45).

Some of the expressions used with ʾĔlōhîm describe God's actions on behalf of His people. He is "God, who brought you out of Egypt, out of the land of slavery" (Deut. 8:14). Some emphasize God's intimacy with His people, as in the words, "Your God in whom you trust" (2 Kings 19:10, NASB), or "my loving God" (Ps. 59:17).

The word *ʾĔlōhîm* is plural. This is usually described as the "plural of majesty." This is remotely like an "editorial plural," in which an author uses the pronoun "we" when speaking of himself. The fact that the Hebrew writers did not regard *ʾĔlōhîm* as a true plural is seen by the fact that they consistently used the term with singular verb forms, adjectives, and pronouns.

William F. Albright has pointed out that in the Canaanite world there was an increasing tendency to employ the plural form with Canaanite deities, as in the title Ashtarot used of Astarte.[1] This was an attempt to emphasize the "totality of manifestations of a deity" or to magnify one of their gods by addressing him as the "totality of gods." While this cultural background may shed some light on the use of the plural, a better reason is found in the Bible itself. The word *ʾĔlōhîm* can speak of the unity of the one majestic God and also allow for a plurality of divine persons within the Trinity (Isa. 48:16; Matt. 28:19). While we recognize that the "plural of majesty" *allows* for the Trinity rather than explicitly stating this doctrine, its use in the Old Testament anticipates the existence of the triune God.

ʾĒl

The term *ʾĒl* means basically the same as *ʾĔlōhîm*. This word may have been the root on which the plural form *ʾĔlōhîm* was constructed. *ʾĒl* can be used as a generic designation for any deity including the true God of Israel. Its discovery among the ancient cuneiform texts found at Ugarit, in present-day Syria, indicates that the term was a very old Semitic name for deity. In fact the supreme god of the Canaanite pantheon was named *ʾĒl*.

Scholars have observed a tendency in Scripture to accompany the designation *ʾĒl* with epithets. It is rarely used in the Bible without some word or description that elevates and distinguishes the true God from other false deities that bear the name *ʾēl* ("god"), and so *ʾĒl* is used to denote the true God's greatness and superiority over all other gods. Translated literally, He is "the great *ʾĒl*" (Jer. 32:18),[2] "*ʾĒl* of *ʾēls*" (Dan. 11:36), "*ʾĒl* of heaven" (Ps. 136:26), and "*ʾĒl* most high" (Gen. 14:18-19).

The term *ʾĒl* is often accompanied by epithets that describe Him as the Savior of Israel. Again, literal translations point to Him as the "faithful *ʾĒl*" (Deut. 7:9), "holy *ʾĒl*" (Isa. 5:16), "almighty *ʾĒl*" (Gen. 17:1),

"Mighty *ʾĒl*" (Isa. 9:6), and "eternal *ʾĒl*" (Gen. 21:33). Some of the epithets are quite personal, as in "*ʾĒl* who arms me with strength" (Ps. 18:32), "*ʾĒl* my rock" (42:9), and "*ʾĒl* is my salvation" (Isa. 12:2, NASB).

In several verses, *ʾĒl* is used in combination with the Hebrew adjective *ʾelyôn*, meaning "high." When used of God, the term has a superlative connotation, "highest." And so in Genesis 14:19 Melchizedek recognized Him as "God Most High" [*ʾĒl ʾelyôn*], Creator of heaven and earth." The psalmist recalled how *ʾĒl ʾelyôn* is the "Rock" and "Redeemer" of His people (Ps. 78:35).

The combination *ʾĒl Šadday* is a familiar designation for God. The origin of *Šadday* is debated. Some have linked it with a word meaning "mountains," thus "God of the mountains." Others suggest it comes from an Akkadian word for "breast," thereby suggesting that God nourishes His own. In the Old Testament the designation stresses the might and power of God (see, for example, Gen. 17:1; 28:3; 35:11; 43:14; 48:3; 49:25). The omnipotent *ʾĒl Šadday* can and will act on behalf of His own to meet their needs and fulfill His promises.

ʾĔlōah

The designation *ʾĔlōah* is used about sixty times in the Old Testament to refer to God. The precise derivation of *ʾĔlōah* is uncertain, although it is clearly related to the terms *ʾĒl* and *ʾĔlōhîm*. Its frequent use in the Book of Job (forty-one times) has led some scholars to suggest that it may have been an ancient term for God.

ʾĔlōah is used three times in parallel with the word "rock" as a descriptive term for God (Deut. 32:15; Ps. 18:31; Isa. 44:8). It is used in Proverbs 30:5 in describing God as a shield to those who take refuge in Him. Its use in Daniel 11:37–39 suggests that the designation conveyed the concepts of strength and might. All this suggests that *ʾĔlōah* is strong and is able to comfort and assure His people in times of need.

ʾĂdōnāy

The word *ʾădōnāy* is derived from an ancient Ugaritic word (*ʾadn*) meaning "lord" or "father." The term *ʾādōn* usually refers to men. Sarah used it with reference to her husband Abraham (Gen. 18:12). The pharaoh of Egypt was called by this title (Gen. 40:1), and Hannah addressed Eli the priest as *ʾādōn* (1 Sam. 1:15). In these verses the term is used as a title of honor and respect, as in "master." Also in numerous passages the term refers to God. In Exodus 34:23 God refers to Himself as "the Lord [*hā ʾādōn*], Yahweh the God of Israel." Deuteronomy 10:17 uses the superlative construction, "Lord of lords" (*ʾădōnêy hā ʾădōnîm*). The Messiah has the title *ʾādōn* in Psalm 110:1.

In about three hundred passages *ʾādōn* appears in a special plural form with a first-person singular suffix (*ʾădōnāy*). In this form, found in Psalms, Lamentations, and the Prophets, the term always refers to God. The plural form *ʾădōnāy* is the plural of majesty, which we also observed in the designation *ʾĔlōhîm* ("God"). It highlights the greatness of God as manifested by His many attributes and allows for the later development of the doctrine of the Trinity.

Ancient of Days

The designation "Ancient of Days" occurs three times in the Aramaic section of Daniel (Dan. 7:9, 13, 22). This phrase, along with other depictions of great age in the context, communicates the impression of "noble venerability."[3] The designation calls attention to the eternality of God, who said, "I am the first and I am the last, and there is no God besides Me" (Isa. 44:6, NASB).

NEW TESTAMENT DESIGNATIONS

There are many designations used for Jesus in the New Testament. John 1 records eight: Word, Lamb of God, Son of God, Rabbi, Messiah, Jesus of Nazareth, King of Israel, and Son of Man. These titles are very significant and are properly discussed in Christology.[4] Here we focus on the more general New Testament designations for God.

Theos

The Greek word *theos* is the most common designation for deity in the New Testament. *Theos* is used in the Septuagint to translate the words

ʾĔlōhîm and ʾĒl. Sometimes it refers to false gods (1 Cor. 8:5; Gal. 4:8), but most frequently it refers to the true God. Some verses use *theos* of Christ (John 1:1; Rom. 9:5; Titus 2:13; 2 Pet. 1:1; 1 John 5:20).

Occasionally *theos* is sometimes joined with other words to describe God's attributes. He is the "God of glory" (Acts 7:2), the "God of all comfort" (2 Cor. 1:3), the "God of love and peace" (13:11), the "God of hope" (Romans 15:13), the "God of peace" (15:33; Phil. 4:9), and the "God of all grace" (1 Pet. 5:10). These phrases do more than describe God; they also indicate that He is the source of these blessings. In addition He is the "God who gives endurance and encouragement" (Rom. 15:5).

Kyrios

The term *kyrios* is derived from the Greek word *kyros*, "power or might." In the New Testament *kyrios* is used as a title of courtesy, as in "lord," "master," "sir." The term occurs more than nine thousand times in the Septuagint. In the vast majority of these cases *kyrios* translates Yahweh, the personal name of God. In the first century some Roman emperors found the title attractive. Nero (A.D. 54–68) is described in an inscription as "*kyrios* of all the world."

Of its many New Testament occurrences *kyrios* sometimes speaks in a general sense of one who has rank or authority, such as a master (Eph. 6:5) or husband (1 Pet. 3:6), or is used as a polite form of address (John 12:21). Most of the occurrences, however, refer to God. He is the Lord, the Master, the ultimate Authority. "The term *kyrios* designates God as the Mighty One, the Lord, the Possessor, the Ruler who has legal power and authority."[5]

In a number of quotations from the Old Testament the New Testament writers substituted *kyrios* for Yahweh in keeping with the Jewish custom of avoiding the use of God's personal name (for example, quoting Rom. 4:8, quoting Ps. 32:2; Rom. 10:16, quoting Isa. 53:1).

Throughout the New Testament, Jesus is recognized as *kyrios*. In Peter's first sermon he acknowledged that God made Jesus Christ "Lord" (Acts 2:36). To Cornelius Peter declared that Jesus Christ "is Lord of all" (10:36). James used *kyrios* to refer to Jesus, his half-brother (James 1:1). Jude wrote of Jesus Christ our "Lord" (Jude 4). Paul regularly used *kyrios* of the Lord Jesus (for example, Rom. 10:9; 14:9; 1 Cor. 1:3; 7:25).

Patēr

The term *patēr,* "father," signifies one who is a "nourisher, protector, or upholder." While this term is frequently used in this normal sense in the New Testament, *patēr* is also used of God in a general sense as Creator and Originator of all things (1 Cor. 8:6; Eph. 3:14-15; Heb. 12:9). The term is also used of the special relationship believers have with God as His spiritual children. By faith we enter into this relationship and become "children of God" (John 1:12). On the basis of this spiritual relationship believers have access "to the Father" (Eph. 2:18). Jesus urged His disciples to be imitators of their "Father in heaven" (Matt. 5:45), their "heavenly Father" (5:48). Paul described God as "the Father of compassion" (2 Cor. 1:3), and the writer of Hebrews addressed the issue of the Father's discipline (Heb. 12:9–10).

Jesus used the term "Father" to express the special relationship He has with God within the Trinity. He was sent by the Father (John 6:37). He did the works of the Father (5:19). He called God His own Father, by which His enemies thought He was "making himself equal with God" (5:18). The Gospel of John emphasizes the Father-Son relationship between Jesus and God the Father, mentioning it about eighty times.

Although God is the Father of believers, He is not their Father in the same way He is the Father of the Lord Jesus. Whenever Jesus spoke of His relationship to God the Father, He always used the singular "My Father" (Matt. 11:27; 25:34; John 20:17; Rev. 2:27). His relationship with the Father has existed for all eternity in the Trinity, whereas our relationship to God is by grace and through regeneration.

Abba

Abba is an Aramaic term for "father"; it is used three times in the New Testament in reference to God (Mark 14:36; Rom. 8:15; Gal. 4:6). In these verses the term is followed by the translation, *ho patēr* ("the Father") to make it clear that God is meant. A*bba* functions as an invocation to God and is expressive of the close personal relationship of the speaker with God.

The Aramaic *abba* stems from what might be called "baby talk." According to the Jewish Talmud, when a child is weaned, "it learns to say *abba* [daddy] and *imma* [mommy]" (*Berakoth* 40a; *Sanhedrin* 70b). In time, the meaning of the word was broadened so that it was no longer a form of address used by little children, but was used by adult sons and daughters as well. The childish character of the word diminished and *abba* acquired the warm, familiar ring which we may feel in such an expression as "dear father."[6]

Nowhere in the Old Testament do we find the term *abba* used in addressing God. The pious Jews sensed too great a gap between themselves and God to use such a familiar expression. Rabbinic Judaism has an interesting example of *abba* being used with reference to God. The Talmud records, "When the world had need of rain, our teachers used to send the schoolchildren to Rabbi Hanan ha Nehba [first century B.C.], and they would seize the hem of his cloak and call out to him: 'Dear father (*abba*), dear father (*abba*), give us rain.' He said before God: 'Sovereign of the world, do it for the sake of these who cannot distinguish between an *abba* who can give rain and an *abba* who can give no rain" (*Taanith* 23b). Note that the rabbi used the respectful invocation, "Sovereign of the world," rather than the term *abba*, in addressing God.

Jesus used *abba* when addressing God the Father in His prayer in the Garden of Gethsemane. "'*Abba*, Father,' he said, 'everything is possible for you. Take this cup from me. Yet not what I will, but what you will'" (Mark 14:36). In using this expression Jesus spoke as a child would speak to its father. This reflects something of the intimacy and trust that characterized His relationship with God.

As the Holy Spirit testifies that believers are God's children (Rom. 8:16), they are invited to cry "*Abba*, Father" (8:15; Gal. 4:6). Believers can address God in this way because of their relationship with God through faith. What an encouragement to know that we can pray to the Father with the same sense of warmth and intimacy in our relationship with God that Jesus enjoyed.

My children know how to ask for favors in such a way that they get a positive response. They know that demanding and nagging don't work. They have learned that I respond best to sweetness, love, and respect. My daughter might say, "Daddy dear, there is a terrific dress on sale at Nordstrom's. Would you split the cost with me?" How can I say anything but yes to that kind of an appeal? God made dads for this very purpose and there is joy in fulfilling our destiny!

As I delight to respond to my children and meet their needs, so God the Father delights to answer those who address Him as *Abba*, "Dear Father." He has both the resources and the resolve to answer our prayers and meet our needs.

These are only some of the many ways by which God, Jesus Christ, and the Holy Spirit are referred to in the Scriptures. Mary Loeks lists one hundred fifty-five names and designations of God![7]

For Further Reading

Lockyer, Herbert. *All the Divine Names and Titles in the Bible*. Grand Rapids: Zondervan Publishing House, 1975.

Sumrall, Lester. *The Names of God*. Nashville: Thomas Nelson Publishers, 1982.

5
GOD'S SELF-REVELATION

And the LORD said, "I will cause all my goodness to pass in front of you, and I will proclaim my name, the LORD, in your presence. I will have mercy on whom I will have mercy, and I will have compassion on whom I will have compassion.

—Exodus 33:19

DURING MY STUDENT DAYS at the University of Oregon, I took a genuine interest in the college coeds, wondering if God was preparing one to be my wife. At a College Life meeting, sponsored by Campus Crusade for Christ, a Christian friend introduced me to her younger sister, Nancy. I liked Nancy from the very start. She had an enthusiasm and spontaneity that attracted me. I remember one of our early dates. When I was taking her home about 11:30 P.M., I suddenly had an inspiration. Instead of going home, why not climb Spencer Butte! Well, Nancy was game!

Half an hour later we set off in the dark on a winding trail that led to the top of the butte south of Eugene. We eventually made it to the summit from which we enjoyed a lovely view of the city lights and the starlit night sky. I was convinced after that experience that I wanted to get to know this girl better.

So I began to ask Nancy about herself. I asked her about her hobbies, her hopes, her dreams. I asked her about her spiritual life. I asked her about her family, her parents, her background. And as she spoke, I listened intently. The more I learned about this dark-eyed beauty, the more I liked her. In time, my "like" became "love." Our relationship grew and several years later I asked her to spend her life with me.

Although we have been married for over twenty-five years, I am still getting to know Nancy. And one of the best ways for me to know her better is to ask her about herself. If I ask the right questions and listen carefully to what she says, I can learn a lot about Nancy's innermost thoughts and character as she reveals more of herself to me.

This chapter examines a passage that records an incident in which God revealed Himself to Moses. I believe this is one of the most important theological texts in Scripture because it is the only passage that actually records God's describing Himself, naming His own attributes. This passage is quoted by later prophets, who recognized its centrality as the fundamental text for knowing God.

If you want to get to know someone better, you need to ask them about themselves. If you want to get to know God better, you need to study God's response to Moses' request, "Now show me your glory" (Exod. 33:18).

THE BREAKING OF THE COVENANT

Exodus 32 recalls one of the spiritual low points in Israel's history. Her sin of idolatry resulted in her breaking the newly established covenant with God.

While the Israelites were camped at Mount Sinai, Moses had ascended the mountain to meet with God and receive the two tablets of the law. When this took longer than expected, the people approached Aaron and requested, "Come, make us gods who will go before us. As for this fellow Moses who brought us up out of Egypt, we don't know what has happened to him" (Exod. 32:1). Three failures of the people can be noted. They failed to recognize their exclusive allegiance to the Lord; they failed to recognize that God, not Moses, had delivered them from Egypt; and they failed to rely on Moses, their covenant mediator.

Aaron yielded to public pressure and fashioned a golden calf, which he then presented to the people. "These are your gods, O Israel, who brought you up out of Egypt" (32:4). The calf Aaron created was reminiscent of the Apis bull cult that was prevalent in Memphis, Egypt, near Goshen where the Israelites had lived. Aaron then built an altar with which the people were to worship the calf! That this image was intended to represent the Lord is suggested by Aaron's words, "Tomorrow there will be a festival to the Lord" (32:5).

Up on Mount Sinai, God informed Moses of that idolatry that had taken place in the camp. The Lord threatened the destruction of the people, promising to raise up a new nation from the seed of Moses (32:10). This was a real test for Moses, but he chose Israel's preservation over his own exaltation. In response to Moses' prayers, God withheld His judgment (32:14).

THE REQUEST OF MOSES

Because of Israel's failure in regard to the golden calf, the Lord withdrew His presence from among the people in the camp (Exod. 33:1–7). He could not dwell among sinful covenant-breakers.

Moses was no doubt discouraged by Israel's failure. He wanted to be with God, and yet God had left the camp. So Moses had a tent set up outside the camp where he could meet with God.[1] Reflecting on this time with God, Moses wrote, "The LORD would speak to Moses face to face, as a man speaks with his friend" (33:11).

More than anything else, Moses wanted to know God better. He prayed, "If you are pleased with me, teach me your ways so I may know you" (33:13). It was great spending time in the presence of God, but Moses wanted to know Him more intimately and intelligently than ever before. With this in mind Moses said, "Now show me your glory" (33:18). *Kābōd*, the Hebrew word for "glory," is related to a verb that means "to be heavy." *Kābōd* is sometimes used with reference to a person's "weighty" reputation or honored position (1 Kings 3:13). It is used in a similar way to refer to the reality and splendor of God's glorious presence. Sometimes His glory was made visible in association with the tabernacle or temple (Exod. 40:34, 1 Kings 8:11; Ezek. 9:3).

What exactly was Moses asking for when he prayed, "Show me your glory"? Moses knew God, but he wanted to know Him better. He wanted to know Him as He is. Moses was asking Him for a full self-disclosure of His glorious person—a revelation that would sustain and encourage him as Israel's leader.

God responded by telling Moses that mortal man cannot see God and live (Exod. 33:20). But He accommodated Himself to Moses' request and told Moses that He would place him in the cleft of a rock, covering him with His hand until He passed by. Then God told Moses, "Then I will remove my hand and you will see my back; but my face must not be seen" (33:23). This text is rich in anthropomorphisms, attributing to God the human features of a hand, back, and face. Since God does not have a physical body (John 4:24), it seems that these terms are used to show that God would be very personally and intimately present with Moses.

THE REVELATION OF GOD'S ATTRIBUTES
IN EXODUS 34:6–7

God fulfilled His promise to give Moses a fresh revelation of His own glory. Once again Moses was called up to Mount Sinai (Exod. 34:1–2). There on that sacred mountain God stood with Moses "and proclaimed his name" (34:5).[2] In the Bible a person's name is closely associated with his or her reputation. Here God revealed Himself to Moses, announcing the attributes most characteristic of His glorious reputation.

Exodus 34:6–7 is unusual in that it is the only place in Scripture in which God lists His own attributes! Here God tells us about Himself. Recognizing the significance of this text, the biblical authors quoted it many times (Num. 14:18; 2 Chron. 30:9; Neh. 9:17; Pss. 86:15; 103:8; 111:4; 112:4; 116:5; 145:8; Joel 2:13; Jon. 4:2; Nah. 1:3). As we examine these attributes and discover what God wanted Moses (and us) to know about Himself, I trust we will join our hearts with the psalmist, who said, "They will speak of the glorious splendor of your majesty, and I will meditate on your wonderful works" (Ps. 145:5).

Compassionate

It never ceases to amaze me that the first thing God revealed about Himself to Moses was His compassion (Exod. 34:6)—not His holiness, sovereignty, or love.

What does it mean to be compassionate? The Hebrew word *raḥûm* ("compassionate") refers to a deep love rooted in a natural bond.[3] This love is usually that of a superior for an inferior being. An associated Hebrew word is rendered "womb" (Jer. 20:17), which suggests that the love and compassion referred to here is like the love a mother has for her child. And yet this tender love is not limited to the female gender. Fathers have compassion too! The psalmist declared, "As a father has compassion on his children, so the LORD has compassion on those who fear him" (Ps. 103:13).

The adjective *raḥûm* appears thirteen times in the Old Testament—twelve times to refer to God and once of man (Ps. 112:4). When used of God, the word *compassionate* conveys the strong bond God has with those He calls His children. God looks on His people as a mother and father look on their own children, with a tender love. Another concept associated with the word *compassionate* is God's unconditional choice. He has compassion on whom He chooses (Exod. 33:19). God's compassion is also linked with His faithfulness. Moses wrote, "For the LORD your God is a merciful God; he will not abandon or destroy you or forget the covenant with your forefathers, which he confirmed to them by oath" (Deut. 4:31). And because He is compassionate, He is also forgiving. The psalmist Asaph declared, "Yet he was merciful; he forgave their iniquities and did not destroy them" (Ps. 78:38). God's compassion is the basis for His sparing a repentant people from deserved judgment. Deuteronomy 30:3 declares that repentance from sin will be met with God's compassion and restoration to blessing (see also 2 Chron. 30:9). Significantly God's compassion provides the basis for Israel's eschatological hope (Isa. 14:1; 49:13; 54:7; Jer. 12:15; 33:26; Mic. 7:19; Zech. 1:16).

Parents love their children. We love them because they are our own. We love them in spite of their disobedience and rebellion. We ache for them when they suffer the consequences of their foolish mistakes. We are committed to them for life and will always try to do what is in their best interests. One winter Sunday afternoon my son came to me and said, "Dad, I'm cold. Would you light a fire in the fireplace?" I could have told him to put on a sweater or do some exercises. But my compassion made me want to fulfill his request and to ease his chill. So I split some wood and built a roaring fire. As a father, I enjoyed responding to my son's request and watching him get warm in front of our fireplace.

The Lord our God is a compassionate Father. He loves us because we are His own. He will never leave us nor forsake us. He will always be there in our time of need, seeking our good for His glory. Although He is infinitely holy, His compassion allows Him to deal gently with weak people. He is full of tender sympathy for our sufferings and the miseries of human frailty. He is always willing to forgive our sins and restore us because of His great compassion.

Gracious

The second character quality God attributed to Himself is graciousness. The adjective *ḥannûn* stems from *ḥānan*, which denotes the stronger coming to help the weaker who stands in need but has no claim for gracious treatment. Such an act is experienced as an undeserved blessing or favor. The overwhelming number of uses of this word in the Old Testament have the Lord as the subject. Jacob explained to his brother, Esau, that the growth of his family and property resulted from the fact that God had dealt "graciously" with him (Gen. 33:5, 11). David explained his prayer and fasting for his dying son by saying, "Who knows? The LORD may be gracious to me and let the child live" (2 Sam. 12:22). Often God's grace is seen in His deliverance of His own from their sins (Mal. 1:9).

The word "gracious" (*ḥannûn*) appears thirteen times in the Old Testament, eleven of which are in combination with *raḥûm*, "compassionate." Like the verbal form, the adjective "gracious" denotes the free and undeserved favor of a superior. All the occurrences of the word except one refer to the Lord being favorable toward the afflicted and needy. The exception, Psalm 112:4, uses the adjective to describe the God-fearing person who shares certain characteristics with God. But with people, this attribute is neither perfected nor permanent. With God, you can always count on His being perfectly gracious. And because He is, He will hear the cry of the poor (Exod. 22:27, NASB), He will not turn from the repentant (2 Chron. 30:9), and He will never forsake His own (Neh. 9:17, 31).

The grace of God is featured throughout both Testaments, emphasizing the theological basis for all God's benevolent dealings with His people. Charles Ryrie wrote, "Christianity is distinct from all other religions because it is a message of grace. Jesus Christ is the supreme revelation of

God's grace; salvation is by grace; and grace governs and empowers Christian living. Without grace Christianity is nothing."[4]

It is so encouraging to know that God deals with us not as we deserve, but rather through grace. While we deserve His judgment, He graciously provided a Redeemer to pay the penalty of our sins. On the basis of grace, we can receive His free gift of salvation and eternal life.

Slow to Anger

God is right in being angry at the sin and disobedience of His people who pain and displease Him (Exod. 32:10). God's anger, though fierce (Jer. 25:37), is not sinful or evil. It has its source in His holy character, which is rightfully offended by the sinful rebellion of His creatures. God's anger often results in His chastising (Ps. 6:1; Isa. 12:1) and punishing His people (2 Sam. 6:7; Jer. 44:6).

The good news for us in studying this attribute of God is that He is not quick to anger. The words "slow to anger" are used nine times in the Bible[5] to refer to God's patience in dealing with those whose sins arouse His wrath. In Hebrew the expression, "slow to anger," includes an adjective meaning "long" and the plural noun "noses." An angry person often displays his emotion in the appearance of his nose (a red nose and flared nostrils). The idea behind the expression, "slow to anger," is that God takes a long time before getting angry. It is as if He takes a long, deep breath before expressing His anger.

Because God is holy, He must respond with wrath and judgment on sin and disobedience. His righteousness demands that He not leave wickedness unpunished. Such lenience would be contrary to His holy character. But God does not hasten to punish the sinner. Instead, He provides him with ample opportunity to turn and repent. God's patience in dealing with the wicked should not be interpreted to mean that sin doesn't matter or isn't serious. Rather, God's patience is intended to lead the wicked to repent. As Peter wrote, God is "not wanting anyone to perish, but everyone to come to repentance" (2 Pet. 3:9).

God is in no hurry to judge sinners. There will be a day when they must stand before His Great White Throne and be judged according to their deeds (Rev. 20:11–15). But in the meantime God continues to demonstrate His patience and grace. His anger is being kindled by humankind's sinfulness, but it is being kindled slowly.

Many of us have experienced the patience of God during times of sin and disobedience. During my freshman year in college I was running from God, living a worldly life. I marvel at His patience and gentle chastening when I deserved a large dose from the cup of His wrath! God's patience with me is a reminder that I need to be patient with others who are weak, immature, and struggling with sin.

Abounding in Love

The next thing God told Moses about Himself is that He is "abounding in loving-kindness and truth." The word "abounding" (literally, great) describes what is present in abundance and clearly applies to God's loving-kindness and His truth. The words "loving-kindness and truth" occur about twenty-five times together and may be an example of a figure of speech in which two words represent one concept or thought. Taken this way "loving-kindness and truth" may refer to God's "true love" or "faithful love." Since we are not certain that the words should be taken together, I will deal with each separately.

The Hebrew word translated "lovingkindness" (NASB), "love" (NIV), "kindness" (JB), or "steadfast love" (NRSV) is *ḥesed*, "unfailing love" or "loyalty." The Septuagint uses the Greek word *eleos* ("mercy" or "compassion") to translate *ḥesed*. The Hebrew word for "stork" is based on the word *ḥesed*, perhaps because the stork is noted for its love and kindness toward its young. For this reason the stork is commonly associated with babies and motherhood. It is clear that a strong, steadfast love is basic to the meaning of *ḥesed*.[6] But there is another Hebrew word for "love," namely, ʾahăbâ. So what is unique and distinctive about *ḥesed*?

In 1927 Nelson Glueck published a doctoral dissertation in German, subsequently translated into English under the title *Ḥesed in the Bible*.[7] Glueck pointed out that ancient treaties used *ḥesed* to describe the covenant relationship between kings and their subjects. As the king is expected to demonstrate *ḥesed* to the people with whom he has entered into covenant, so the subjects are to show *ḥesed* toward their king. This love is mutual and is pledged in the covenant—a "covenantal love." It includes the ideas of loyalty, service, and obedience. As ancient kings entered into a relationship with their subjects expressed in terms of covenantal love, so the Lord in establishing His covenant with Israel promised loyalty to His covenant promises and called for loyalty on the part of His people.

Not all have agreed with Glueck's analysis of *ḥesed*. Others hold that *ḥesed* expresses love in a more general sense, emphasizing God's freedom to love without any sense of obligation as in a covenant relationship. I am not convinced that it has to be all one way or the other. Certainly God's relationship with His people Israel was formalized and defined by a covenant (Exod. 19:5; 24:8; 31:16; 34:10). But there is also a freedom, initiative, and grace in God's *ḥesed*. All of God's favor is based on His love (Deut. 7:8). God entered into a covenant with His people which guarantees the perpetuity of this love.

His love is an undeserved, selective affection by which he binds Himself to His people in a way that precipitates their redemption and blessing. He sovereignly grants His gifts and blessings beyond anything for which we might hope and in spite of what we might deserve. Yahweh's *ḥesed* will never diminish or cease, for it is founded on His covenant commitment. And so the psalmist encouraged us to "give thanks to the LORD, for he is good, His love [*ḥesed*] endures forever" (Ps. 136:1).

Abounding in Faithfulness

Besides being "great" in His steadfast love, God also abounds in faithfulness. The word *ʾĕmet*, based on the verb *ʾāman*, means "to support, establish, confirm." The basic idea is that of firmness, certainty, and dependability. The Old Testament frequently applies the word *ʾĕmet* to God as a characteristic of His nature. It describes God who led Abraham's servant to the right wife for Isaac (Gen. 24:27). Also the term is fittingly applied to God's words (Ps. 119:142, 151, 160). As a characteristic of God, *ʾĕmet* becomes the means by which people come to know and serve God (1 Kings 2:4; Pss. 25:5; 26:3).

Many people cannot be relied on to keep their promises. They break appointments, fail to show up at meetings, and neglect to follow through with their commitments and obligations. How encouraging it is to know that there is One who is forever reliable, whose word can be trusted, whose promises will always be fulfilled. God is eternally true to Himself and His own attributes. He is like the Rock of Gibraltar in a world shaken by uncertainty. He is the One you can count on to always be there at your time of need.

Maintaining Love to Thousands

The love that so characterizes God's person is not a mere attribute to discuss and admire. It is actively involved in extending divine mercies to those in need. In Exodus 34:7 the word translated "love" is the same word *hesed* we considered earlier in this chapter. It speaks of God's steadfast love, which is frequently shown to His people as covenant loyalty. Here we see that Yahweh extends His abounding loyal love to the multitudes. The word translated "maintaining" means that God extends this attribute in ministry to those in need. The participial form indicates that the action of the verb is continuous. God keeps on extending His love to the thousands who need His tender touch.

Forgiving Wickedness, Rebellion, and Sin

Another fact God wants us to know about Himself is that He is willing to forgive the sins of His people. The word "forgive" (*nāsāʾ*) means "to lift up, carry, to take away." Exodus 34:7 uses it figuratively of God's "taking away" sin. The concept of God's removal of our sins is powerfully emphasized in Psalm 103:12, "As far as the east is from the west, so far has he removed our transgressions from us."

God used three words in this passage to refer to those actions and attitudes which He forgives. The first word, "wickedness," is from a verb meaning "to bend or twist." Wickedness, then, refers to crooked behavior, a turning away from the straight and narrow way. This word is used in the Bible to identify various kinds of civil, social, and moral violations. The second word, "rebellion," refers to a breach of relationships, civil or religious, between two parties. In a context of international relationships, the verbal form designates a revolt against rulers. In a religious sense it refers to rebellion against God's authority. The third word, "sin," is related to the verb "to miss the way." Missing God's standard or failing to fulfill His requirements constitutes an act of sin. All sin is serious and separates humankind from God. Since God is holy, sin cannot be ignored. It has to be dealt with. This is where forgiveness comes in.

"Forgives" is a participle, which emphasizes the ongoing and continuous nature of God's forgiveness. He keeps on forgiving those who acknowledge their sins and repent. Micah contemplated God's attribute of forgiveness when he said, "Who is a God like you, who pardons sin and forgives the transgression of the remnant of his inheritance? You do not stay angry forever but delight to show mercy [*hesed*]" (Mic. 7:18). It is fortunate for us that "he does not treat us as our sins deserve or repay us according to our iniquities" (Ps. 103:10). How thankful we are for that! Because of God's forgiveness David could exclaim, "Blessed is he whose transgressions are forgiven, whose sins are covered!" (32:1).

Not Leaving the Guilty Unpunished

This next attribute features the other side of God's forgiving grace. Because of His infinite mercy and grace, the Lord delights in forgiving and restoring sinners to Himself. But His grace cannot abrogate His justice. There is stern accountability before a holy, wrathful God for those who refuse to repent.

Literally the sentence reads, "He will most certainly not acquit [the guilty]." "Acquit" (*nāqâ*) means "to be clean, pure or spotless." In a judicial context it means "to go unpunished." A husband is "acquitted" of any guilt if he, in declaring his wife unfaithful, follows the legal procedures required by law (Num. 5:31). The word is sometimes used with a negative, yielding a strong warning or reprimand. An example of this is in Proverbs 6:29, which states that the one who sleeps with another man's wife will not go "unpunished." In Exodus 34:7 the verb is used with the negative "not" to intensify the warning: God will not regard the unrepentant sinner as innocent.

God's grace is so rich and free, one wonders why anyone would refuse His pardon and forgiving love. But people are so depraved and deluded that they refuse God's ultimate gift. Because He is holy and just, as well as loving and forgiving, the unrepentant wicked face the most serious consequences of their sin and rebellion.

Not Erasing the Consequences of Sin

The last phrase in God's self-revelation to Moses in Exodus 34:6–7 addresses the consequences of sin. While it is God's nature to forgive, it is not His nature to remove the natural consequences that follow foolish and sinful behavior. The clause, "He punishes the children and their children for the sin of the fathers to the third and fourth generation" is sometimes misunderstood to mean that God punishes children for the specific sins of their parents and forefathers. However, other verses show this is not the meaning.

Certainly it would be unjust for God to punish children for the sins of their parents. Yet this is exactly what some people were saying in Ezekiel's day. The people had composed a proverb, "The fathers eat sour grapes, and the children's teeth are set on edge" (Ezek. 18:2). They felt that by allowing the Babylonians to destroy Jerusalem, God was punishing the people for their ancestors' sins. God responded by saying that they should not use that proverb anymore. He announced, "The soul who sins is the one who will die. The son will not share the guilt of the father, nor will the father share the guilt of the son. The righteousness of the righteous man will be credited to him, and the wickedness of the wicked will be charged against him" (18:20).

Exodus 34:7, then, does not mean God will punish children for their parents' sins. Instead God allows the *consequences* of sinful behavior to be experienced by children and other descendants. While God is most willing to forgive and pardon, He does not erase the consequences of sinful behavior. Many a child has suffered the consequences of growing up in a family with an alcoholic or abusive parent. When a parent is sent to prison, the children do suffer. God does not reverse the natural consequences of our foolish and sinful actions. Unfortunately children often do reap what their sinful parents sow.

THE RESPONSE OF MOSES

Moses' prayer "Show me your glory" (Exod. 33:18) had been answered. God had revealed Himself to Moses in a unique way. God had passed in front of Moses and proclaimed His own attributes. How did Moses respond?

He did not immediately reach for the nearest clay tablet to write down what God said about Himself. Nor did he begin to exegete these attributes to understand them better, discuss them with Joshua and Aaron, or debate them with other leaders. He responded to God's self-revelation in worship. "Moses bowed to the ground at once and worshiped" (34:8).

When Moses saw God as He is, he saw himself with new insight. He immediately prostrated himself on the ground and worshiped the Lord. May we follow Moses' example as we are getting to know God better. May we draw near to Him in worship, submission, and service as He discloses Himself to us through His Word.

6

WHAT THE PENTATEUCH
TEACHES ABOUT GOD

The LORD [is] God Most High, Creator of heaven and earth.
— Genesis 15:22

OFTEN DURING THE EARLIEST PERIOD of a budding relationship one makes some of the most significant discoveries about another person. This is true of a fishing buddy with whom I attended seminary. I met Mike at church and was immediately drawn to him. Before long we found ourselves and our wives getting together for fun evenings. This gave me an opportunity to get to know Mike better. One time Mike invited me to join him on a backpacking and fishing weekend at one of Oregon's mountain lakes. That experience sealed our relationship. Over the years we have spent countless weekends sitting in a rubber raft, wet from cold rain, waiting for the next brook trout to bite.

I have been friends with Mike for about twenty-five years now. But most of what I know about his personality, I learned during those first years as we spent time together. I learned in those first years of our friendship that Mike is a godly, committed Christian. He is a man of action who has firm convictions about moral and doctrinal issues. Nothing I have seen in his life since those first years of getting acquainted has altered this opinion.

As with friendships, I believe we get to know some major aspects of God's character in the earliest books of the Bible. These books record God's encounters with Abraham, Moses, and the people of Israel. This period might be looked on as the beginning stages of a friendship. What we discover about God in the earliest books of the Bible is confirmed and amplified throughout the Word of God.

This chapter discusses what the first five books of the Bible reveal about God. These books, written by Moses, record the time period from the creation of the world to Israel's preparations for the conquest of Canaan. Christians often call these books the "Pentateuch," a Greek term meaning "five books." These five—Genesis, Exodus, Leviticus, Numbers, and Deuteronomy—reveal foundational truths about God. Each book highlights a particularly significant attribute of God which helps us know Him better.

GENESIS: THE SOVEREIGNTY OF GOD

The theological theme of Genesis is the sovereignty of God, that is, His supreme and absolute authority as Ruler over all His creation. Jeremiah affirmed, "But the LORD is the true God; he is the living God, the eternal King" (Jer. 10:10). While earthly monarchs rule a particular dominion for a limited duration, God's rule is both universal and eternal. David declared, "The LORD has established his throne in heaven, and his kingdom rules over all" (Ps. 103:19). And another psalmist said, "The LORD is King forever and ever" (10:16). While Genesis does not contain the statement, "God is sovereign," this truth is highlighted throughout the book.

The first evidence of God's sovereignty in Genesis is His creation of the physical universe, "the heavens and the earth" (Gen. 1:1). God did not need to ask anyone if it was okay to create the universe. He did not have to report to anyone when He was finished. He did not have to depend on anyone to supply the needed materials. God simply spoke the word and the universe came into existence! The light, the atmosphere, the dry land, the plants, the stars, the animals, and humankind all came into being in response to His almighty, authoritative word.

God's sovereignty is also evidenced in Genesis by His regulation of humans. He commanded Adam and Eve, "You are free to eat from any tree in the garden; but you must not eat from the tree of the knowledge of good and evil" (2:16–17). He also exercised His sovereignty by condemning and judging their sin (3:14–19). God's sovereignty over His creation is further evidenced by His judgment on the wicked world in the time of Noah. Only a sovereign God could say, "I will wipe mankind, whom I have created, from the face of the earth" (6:7).

God's sovereignty is powerfully illustrated in His choice of Abraham to father a people who would bring blessing to the nations of the world (12:1–3). God not only sovereignly chose Abraham, but He also demonstrated His sovereignty by making unconditional promises to Abraham and his descendants—promises that would impact all nations forever. The sovereignty of God was displayed on Mount Moriah where at a critical moment, God provided a ram to take Isaac's place (22:8, 13–14), which illustrates His provision of a Lamb, Jesus Christ, to take our place.

One of the greatest illustrations of the sovereignty of God is the story of Joseph. The sale of Joseph into Egypt, his imprisonment, his eventual promotion to a high position in Egyptian government, and his provision for Jacob's family during a terrible famine, were all part of God's sovereign plan and purpose. God made Joseph prosper in whatever he did (39:23), and Joseph acknowledged that it was God who sent him to Egypt to preserve life (45:5).

One of the grandest statements in Scripture about God's sovereignty appears in Genesis 50 after Jacob's death. Joseph's brothers were afraid he might punish them for wronging him. Joseph replied, "Don't be afraid. Am I in the place of God? You intended to harm me, but God intended it for good to accomplish what is now being done, the saving of many lives" (50:19–20). Joseph acknowledged that what his brothers did was evil, but he would not act as their judge. Yet he recognized that God used their evil actions to accomplish good! Amazingly, God can accomplish His sovereign purposes through people's sinful actions.

This is not to say that people bear no responsibility for their actions. The sovereignty of God does not abrogate our responsibility to do what is right. In other words, when we do wrong, we can't blame God for it. But He may use a wrong to accomplish something good. A helpful illustration of this fact is Christ's crucifixion. Preaching to the people of Jerusalem about Jesus' death, Peter declared, "This man was handed over to you by God's set purpose ['predetermined plan,' NASB] and foreknowledge; and you, with the help of wicked men, put him to death" (Acts 2:23). The crucifixion was according to God's predetermined plan, but it was a wicked deed done by godless men. In the crucifixion of Christ, evil accomplished good, but those who crucified Him bore responsibility for it. God is sovereign over evil, but He is not to be blamed for it.

The truth of the sovereignty of God is emphasized throughout the Bible. Perhaps the classic New Testament text is Romans 8:28, "And we know that in all things God works for the good of those who love him, who have been called according to his purpose." And Paul referred to God as the One "who works out everything in conformity with the purpose of his will" (Eph. 1:11). Both verses point out that His sovereignty extends over "all things." Nothing is left out of God's sovereign authority and absolute control.

The sovereignty of God is a very practical doctrine, providing believers with great comfort and encouragement in the face of difficult or even tragic circumstances. When my brother was killed in an automobile accident at age fifteen, the truth of God's sovereignty sustained our family through our sorrow and grief. This was not an "accident" or unfortunate circumstance in which God lost control and my brother was outside His care. Not at all! My brother's death was part of God's sovereign and loving plan—a plan which I don't understand, but one I can trust to a sovereign God who knows and does what is best.

EXODUS: THE SALVATION OF GOD

The salvation God provides is one of the grand themes of the Bible. This is highlighted in the Book of Exodus, in which He is presented as the God who acts in salvation to deliver His own. We find this theme introduced in God's declaration to Moses, "So I have come down to rescue them from the hand of the Egyptians and to bring them up out of that land into a good and spacious land, a land flowing with milk and honey" (Exod. 3:8). Yahweh is not like the gods of Canaan who are impotent and unavailable (1 Kings 18:27). He is the powerful God who intervenes and saves. As Moses sang, "The LORD is my strength and my song; he has become my salvation" (Exod. 15:2).

The theme of salvation is powerfully presented in Exodus through its record of the birth of the nation Israel. The Lord miraculously delivered His people from bondage in Egypt, made a way for them through the Red Sea, provided for them in the wilderness, gave them the Law, and instructed them concerning the tabernacle. All these actions reveal the redemptive character of God. He is able and willing to save.

The first Passover (recorded in Exodus 12) was a highly significant event in Israel's history. Here God laid out a pattern for redemption which He followed in future dealings with His people. The Passover teaches the basis of God's redemption and looks ahead to Christ's redemptive work at the cross. The Passover must be understood in the context of a death sentence that fell on all Egypt because of the pharaoh's stubborn refusal to let the Israelites depart (11:4–8). God announced that all the firstborn in the land of Egypt would die. That included Egyptians, slaves, and Israelites. But the God of judgment is also the God of salvation, and He provided a way for the Israelite firstborn children to be delivered from the sentence of death.

Each family, God said, was to prepare a small animal from their herd for sacrifice. In celebrating the Passover each year since then, Jews have usually sacrificed a lamb, but a goat could also be used on that first Passover. After being killed, the blood of the animal was to be applied to the doorposts and lintels of the Israelite homes (12:7). The blood served as a symbol of the death of the substitute. Then God announced, "The blood will be a sign for you on the houses where you are; and when I see the blood, I will pass over you. No destructive plague will touch you when I strike Egypt" (12:13). This makes a profound theological statement about redemption. God said that the blood of the animal would be accepted in the place of the blood of the firstborn. This act of substitution anticipated the work of Christ, who died in the place of all of us who are under the sentence of eternal death.

The Passover sacrifice should not be interpreted as a work by which the Israelites earned their deliverance. God's salvation is always a gift of His grace and is never the result of human effort or works of merit. Later, when the Israelites confronted the Red Sea and the Egyptian army was closing in from behind, Moses said, "Do not be afraid. Stand firm and you will see the deliverance the LORD will bring you today. The Egyptians you see today you will never see again. The LORD will fight for you; you need only to be still" (14:13–14). God did not ask the Israelites to help Him save them. He simply said, in essence, "Stand back and watch Me do it." And so the sacrifice and application of blood was not a "work," but a demonstration of the faith response by those who heard God's plan for deliverance and believed it. The Israelites were saved by faith, not by their own works. And that pattern is demonstrated throughout the Bible. Salvation is always by grace, through faith, based on blood—ultimately the blood of Christ (Heb. 10:4, 10–14).

Yahweh's salvation came to its culmination in redemptive history when Jesus, the Lamb of God, shed His blood for a world of lost and dying sinners. All the previous Passovers pointed to this singular event. Reflecting on Christ's sacrifice at the cross, Paul wrote, "For Christ, our Passover lamb, has been sacrificed" (1 Cor. 5:7). The "good news" of the gospel is that there is salvation through Christ, the Savior of the world.

LEVITICUS: THE HOLINESS OF GOD

God's holiness and the consequent separation of His chosen people from sin and defilement are the central theme of Leviticus. But what does the Bible mean when it uses the term *holy*? *Qōdeš*, the Hebrew word for holiness, conveys the idea of "separateness" (Lev. 20:26). The word *qōdeš* does not mean primarily moral rectitude, though ethical or moral holiness does stem from the idea of being separate (11:44; 19:2). What is "holy" is marked off, separated, and withdrawn from ordinary use. Holiness is considered the opposite of *ḥōl*, "profaneness," that is, "commonness" (10:10; Ezek. 22:26). The fact that holiness does not necessarily refer to moral purity is seen in that a Canaanite temple prostitute was separated for religious service and called a *qᵉdēšâ* (Deut. 23:18), but of course in an unholy relationship.

When we read that the Lord is holy, we are to understand that He is totally and absolutely *separated* from anything defiling or contrary to His character. While the attribute of "holiness" emphasizes God's transcendence, we discover that His holiness is not exclusive, but draws others to be "separated" to Him. To the people of Israel, He said, "You are to be holy to me because I, the LORD, am holy, and I have set you apart from the nations to be my own" (Lev. 20:26). Even inanimate objects, like a grain offering (2:3) or a house (27:14), may be considered "holy" if they are separated to God. When people are said to be separated or set apart to God, who is righteous, holiness takes on the meaning of moral purity—conformity to God's righteous standards and statutes (20:7–8).

One of the most powerful lessons regarding the holiness of God is found in Leviticus 10. On the very day the priests were consecrated and daily sacrifices began, two of Aaron's sons, Nadab and Abihu, lost their lives for violating the priestly ritual. In their excitement over the descent of the fire from heaven which consumed the sacrifice on the altar, Nadab and Abihu took some personal liberties, offering incense at an improper time and in an improper way (10:1). The fire was "unauthorized" since it was contrary to the prescribed priestly service. As a result, Nadab and Abihu were slain by the Lord in the tabernacle court.

What was so bad about these priests' actions that it cost them their lives? Moses explained their deaths to Aaron: "This is what the LORD spoke of when he said: 'Among those who approach me I will show myself holy; in the sight of all the people I will be honored'" (10:3). Nadab and Abihu's sin was their failure to treat God as holy. If this attribute is ignored or neglected, He will demonstrate His holiness through judgment on sin.

Leviticus 20:22–26 contains central truths of the book relating to the holiness of God. First, God is holy, being both transcendent and separated from all moral impurity. Second, Israel had been separated from the other nations by God's sovereign choice. Third, because Israel was separated from the other nations to serve and glorify God, the people were to observe Yahweh's commands, which prescribed the path for a separated and morally pure life. The Israelites were to lead holy, separated lives because Yahweh is holy and His people are intimately related to Him. Moral purity is a logical outgrowth of the concept of holiness. Those who are separated to the Lord must live in conformity with His righteous standards.

Like God's sovereignty and salvation, His holiness is a theological theme that is developed throughout Scripture. Moses spoke of God as being "majestic in holiness" (Exod. 15:11). Peter confessed Jesus as "the Holy One of God" (John 6:69), and he referred to Jesus as "the Holy and Righteous One" (Acts 3:14). The holiness of God is recognized by the four "living creatures" in John's vision, who declare "Holy, holy, holy is the Lord God Almighty" (Rev. 4:8). And in Revelation 15:4 saints in heaven sing a song that includes the words "You alone are holy." Peter summoned God's children to be like their Father in purity of heart and life: "But just as he who called you is holy, so be holy in all you do; for it is written: 'Be holy, because I am holy'" (1 Pet. 1:15–16).

NUMBERS: THE WRATH OF GOD

The Book of Numbers introduces us to an easily misunderstood aspect of God's character—His divine wrath. In the Old Testament the expressions "the wrath of the LORD," "the wrath of God," and "the anger of the LORD" occur with surprising frequency—about 375 times. In fact, the Bible includes more references to God's anger, fury, and wrath than to His love and tenderness.[1]

God's wrath is the logical and necessary response of His holiness and righteousness to the presence of sin. Yahweh's wrath is the natural expression of His holiness manifesting itself against willful sin and rebellion.

An example of God's holy wrath against sin is seen in Numbers 11:1–3. After just three days of travel from Mount Sinai, the Israelites began to murmur and complain about their circumstances. This reflected their ingratitude to God for His past mercies and their lack of faith in His provision for present needs. The Lord's "anger was aroused. Then fire from the LORD burned among them and consumed some of the outskirts of the camp" (Num. 11:1). Moses named the place *Taberah* ("burning") because of the burning judgment of the Lord (11:3).

God's wrath was displayed again when the Israelites began eating the quail God had sent into the camp. Moses reported, "While the meat was still between their teeth and before it could be consumed, the anger of the LORD burned against the people, and he struck them with a severe plague" (11:33). Moses named the place *Kibroth-Hattaavah* ("the graves of greediness"), suggesting perhaps that they lacked faith in the adequacy of God's provision (Num. 11:34). God's wrath is seen again in the judgment on Miriam (12:9–10) and the destruction of the followers of the rebel Levite Korah (16:31–33).

Numbers teaches us that because of His mercy and patience (14:18) the Lord can let His wrath operate gently, providing opportunity for sinners to repent. God's wrath can also be propitiated or turned aside by an offering or by intercession. When the Israelites rebelled against the Lord at Kadesh Barnea and sought a leader to take them back to Egypt, Moses' intercessory prayer staved off God's judgment (14:11–20). When the Israelites complained that Moses and Aaron had caused the deaths of Korah and his followers, the plague manifesting God's wrath was checked by Moses' sacrifice (16:46–48).

The psalmist Asaph recalled God's anger against Israel: "God's anger rose against them" (Ps. 78:31). In Psalm 90, the only psalm written by Moses, the great leader of Israel spoke of God's wrath: "Who knows the power of your anger? For your wrath is as great as the fear that is due you" (90:11). Many other verses speak of God's wrath, including Psalms 21:9; 95:11; 106:23; Isaiah 10:6; 60:10; Jeremiah 7:29; 10:10; Hosea 5:10; 13:11. Some have questioned whether the wrath of God is compatible with His divine love. Actually there is no inconsistency in affirming both. Leon Morris offers this helpful comment: "The love of God is a love which is so jealous for the right and for the good of the loved one that it blazes out in fiery wrath against everything that is evil."[2] Without His wrath, "Yahweh would cease to be fully righteous and His love would degenerate into sentimentality."[3] In addition, as J. I. Packer points out, God's wrath "is always judicial—that is, it is the wrath of the Judge, administering justice."[4] Romans 2:5–6 underscore that His wrath is based on justice, not unfair cruelty.

While the wrath of God is prominent in the Old Testament, it is revealed in the New Testament as well.[5] Only faith in God's Son, who has satisfied God's wrath (Rom. 3:25; 1 John 2:2), can save sinners from divine judgment.

DEUTERONOMY: THE LOVE OF GOD

Deuteronomy most clearly presents Yahweh's love for His people and the necessity for His people to love Him in return. William Moran has pointed out that this love of God in Deuteronomy is a love defined by and pledged in the covenant—a "covenantal love."[6] Extrabiblical texts dating from the eighteenth to the seventh centuries B.C. use the term *love* to describe the loyalty and friendship that unites independent kings, as well as kings and their subjects. As the sovereign was expected to love his subjects, so the people were to love their sovereign.

A key passage on the love of God in Deuteronomy is 7:7–11. Yahweh did not love Israel because they were more or better than the people of the other nations (7:7). Rather, God chose to commit Himself to the people in keeping with His covenant to their forefathers. Yahweh's love is His undeserved, selective affection by which He binds Himself to His people and which results in their redemption from bondage. The redeemed are thus obligated to demonstrate their love for God in return.

The ancient kings demanded an oath of allegiance from their subjects, expressed in terms of love. And so Yahweh, in establishing His covenant with Israel, demanded love and obedience on the part of His people. God told them, "Love the LORD your God with all your heart and with all your soul and with all your strength" (6:5). This is a love which can be commanded and may be defined in terms of loyalty (11:1, 22), service (10:12; 11:13), and obedience (10:12; 19:9).

The concept of God's love in Deuteronomy clarifies the fact that His relationship with His people under the covenant was one of love rather than legalism (4:37; 7:13; 33:3). This love is a personal devotion created and sustained by God in the human heart (30:6). Love for Yahweh involves the heart, soul, and might—one's total personality. This love cannot be demonstrated in superficial obedience that is not a result of heartfelt conviction (6:5; 13:3). In light of this background, the words of Jesus have greater meaning: "If you love me, you will obey what I command" (John 14:15).

While the love of God is introduced in Deuteronomy, this theme is highlighted throughout the Bible. The Book of Hosea uses the tragedies of the prophet's marriage and family life to illustrate God's unceasing love for His people in spite of their unfaithfulness (Hosea 1–3). God keeps on loving even when His people are unfaithful. Sin and failure do not decrease God's love, although they may result in unpleasant consequences for us.

John 3:16 teaches that God loves men and women so much that He gave His Son Jesus to die for our sins. God's love is a giving, sacrificing love. In Romans 5:8 Paul emphasized that God took the initiative in exercising love. "But God demonstrates his own love for us in this: While we were still sinners, Christ died for us." Paul presented God's example of sacrificial love as a pattern for believers to follow (Eph. 5:1–2).

In his classic exposition on love, John wrote, "God is love" (1 John 4:8), a love that was profoundly demonstrated in the incarnation of Jesus Christ (4:10). As believers, we are to love because He first loved us (4:11, 19). In Dostoevsky's *The Brothers Karamazov*, Father Zossima said that the lack of love is the punishment as well as the substance of sin. To the question "What is hell?" Father Zossima replied, "I maintain that it is the suffering of being unable to love." He then presented the appeal: "Love a man even in his sin, for that is the semblance of Divine love and is the highest love on earth."[7]

LESSONS FROM THE PENTATEUCH

The first five books of the Bible teach us some fundamental lessons about God. These are basic truths that anyone who wants to know God better must recognize and apply. They are so important that I ask my seminary students to memorize them.

- Genesis: God is the supreme Sovereign.

- Exodus: God is the powerful Savior.

- Leviticus: God is absolutely holy.

- Numbers: God is a wrathful Judge.

- Deuteronomy: God is rich in love.

Taken together, these truths reveal much about God and His purposes: The sovereign God, being absolutely holy, must respond with wrath to displays of sin. But being rich in love, he provides a way of salvation to those who submit themselves to Him by faith.

For Further Study

Merrill, Eugene H.. "A Theology of the Pentateuch." In *A Biblical Theology of the Old Testament.* Edited by Roy B. Zuck. Chicago: Moody Press, 1991.

Packer, J. I. *Knowing God.* Downers Grove, Ill.: InterVarsity Press, 1975.

7

THE GREATNESS OF GOD

Great is the LORD and most worthy of praise; his greatness no one can fathom. . . . They will speak of the glorious splendor of your majesty, and I will meditate on your wonderful works. They will tell of the power of your awesome works, and I will proclaim your great deeds.

—*Psalm 145:3, 5–6*

PEOPLE OFTEN USE certain terms to describe other individuals' personalities. We say a person is shy or reserved, and we refer to another person as optimistic and outgoing. Someone else might be described as sullen or easily depressed. Psychologists have developed this approach into quite a science, constructing personality tests that can often tell us more about what a person is really like. Such examination can give us insights into a person's character beyond what may be a superficial exterior.

No one has constructed a personality test to help us get to know God. But He has given in the Bible many descriptions of His most fundamental character traits. These are usually referred to as His "attributes." One theologian has defined God's attributes as "those distinguishing characteristics of the divine nature which are inseparable from the idea of God and which constitute the basis and ground for his various manifestations to his creatures."[1] Of course, God's attributes are distinguishable from His works, but they are not unrelated. Obviously, what God *is* constitutes a key factor in what He *does*. Also God's attributes do not add anything to Him. Rather, they reveal His nature, what He is like.

Many theologians have sought to categorize or group the attributes of God. Herman Bavinck, Louis Berkhof, Charles Hodge, William Shedd, and others follow with some variations the categories that appear in the

Westminster Confession. Others, such as J. Oliver Buswell Jr., and Charles Ryrie, don't categorize the attributes. Most often God's attributes are classified under two categories that stand in contrast to each other. Frequent classifications include *absolute* and *relative* (A. H. Strong), *incommunicable* and *communicable* (William G. T. Shedd, Louis Berkhof), *moral* and *nonmoral* (Henry C. Thiessen).[2] These categories are not hard and fast, and theologians continue to debate which attributes fall into which category. More important than the categories are the attributes themselves and what they reveal about God.

Two things stand out in the Bible concerning God. He is *great* (Neh. 9:32; Ps. 77:13) and He is *good* (34:8; 100:5; Nah. 1:7). His greatness and goodness form the basis of the praise that His people present to Him (Ezra 3:11; Pss. 48:1; 96:4). I suggest that these two characteristics serve as the most basic categories within which God's attributes may be considered. The validity of this grouping has been recognized by other theologians as well.[3]

This chapter examines the attributes that emphasize God's greatness and uniqueness, and the following chapter focuses on God's goodness and those attributes that provide the basis of His benevolent dealings with humanity. The order in which these attributes are discussed is not intended to reflect their priority or importance.

GOD IS SPIRIT

Among the most basic of God's attributes is the fact that He is a spiritual being. God is not composed of physical material. In Jesus' discussion with the Samaritan woman He spoke of this attribute: "God is spirit, and his worshipers must worship in spirit and truth" (John 4:24). The spiritual nature of God is also suggested by various references to Him as "invisible" (Col. 1:15; 1 Tim. 1:17; Heb. 11:27). Also Jesus said that no one has seen God the Father (John 1:18; 5:37; 6:46).

The fact that God is spirit distinguishes the true God from idolatrous forms of worship that were so prevalent in biblical times. The true God, being spirit, cannot be likened to any physical form. So the Israelites were instructed in the first of the Ten Commandments not to make any idol or physical likeness of God (Exod. 20:4). Isaiah mocked the idolater who makes an image for worship and then fastens it with nails so it won't fall over (Isa. 41:7). To represent God physically is to misrepresent Him and to mislead and deceive others.

One might object to this attribute by citing references to God's physical features such as His face, hands, and back (Exod. 33:20–23). But these are simply a way of expressing spiritual truths about God through human analogy. When God said of Israel, "See, I have engraved you on the palms of my hands" (Isa. 49:16), He was simply saying by analogy that His people will not be forgotten or neglected. It is as if God tied a string around His finger to remind Himself to care for Israel. Any references to God's physical features (for example, His eyes, face, arm) are anthropomorphisms and should not be taken literally.

The fact that God is a spiritual being has implications for worship. The point Jesus was making with the Samaritan woman is that it doesn't matter whether you worship on Mount Gerizim or at the temple mount in Jerusalem. Worship must focus on spiritual realities, not physical formalities, and should not be limited by time or place. As Christians, we must worship God "in spirit and in truth" (John 4:24), that is, in a manner consistent with His true, spiritual nature.

GOD IS LIVING

Contrary to the teachings of German philosopher Friedrich Nietzsche (1844–1890), God is *not* dead. According to the Bible, He is very much alive and active. The psalmist cried out, "My soul thirsts for God, for the living God" (Ps. 42:2). Jeremiah said, "But the LORD is the true God; he is the living God, the eternal King" (Jer. 10:10). Peter confessed that Jesus is the Messiah, "the Son of the living God" (Matt. 16:16). Paul acknowledged that the Thessalonians turned from their idols to serve the "living and true God" (1 Thess. 1:9). He reminded Timothy that we believers "have put our hope in the living God" (1 Tim. 4:10). The divine Being in John's apocalyptic vision declared, "I am the First and the Last. I am the Living One; I was dead, and behold I am for ever and ever!" (Rev. 1:17–18).

The life God possesses differs from the life enjoyed by other living things.

Our physical lives have a beginning and an end. But the life God possesses is eternal. Life is intrinsic to His very nature. Jesus said He "has life in himself" (John 5:26). His life has neither a beginning nor an ending. Another significant feature about God's life is that it does not depend on anything or anyone. Our lives depend on food, water, sleep, oxygen, and a host of other necessities. Paul pointed out to the Athenians that God is neither "served by human hands, as if he needed anything, because he himself gives all men life and breath and everything else" (Acts 17:25).

The fact that God possesses the attribute of life has significant implications for us. As Creator, God has life in Himself and is able to impart that life to others (Gen. 2:7). Jesus drew on this truth when He told His accusers, "For just as the Father raises the dead and gives them life, even so the Son gives life to whom he is pleased to give it" (John 5:21). Both the Father and Son have life in themselves and therefore can extend eternal life to those who are spiritually dead (5:24) and resurrection life to those who are physically dead (5:28–29). The fact that God is living means that those who place their faith in Him enter into His own eternal life. Those who reject Him miss out on that opportunity forever.

GOD IS ETERNAL

God is eternal, that is, He has always existed and always will. Genesis 1:1 affirms God's existence at the very beginning of time, "In the beginning God . . . " While creation had a beginning point in time, God had no such beginning. Moses referred to God as "the eternal God" (Deut. 33:27) and Paul did the same (Rom. 16:26). Although it is impossible to comprehend, God existed from eternity past and will continue to exist throughout eternity future. In Psalm 90:2 Moses declared, "Before the mountains were born or you brought forth the earth and the world, from everlasting to everlasting you are God." And Isaiah referred to Him as the "everlasting God" (Isa. 40:28). The fact of God's eternal existence is intrinsic to His own name, Yahweh, which probably means, as discussed earlier, "The One Who Is."

God's eternality has significant implications. Because He is eternal, He is not bound by the limitations of time. He is able to look back forever and forward forever. He sees the past and the future as if they are the present. And while human beings are limited in their knowledge by succession of events, God knows no such limitation. For example, I can't know who my daughters-in-law will be since my sons are not yet married. But God knows who my daughters-in-law will be because He sees the future as I see the present. The fact that God is eternal gives me confidence in His plan for my life. Nothing ever takes Him by surprise. He is "the First and . . . the Last," "the Alpha and the Omega," "the Beginning and the End" (Isa. 44:6; Rev. 1:8; 21:6). He knows "the end from the beginning" (Isa. 46:10) and everything in between.

GOD IS ALL-KNOWING

The Bible teaches that God knows everything. As the apostle John wrote, "God is greater than our hearts, and he knows everything" (1 John 3:20). Peter referred to this attribute when he said to Jesus, "Lord, you know all things; you know that I love you" (John 21:17). Theologians call this attribute omniscience, from the Latin *omni*, "all," and *scientia*, "knowledge." The biblical doctrine of omniscience means that God—by His divine nature and without the effort of learning—knows all things, past, present, and future. Several things can be said about His omniscience.

First, God knows all things that exist in actuality. The writer of Hebrews declared, "Nothing in all creation is hidden from God's sight. Everything is uncovered and laid bare before the eyes of him to whom we must give account" (Heb. 4:13). David prayed, "You discern my going out and my lying down; you are familiar with all my ways. Before a word is on my tongue you know it completely, O LORD" (Ps. 139:3–4). Jesus said that our heavenly Father "knows what you need before you ask him" (Matt. 6:8). God knows when a sparrow falls to the ground (10:29). He even knows the number of hairs on our heads (10:30), and He knows what is in our hearts (1 Sam. 16:7; Luke 16:15; John 2:25) and thoughts (Ezek. 11:6).

Second, God knows all future events. This is the basis for predictive prophecy. Because God knows the future, Isaiah was able to announce the coming of Cyrus to deliver the Jews from Babylon about 150 years before the event (Isa. 45:1–3). Because God knows the future, Daniel was able to predict the rise and fall of nations that would dominate Israel (Dan. 2:36–43; 7:4–8). Because God knows the future, Zechariah was able to predict that Jesus would ride into Jerusalem on the colt of a donkey (Zech. 9:9; Matt. 21:1–7). Because God knows the future, the authors of Scripture have been able to announce the coming of such eschatological events as the Rapture, the Tribulation, the millennial kingdom, and the new heavens and new earth. God knows the future because He *controls* the future. He "works out everything in conformity with the purpose of his will" (Eph. 1:11).

Third, God knows things that might have happened had the variables been different. For example, He knew that the people of Tyre and Sidon would have repented had they witnessed the miracles that occurred in Chorazin and Bethsaida (Matt. 11:21).

Because God is able to see beyond the surface and has access to all information, we know that His judgments and decisions are wise and just. Because God knows everything, He can hold us accountable for our unseen attitudes as well as our actions. Because God knows all potential outcomes of our possible actions, we must trust His leading along the path of life.

Some might wonder why believers should be encouraged to bring their prayer concerns to God if He already knows our needs. Good question! It is important to realize that prayer involves much more than giving God a wish list. If the only time my children communicated with me was to send me their Christmas list, I would be disappointed. Prayer is communication with God. And He delights in the communication and the fellowship it involves. God knows our needs, but He still invites us to pray (Phil. 4:6; 1 Thess. 5:17). I am pleased when my children approach me with their requests. It gives us a chance to talk and an opportunity for me to express my love. I am confident that God delights in hearing our prayers, even though He knows our needs even before we tell Him.

GOD IS ALL-POWERFUL

Another fact about God is that He is all-powerful or omnipotent. The word omnipotent comes from the Latin words *omni,* "all" and *potens,* "powerful." God's omnipotence means that He is able to do anything that is according to His will. Gabriel announced this truth when Mary was told that she would become the mother of the Messiah: "For nothing is impossible with God" (Luke 1:37). Jesus Himself told His disciples, "with God all things are possible" (Matt. 19:26). God describes Himself as "the Almighty" (Rev. 1:8).

God's omnipotence is displayed in the biblical account of creation. When God said, "Let there be light" (Gen. 1:3), light came into existence. This pattern is evident in the six days of creation as God spoke creation into existence. He did this all by His almighty power. David acknowledged, "The voice of the LORD is powerful" (Ps. 29:4). Reflecting on the power of God, Jeremiah prayed, "Ah, Sovereign LORD, you have made the heavens and the earth by your great power and outstretched arm. Nothing is too hard for you" (Jer. 32:17).

Israel's exodus from Egypt serves as another display of God's great power (Exod. 14:31). After delivering Israel across the Red Sea and destroying the Egyptians, Moses exclaimed, "Your right hand, O LORD, was majestic in power" (15:6). When the Israelites in the wilderness were worried about where they would get their next meal, God asked Moses, "Is the LORD's power limited?" (Num. 11:23, NASB). The implied answer is no. The all-powerful God is able to meet the needs of His people.

God's absolute power is evident in His ability to move the events of history (Isa. 14:26–27). He is able to bring all events and all people to their predetermined end (Eph. 1:11; Rom. 8:29–30). Even in the face of sin and disobedience, God's eternal purposes are not frustrated by human rebellion. Instead, His purposes are fulfilled (John 12:37–40; 17:12; Acts 2:23; 4:27–28).

While God's power is displayed in creation, the Exodus, and in His control of history, the greatest display of His omnipotence is in our salvation. The gospel is the "power of God" for salvation (Rom. 1:16). Jesus was anointed "with the Holy Spirit and power" (Acts 10:38). His resurrection displayed God's power (Phil. 3:10). And God's power is displayed in His ability to save those who believe in Christ and to keep them saved (1 Cor. 1:18; 6:14; 1 Pet. 1:5).

While God is omnipotent, the Bible says there are some things He cannot do. These are the things which are not in harmony with His nature. God cannot sin or approve evil (Hab. 1:13; James 1:13), He cannot lie (Heb. 6:18), and He cannot be unfaithful or break His promises (2 Tim. 2:13; Heb. 13:5). Nor can He do anything that by definition is impossible such as making a square circle, a round rectangle, or a four-sided triangle.

When we face insurmountable difficulties and threatening circumstances, it is good for us to remember that nothing is too difficult for the Lord, just as an angel reminded Abraham (Gen. 18:14). How encouraging to know that the all-powerful God imparts His strength to His people. Those who rely on the Lord will "soar on wings like eagles" (Isa. 40:31). They will be able to do "everything" through Christ who strengthens them (Phil. 4:13).

Once a man approached Jesus, asking Him to deliver his son from an evil spirit that caused epilepsy. He had asked Jesus' disciples to cast out the demon, but they were unable to do so. So in desperation, the boy's father appealed to Jesus, "But if you can do anything, take pity on us and help us" (Mark 9:22). Jesus answered, "'If you can'? . . . Everything is possible for him who believes" (9:23). The boy's father was wondering if Jesus had the power to deliver the demon-possessed boy. Jesus pointed out that it was not an issue of His divine power, but an issue of the father's belief. God is unlimited in His ability to accomplish great things for those who will approach Him with belief. What an encouragement to know that we serve the all-powerful God!

GOD IS EVERYWHERE PRESENT

Because God is spirit, rather than a physical being, He is able to be everywhere at once. David was reflecting on this truth when he wrote, "Where can I go from your Spirit? Where can I flee from your presence? If I go up to the heavens, you are there; if I make my bed in the depths, you are there. If I rise on the wings of the dawn, if I settle on the far side of the sea, even there your hand will guide me, your right hand will hold me fast" (Ps. 139:7–10). This is the doctrine of God's omnipresence, which means that God is present everywhere. God, in the totality of His existence, is present throughout the universe.

It is important to distinguish the biblical doctrine of God's omnipresence from the false view of pantheism. Omniscience states that God is present everywhere, though separate from the world and the things in it. Pantheism, on the other hand, teaches that God is *in* everything. The Bible affirms that God is present with you as you read this book, whereas pantheism teaches that God is in the chair in which you're sitting. Pantheism distorts the doctrine of God's immanence (presence) by failing to recognize that God is active in His creation, but is not to be identified with it.

David recognized that there is no place where he could go where God could not be found. Nowhere in His creation is God absent or inaccessible. Jeremiah quoted God as saying, "Am I only a God nearby. . . . and not a God far away?" (Jer. 23:23). The implication seems to be that God is both "near" and "far off." The Lord points out in the next verse that there is no place in creation where a man can hide from the presence of God. "Do not I fill heaven and earth?" (23:24).

The doctrine of God's omnipresence is revealed in the name "Immanuel," a designation ultimately fulfilled in Christ (Isa. 7:14; Matt. 1:23). The Hebrew name literally means "God with us." In Jesus Christ, God is present among His people. Jesus advanced this thought when He told His disciples, "For where two or three come together in my name, there am I with them" (Matt. 18:20). At the end of His earthly ministry, He commissioned the apostles to "make disciples" (28:19) and He promised them, "Surely I am with you always, to the very end of the age" (28:20). He would be with each of the disciples as they dispersed from Jerusalem for ministry throughout the world.

When danger threatens or calamity strikes, we can be assured of God's personal presence to comfort and calm us. How comforting are His words, "Never will I leave you; never will I forsake you" (Heb. 13:5). Jesus is the Good Shepherd who never leaves His sheep in a time of danger (John 10:11–12). The doctrine of God's omniscience also serves as a warning for those who would contemplate sin and disobedience. God does not absent Himself from those who displease Him. He is present at every lie, theft, and adultery. He is present when we are watching television, telling a joke, and completing our income-tax forms. I wonder how differently believers would behave if they truly believed God is personally present with them everywhere and at all times.

GOD IS CONSTANT

In a world that is so characterized by change, it is reassuring to know that there is at least One who is constant. God doesn't change. He is unchanging and unchangeable. Theologians call this the attribute of immutability. James wrote that God consistently gives only good gifts. "Every good and perfect gift is from above, coming down from the Father of the heavenly lights, who does not change like shifting shadows" (James 1:17). In Malachi 3:6, God declared through the prophet, "I the LORD do not change. So you, O descendants of Jacob, are not destroyed." If God were liable to change, He might have been willing to break His promise and destroy a sinful nation (Ps. 89:34). But Israel owes her continued existence to the unchanging purpose and character of God! An anonymous psalmist declared that while the heavens and the earth will "perish," "wear out," and "change," God remains the same forever (102:26–27).

However, does the Bible teach that God changes His mind? Exodus 32:14 records that "the LORD changed His mind about the harm which He said He would do to His people" (NASB). In 1 Samuel 15:11 the Lord said, "I regret that I have made Saul king" (NASB). Jonah 3:10 (NASB) records that God "relented concerning the calamity which He had declared He would bring upon" the people of Nineveh. The Hebrew verb used in each of these passages is *nāham* ("to be sorry, repent, regret"), attributing to Him a human kind of response. From our limited vantage point, it may *seem* that God's purposes have changed. When people repent in response to prophetic warnings, He withholds judgment. But He has not actually changed His mind or purposes; He has simply responded to repentance with a manifestation of grace. For further discussion on this issue see chapter 20, "Answers to Tough Questions about God."

The fact that God does not change provides a strong theological basis for the believer's security and hope. God's immutability means that His plans and purposes are not subject to alteration or modification. When Balaam was hired to curse Israel, God directed him to declare, "God is not a man, that he should lie, nor a son of man, that he should change his mind. Does he speak and then not act? Does he promise and not fulfill? I have received a command to bless; he has blessed, and I cannot change it"

(Num. 23:19–20). What God has purposed to do will in fact be accomplished. The promises and covenants of God will be fulfilled.

GOD IS INDEPENDENT

God is completely free and independent. He "has life in himself" (John 5:26), and this life is totally independent of others. He has no needs that must be fulfilled by His creation or by humanity. He has no plans that have been imposed by others. His works are self-determined instead of being influenced by the thoughts, feelings, and plans of anyone else. Isaiah had this attribute of God in mind when he wrote, "Who has understood the mind of the LORD, or instructed him as his counselor? Whom did the LORD consult to enlighten him, and who taught him the right way? Who was it that taught him knowledge or showed him the path of understanding?" (Isa. 40:13–14). Apparently drawing from Isaiah's thought, Paul wrote, "Who has ever given to God, that God should repay him?" (Rom. 11:35). In other words, is God anyone's debtor? Is He under obligation to anyone? The answer is no. God is absolutely free.

God is free to accomplish good according to His will (Eph. 1:5). He is also free to permit evil, though with divine displeasure (Acts 2:23). God is free to choose some for Himself (Mal. 1:2; Eph. 1:4), and He is free to pass over others (Mal. 1:3; Rom. 9:22). He is free to kill and free to give life (1 Sam. 2:6). He is free to exalt the lowly and free to humble the proud (2:7–8). He is free to raise dead saints and give them life (John 5:21), and He is free to raise the dead and execute judgment (5:27, 29).

While God is absolutely independent and free, there are some things He cannot do because they are contrary to His own nature. For example, He cannot lie (Heb. 6:18), be unfaithful (2 Tim. 2:13), or do evil (Hab. 1:13; James 1:13). The inability to sin should not be viewed as weakness in His nature; instead it reflects divine consistency of His character and attributes.

Because God is free and independent, there is nothing He needs that we might offer Him. In no way have we contributed anything to God so as to merit His attention or concern. Nothing God has done for us has been done out of a sense of obligation. All that He has done for us is out of His love and compassion. And there is no way we can pay Him back for these blessings since He has no needs. Understanding the freedom of God helps us appreciate the greatness of divine grace.

GOD IS INSCRUTABLE

One of the most important attributes to reflect on when considering the nature of God is His inscrutability. When we affirm that God is inscrutable we are saying that there remains a mystery about His person which is beyond our comprehension in spite of careful study. Paul addressed this fact when he wrote, "Oh, the depth of the riches of the wisdom and knowledge of God! How unsearchable his judgments, and his paths beyond tracing out! Who has known the mind of the Lord" (Rom. 11:33–34).

God has revealed so much of Himself to humans through both general and special revelation. This revelation enables us to know Him and to know Him well. But there remains much of God that is hidden. Job recognized that God "performs wonders that cannot be fathomed, miracles that cannot be counted" (Job. 9:10). To Zophar's questions, "Can you fathom the mysteries of God? Can you probe the limits of the Almighty?" we must answer a resounding no. While God is "a revealer of mysteries" (Dan. 2:47), He retains some mystery about Himself. God can be known, but not dissected and analyzed. He can be comprehended, but not completely. Some things belong to Him as secrets (Deut. 29:29).

Too often budding theologians analyze God to such an extent that they attempt to remove the mystery of His divine being. Unfortunately they end up with something that is far less than God. They end up with a mini-God, a God who is limited by their own finite understanding. As Christians, we must pursue our knowledge of God. But at the same time we must take care that our theological analysis does not diminish the mystery of His divine being.

For Further Study

Erickson, Millard J. *God the Father Almighty.* Grand Rapids: Baker Book House, 1998.

Packer, J. I. *Knowing God.* Downers Grove, Ill.: InterVarsity Press, 1973.

Pink, Arthur W. *Gleanings in the Godhead.* Chicago: Moody Press, 1975.

Tozer, A. W. *The Knowledge of the Holy.* New York: Harper & Brothers, 1961.

8

THE GOODNESS OF GOD

Taste and see that the LORD is good; blessed is the man who takes refuge in him.

—Psalm 34:8

I RECENTLY BEGAN A MAJOR PROJECT in my garage. I am restoring a 1944 Ford GPW, commonly known as a military jeep. My dad purchased the vehicle in 1967 for me to drive while attending college. It had been modified by the previous owner into a hunting rig. With some further additions, like a roll bar and canvas top, our jeep became a classy means of transportation during my four years at the University of Oregon. Each of my brothers drove the family jeep during their college days, but since then it has been parked and is collecting rust.

While surfing the Internet, I discovered that such jeeps are highly prized by those with an interest in military vehicles. After some reading on the subject, I decided to restore our family jeep to its original 1944 condition and thus preserve a bit of American military history. What a project this has become! First, I had to strip away all the modifications that had been added over the years. Off came the roll bar, wide tires, and white vinyl top. Then I began my search for original or replacement parts. After a long search I found four combat rims with military tires. I located a man in Australia who manufactures new gas tanks for old military jeeps. Through the Internet I ordered a replacement bumper, a new gas line, and a mounting bracket for the spare tire.

Although the jeep was in fairly good shape, the underside was coated with a mixture of greasy grime, hard mud, and heavy rust. I have spent hours under the vehicle with a face mask and eye guards, grinding, sanding, and cleaning. A friend helped me rebuild the carburetor. Every gas jet was removed and cleaned. We replaced the float, springs, and gaskets.

I hesitate to guess the hours I have spent in my garage working on this jeep. One thing is for sure: I am really getting to know this vehicle. I have read books and articles about the development and history of military jeeps. I have studied the maintenance manual and wiring charts. I have spent more hours under the jeep than under any other vehicle I have owned. I know the parts, the specifications, and the problems with my jeep. I know this jeep because I have spent time with it. And in my labors I have grown rather fond of this old vehicle. I wouldn't trade it for anything—not even a new Jeep Wrangler!

What's my point here? Well, this book is about knowing God better. And it is my strong conviction that we'll not get to know Him better unless we are spending time with Him, studying His attributes, learning about His plans and purposes, and discovering His will for our lives. Sadly, there are people who spend years getting to know their car, their boat, or their mountain cabin, and never spend any time getting to know their own Creator! In this chapter we want to get to know God better by studying those attributes that reflect His goodness toward humankind.

In the previous chapter we discussed attributes that are uniquely true of God, like His omnipotence, omnipresence, and omniscience. These attributes reflect the fact that He is a unique, supernatural being. The attributes discussed in this chapter can in some measure also be ascribed to people. These are sometimes referred to as God's communicable attributes. They are qualities that God exhibits in absolute perfection that believers are called on to emulate (Matt. 5:48). God's moral attributes provide a pattern or example for godly Christian living. As Paul said, "Be imitators of God . . . as dearly loved children" (Eph. 5:1).

GOD IS GOOD

In the Bible the concept of "good" is indissolubly linked with God. God is good. He does what is good, and He is the ultimate Source of all that is good. The psalmist frequently affirmed that the Lord is good (Pss. 34:8; 86:5; 100:5; 118:1, 29; 135:3; 136:1). The prophets too recognized God's goodness (Jer. 33:11; Nah. 1:7). In His conversation with a ruler of the Jews, Jesus said that in fact only God is truly good (Luke 18:19).

The Hebrew word for "good" describes what is pleasant, agreeable, and beneficial. Besides describing God's character, it also describes His actions. In Psalm 119:68, the psalmist wrote, "You are good, and what you do is good." That God is a source of good is evident from the biblical account of creation. With each act of creation God said it was "good" (Gen. 1:4, 10, 12, 18, 21, 25, 31). That God intended good for His creation is evidenced in the creation account by the repeated reference to blessing. God "blessed" the first couple (1:22, 28), and He blessed the "seventh day" (2:3). Contemplating the goodness of God, David exclaimed, "How great is your goodness, which you have stored up for those who fear you" (Ps. 31:19).

James, the brother of our Lord, remarked that since God does not change, He will never alter His pattern of giving only good gifts. "Every good and perfect gift is from above, coming down from the Father of the heavenly lights, who does not change like shifting shadows" (James 1:17). The expressions of God's goodness are not limited to believers. Paul told the unbelieving people at Lystra that God "did good and gave you rains from heaven and fruitful seasons, satisfying your hearts with food and gladness" (Acts 14:17, NASB).

The goodness of God is particularly featured in His Son Jesus who identified Himself as "the good shepherd" (John 10:11, 14). His benevolence as our Shepherd is seen in the fact that He laid down His life for us, the sheep. Unlike the hired hand who has little personal interest in the lives of the sheep and flees at the first sight of danger, Jesus gave Himself sacrificially on the cross for the ultimate good of His people. This selfless act resulted in the good gift of our salvation.

As the Israelites "reveled" in God's "great goodness" (Neh. 9:25), so should we. Not a day should pass without God's people pausing to acknowledge that the Lord is good and that they are the recipients of His good gifts. We have so much of God's goodness for which to be thankful—our lives, our salvation, our food and shelter, our families and friends, our church, our opportunities for ministry.

Sometimes a person who has just received a blessing will say, "Isn't God good?" But we should remember that God is good even when we don't experience His benefits. In other words God doesn't change. He is still good when my car doesn't start, when my roof leaks, and when a loved one dies of cancer. We can demonstrate the depth and genuineness of our faith when we affirm God's goodness even in the midst of difficult times. When Job lost everything, he still blessed God, acknowledging that His intrinsic goodness transcends human experience.

GOD IS HOLY

God is infinitely and absolutely holy. Although we have already considered this attribute in chapter 6 when examining the message of Leviticus, let's take another brief look at this truth.

When we say "God is holy," we mean He is totally separated from all that is unholy, defiling, or contrary to His nature. God's holiness is unique and distinctive in that it is without any contamination or impurity. As Hannah said in her prayer of praise, "There is no one holy like the LORD" (1 Sam. 2:2). So infinitely holy is Yahweh that the angelic creatures called seraphs in Isaiah's vision used the term three times to describe God: "Holy, holy, holy is the LORD Almighty" (Isa. 6:3).

The Levites, the priests, the tabernacle, the altar, and even the land of Israel were set apart for the service of Yahweh and thus were regarded as "holy." Beyond that, the people who were associated with the holy God were called on to be holy. God told His people, "Be holy, because I am holy" (Lev. 11:44–45; see also 14:2; 20:8, 26).

Closely associated with the idea of God's holiness is that of His purity. God's moral purity means He is absolutely free from anything wicked or evil. Habakkuk remarked, "Your eyes are too pure to look on evil" (Hab. 1:13). Since God is pure, all that is associated with Him must be pure. David described God's words and commandments as "pure" (Pss. 12:6; 19:8, NASB). The articles of the tabernacle were to be overlaid with "pure gold" (Exod. 25:11, 17, 24). It seems that our holy God delights in what is pure. Jesus said, "Blessed are the pure in heart, for they will see God" (Matt. 5:8). Our Savior is the ultimate earthly example of a pure and sinless life. And contemplation of His person should have a purifying effect on His people. As John wrote, "Everyone who has this hope in him purifies himself, just as he is pure" (1 John 3:3).

GOD IS RIGHTEOUS

God's righteousness is another dimension of His moral purity. Intrestingly the first one in the Bible to acknowledge that God is righteous was Pharaoh. After being confronted with seven of the ten plagues, he said, "I have sinned this time; the LORD is the righteous one" (Exod. 9:27, NASB). Later Moses told the people of Israel "Righteous and upright is He" (Deut. 32:4, NASB). After God's judgment through the invasion by Shishak, the leaders of Israel acknowledged, " The LORD is righteous" (2 Chron. 12:6, NASB). David declared, "For the LORD is righteous, he loves justice" (Ps. 11:7).

The root meaning of the Hebrew *ṣaddîq* is "straight." What is righteous conforms to a right ethical or moral standard. God's attribute of righteousness means He will always do what is right in His relationships and dealings with others. God's deeds are often described in the Bible as "righteous acts" (1 Sam. 12:7) or "righteous deeds" (Ps. 103:6, NASB). His laws and ways are righteous (119:75; 145:17). What else could we expect of the Lord God whom Isaiah called "the Righteous One" (Isa. 24:16)?

God's righteousness is sometimes expressed through His judgment on sinners and vindication of the innocent (Ps. 7:8–11). But because God is righteous, always measuring up to the standard of His holiness, we may trust His decisions. He will be completely just and fair in His dealings with us. Nebuchadnezzar, after experiencing God's discipline, was able to say that God's works are true and "his ways are just" (Dan. 4:37). And although His sinful people may rightly require His discipline, it is tempered with mercy based on repentance (Ps. 51:14; Hab. 3:2).

The title "the Righteous One," was used by the early church as an appellation for Jesus (Acts 3:14; 7:52; 22:14). John declared that believers have an Advocate with the Father, "Jesus Christ, the Righteous One" (1 John 2:1). In His vision of the final series of judgments in Revelation, John heard an angel say of Christ, "Righteous art Thou, who art and who wast, O Holy One, because Thou didst judge these things" (Rev. 16:5, NASB).

As God's people we can be assured that right will prevail over all that is wrong because God is righteous.

GOD IS LOVE

Although we considered this attribute in chapter 6, we come back to it as one of the major characteristics of our good God. The love of God is fundamental to much of what is true about Him. For out of His love flow His benevolence, grace, mercy, and goodness.

John wrote, "Whoever does not love does not know God, because God is love" (1 John 4:8). *Agapē*, the Greek word used here for "love," refers not to a fleeting feeling or emotional attraction, but to a sacrificial commitment to the ultimate good of another person. This sacrificial *agapē* love was the basis for God's giving His Son to be the Savior of the world. "For God so loved the world that he gave his one and only Son, that whoever believes in him shall not perish but have eternal life" (John 3:16). It is encouraging to know that God's love for us is not conditioned on our moral virtues or obedience to His commands. God did not say, "I'll love you when you repent and become good." If this were the case, none of us could experience God's love. Instead, God said, "I love you just like you are, with your blemishes, faults, and sins." This is clearly evidenced by Paul's words to the Romans: "God demonstrates his own love for us in this: While we were still sinners, Christ died for us" (Rom. 5:8).

Because God's love is based on His unchanging nature rather than our personal behavior, He will never stop loving us. Perhaps you have heard someone say these sad words, "I don't love you anymore." These words would be impossible for God to speak. He told His people Israel, "I have loved you with an everlasting love" (Jer. 31:3). This is equally true of His relationship with the body of Christ, His church (Eph. 5:25). His love is so vast and inexhaustible that, as F. B. Meyer once wrote, "The love of God toward you is like the Amazon River flowing down to water a single daisy."[1]

Sacrificial love elicits a response of love. Stacy Sewell knows this to be true. As a cystic fibrosis patient, she was within weeks of death. Her disease had left her lungs scarred and nearly useless. But she can breathe freely today because of the sacrificial love of her parents. Doctors removed one lobe each from James and Barbara Sewell and then implanted them in their daughter. The lobes act like a full pair of lungs for Stacy. "I feel wonderful," she said after recovering from the surgery. She thanked her parents for undergoing surgery to save her life. "I could not love them any more than I do," she said. "I'll take every breath for them because it's their lungs."[2]

In a similar way God's love for us elicits a response in the hearts of His people. We love Him because of all He has done for us. "We love because he first loved us" (1 John 4:19). And our love for God is demonstrated by our love for others (4:21).

GOD IS FAITHFUL

Moses told the people of Israel, "Know therefore that the LORD your God is God; he is the faithful God, keeping his covenant of love" (Deut. 7:9). The word "faithful" (from the verb ʾāman) carries the idea of being firm or certain. It is used to describe the strong arms of a parent holding a small child. Just as a parent holds a child tightly to prevent injury in a dangerous situation, so our faithful God holds us tightly to Himself with arms that will never let us go.

Pistos, the New Testament word for faithful, has a similar emphasis on what is trustworthy, dependable, and reliable. Writing to the Corinthians, Paul declared three times that God "is faithful" (1 Cor. 1:9; 10:13; 2 Cor. 1:18). Because of His great love for us, we can have full confidence in His protection and care. As with God's love, His faithfulness does not depend on the actions or behavior of His people. Paul wrote to Timothy, "If we are faithless, he will remain faithful, for he cannot disown himself" (2 Tim. 2:13).

One aspect of God's faithfulness is the fact that He is totally dependable. How often have you been disappointed by people who did not fulfill what you expected of them? People are late for appointments or miss them altogether. People say they have forgiven someone only to bring up the matter weeks later. People promise to help on a project and then don't follow through. People disappoint us because they are marked by weakness and sin. But God can always be counted on! You will never be disappointed when you rely on Him (Isa. 28:16; Rom. 10:11).

Because God is faithful, we can count on Him to keep His promises (Heb. 10:23; 11:11). Because God is faithful, we can count on Him to forgive our sins (1 John 1:9). Because God is faithful, we can believe what He has revealed in His Word (Rev. 1:5). Because God is faithful, we can be assured that there is a way out of every temptation (1 Cor. 10:13). Because God is faithful, we know that He can be relied on to complete that spiritual work He has begun in our lives (1 Thess. 5:24). Because God is faithful, we can count on Him to strengthen us and protect us from the evil one (John 17:15). What an encouragement to know the implications of God's faithfulness!

Since God is faithful, He desires that those who are associated with Him emulate His faithfulness. Like God, we must be people who are true to our word (Ps. 15:4; Eccles. 5:4–5). We need to live in such a way that people can trust us because they know we are faithful.

GOD IS TRUE

Yahweh, in contrast with the false deities worshiped by pagan people, is "the true God" (Jer. 10:10). Jesus prayed that His disciples might know "the only true God" (John 17:3). In a world filled with pseudodeities and impostors, there is only one true God. This is the God of Abraham, Isaac, and Jacob. This is the God who has revealed Himself in Jesus, His divine Son. Paul rejoiced over the Thessalonians who "turned to God from idols to serve the living and true God" (1 Thess. 1:9). John identified "the true God" with His Son, Jesus Christ (1 John 5:20). Jesus is the "true vine" in God's vineyard (John 15:1)

Not only is our God the one true God; He Himself is true. Jesus said "But he who sent me is true" (John 7:28; see also 8:26). The Greek word translated "true" (*alēthinos*) denotes what is real or genuine. When used of God, it affirms the reality of His existence. God is not the result of one's imagination, created in the human mind by some spiritual longing or deep-seated sense of inadequacy. God is just as true and real as my very own existence. Although invisible and without a physical body (John 4:24; Col. 1:15), God is very true and authentic.

Because He is true, He alone is worthy of our worship. No person, thing, or activity should usurp His place in our lives (1 John 5:21). Because God is true, He will never tell a lie (Titus 1:2). Because He is true, He is the perfect expression of truth, embodied in Jesus who said, "I am . . . the truth" (John 14:6).

The fact that God is true has implications for believers. Those who worship God "must worship in spirit and in truth" (John 4:24). This means our worship must involve spiritual rather than physical realities and must reflect what is true about God. This speaks of the importance of true doctrine in our hymns and other expressions of worship. The fact that God is true suggests that those who identify themselves with Him by faith need to be real, genuine, and truthful in their relationships with others. Avoiding manipulation and "double-speak," they must "speak truth" to each other (Eph. 4:25, NASB). Also we need to represent God truly in our actions and in our behavior.[3]

GOD IS GRACIOUS

God is characterized in Scripture by His infinite grace, whereby He bestows the riches of mercy and blessing on the most unworthy creatures. The Greek word *charis* speaks of a free gift or favor. Grace, simply stated, is God's unmerited favor granted to those who deserve His wrath. God's grace is the basis for our salvation and all the spiritual blessings believers enjoy in Christ. Paul wrote, "For it is by grace you have been saved" (Eph. 2:8). So important was the grace of God to Paul that he generally began his letters, "Grace and peace to you," and concluded with "Grace be with you" (for example, Col. 1:2; 4:18).

Since God is a God of grace, the Bible describes Him as "gracious." This attribute is one of the first revealed by God Himself in Exodus 34:6. The psalmists repeatedly emphasized that Yahweh is gracious (Pss. 86:15; 111:4; 112:4; 116:5; 145:8).

God is gracious in extending to us the free gift of salvation while requiring nothing from us. Indeed, it is only by His grace that our depraved minds and hearts could respond to His gracious offer. But the graciousness of God extends beyond our salvation. God's grace enables us to grow in the Christian life and to serve. Even the services believers perform are opportunities which "God prepared in advance for us to do" (Eph. 2:10). Paul referred to the offering being collected by the Corinthians for the Jerusalem church as "this act of grace" (2 Cor. 8:6; see also 8:7). Salvation by grace; sanctification by grace; service by grace—it seems clear that God's entire program for His people is one of grace from start to finish (see John 1:16).

How should we respond to God's graciousness toward us? We certainly can't "pay Him back." Nor can we give Him anything He doesn't already have. But we can give Him our hearts, our love, and our praise. When I bought a home for my family, my dad did something I wasn't able to do for myself. He helped me come up with money for the down payment. He didn't ask for anything in return. He gave me the money because of his love. All I could do was to say "Thanks, Dad." As I reflect on this situation and my own experience as a father, I think my dad took some pleasure in my expression of gratitude. I believe this is also true with God. The writer of Hebrews invites us to "offer to God a sacrifice of praise . . . for which such sacrifices God is pleased" (Heb. 13:15–16).

GOD IS WISE

The Bible teaches that God is wise and that He imparts His wisdom to those who fear Him. The apostle Paul concluded his letter to the Romans with a benediction: "To the only wise God be glory forever through Jesus Christ! Amen" (Rom. 16:27). The wisdom of God is a major teaching in the Old Testament. The Hebrew word for wisdom (*hokmâ*) initially meant skill or ability. So wisdom is the ability to achieve success or skill by doing things God's way. When the Israelites witnessed the discerning judgment of their king regarding two harlots disputing over the child, they saw that Solomon "had wisdom from God" (1 Kings 3:28). Although confused about the reason for his suffering, Job acknowledged God's wisdom (Job 12:13; 28:20, 23). When God gave Daniel the answer to his prayer for understanding Nebuchadnezzar's dream, he responded, "Praise be to the name of God for ever and ever; wisdom and power are his" (Dan. 2:20).

The attribute of wisdom is seen in Jesus Christ as well. Isaiah spoke of the messianic "Branch" from "the stump of Jesse," on whom will rest "the Spirit of wisdom and of understanding" (Isa. 11:1–2). In His youth Jesus grew in wisdom (Luke 2:40, 52). When He spoke in the synagogue at Nazareth, the astonished people asked, "Where did this man get this wisdom and these miraculous powers?" (Matt. 13:54). Jesus is not only foreshadowed in the divinely established functions of the prophet, priest, and king spoken of in the Old Testament, but He is also the ultimate "wise man"—One with greater wisdom than Solomon (12:42). In Him "are hidden all the treasures of wisdom and knowledge" (Col. 2:3). Jesus is wisdom incarnate and wisdom personified.[4]

In 1 Corinthians 1:18–2:8, Paul contrasted the world's wisdom with God's wisdom. The world through its wisdom did not come to know God. But God has imparted His wisdom to the world in the person of Jesus Christ. Paul wrote that "Christ Jesus . . . has become for us wisdom from God" (1:30). God's wisdom is epitomized in the mystery of the crucified, resurrected Christ (1:23–24; 2:7).

While God is infinitely wise, He graciously imparts a measure of wisdom to those who seek it from Him. As already noted, God gave Solomon wisdom (1 Kings 4:29), and He gave Daniel wisdom (Dan. 2:23). Solomon taught that "the LORD gives wisdom, and from his mouth come knowledge and understanding" (Prov. 2:6). James encouraged his readers to ask God for wisdom: "If any of you lacks wisdom, he should ask God, who gives generously to all without finding fault, and it will be given to him" (James 1:5).

GOD IS MERCIFUL

One of the most comforting of God's moral attributes is His mercy. David declared, "The LORD is gracious and merciful . . . and His mercies are over all His works" (Ps. 145:8–9, NASB). In the New Testament the Greek word translated "mercy" (*eleos*) is used most frequently of the compassion or pity shown by God in Christ. This attribute "assumes the need on the part of him who receives it, and resources adequate to meet the need on the part of him who shows it."[5] We enjoy forgiveness of our sins "because of the tender mercy of our God" (Luke 1:78). Paul acknowledged that our salvation is not based on our wills or abilities, "but on God's mercy" (Rom. 9:16). He spoke of God's mercy when sharing his own testimony. "Even though I was once a blasphemer and a persecutor and a violent man, I was shown mercy" (1 Tim. 1:13). Paul wrote of God being "rich in mercy" (Eph. 2:4), and Peter spoke of God's "great mercy" (1 Pet. 1:3).

Believers are called on to demonstrate mercy in our dealings with others. Jesus said, "Be merciful, just as your Father is merciful" (Luke 6:36). As believers, we must be ready to demonstrate compassionate intervention to people in need. Their needs might be physical, emotional, or spiritual. In some cases we have the resources and abilities to meet such needs. As Jesus responded to those in need of His mercy (Matt. 9:27–31; 20:30–34), we should do the same. And a blessing will be ours, for Jesus said, "Blessed are the merciful, for they will be shown mercy" (Matt. 5:7).

For Further Study

Packer, J. I. *Knowing God*. Downers Grove, Ill.: InterVarsity Press, 1973.

Pink, Arthur W. *Gleanings in the Godhead*. Chicago: Moody Press, 1975.

Tozer, A. W. *The Knowledge of the Holy*. New York: Harper & Brothers, 1961.

9

IMAGES OF GOD

To whom, then, will you compare God?
—Isaiah 40:18

IT IS INTERESTING TO DISCOVER what people think God is like. C. S. Lewis told a humorous story about a schoolboy who was asked what he thought God was like. He replied that, as far as he could determine, God was "the sort of person who is always snooping round to see if anyone is enjoying himself and then trying to stop it."[1]

What is God *really* like? The ancient writers of Scripture wanted the Israelites to know, but they lived during a time when methods of communication were quite limited. Can you imagine living in a world without television, radio, overhead projectors, slide projectors, video players, and computer graphics? The people living in the world of the Bible had none of these media. What they did have were words. And so they used words to create mental images of what God is like. These "word pictures" are particularly prominent in the poetic sections of the Bible where imagery and metaphor abound.

Using images is a great way to communicate truth about God, for several reasons. First, the mental images seem to remain in our memories better than abstract precepts. Think of an advertisement you have seen recently. You can't get some ads out of your mind! Second, mental images appeal to the emotions as well as the mind. People are informed by words, but are moved by word pictures. Third, images that present truth about

God can easily be passed on to others. For example, children, teens, and adults can appreciate the image Jesus used in his words, "I am the good shepherd." In this chapter we will see how the imagery of the Bible helps us learn more about God.

GOD OUR ROCK

Of the seventy-five occurrences of the word "rock" in the Bible, thirty-three are figurative references for God. Moses was the first to refer to God as "the Rock" (Deut. 32:4; 32:15), but concerning the pagan nations Moses said, "Their rock is not like our Rock" (32:31). David declared, "The LORD is my rock, my fortress and my deliverer; my God is my rock, in whom I take refuge" (2 Sam. 22:2–3). The rock imagery is also prominent in the Psalms.[2]

The Hebrew word *ṣûr*, "rock," refers not to a small rock or pebble, but to a large boulder, block of stone, cliff, or possibly mountain. What do we know about rocks that would lead the biblical writers to use them as an image for God? First, large rocks are immovable. They tend to stay put. Second, rocks last a long time. Under the Dome of the Rock on Jerusalem's temple mount is the rock of Mount Moriah where Abraham offered Isaac (Genesis 22). After nearly four thousand years, that rock is still there. You can see that rock when you visit Jerusalem. Third, rocks can provide protection. You can hide behind them when your enemy attacks. Neither arrows nor sling stones can penetrate a fortress made of solid rock. Large rocks can also provide shade from the intense heat of the sun in a rocky, barren wilderness.

With these facts in mind, we can see why the biblical writers would refer to God as "our Rock." He is sure, solid, immovable, and provides protection. He is totally reliable. He will not erode away or diminish over time. While man-made fortresses crumble and fall, God is "the Rock eternal" (Isa. 26:4). After thousands of years, He will still be there. As a rock, God is our fortress and place of refuge (Ps. 18:2). He is the One to whom we can flee when we are under attack or in times of suffering and difficulties. As "the rock of my salvation" (89:26, NASB), He is our sure Source of strength and deliverance. The one who relies on God as his Rock will be secure (62:2, 6).

Isaiah referred to the Messiah as "a stone that causes men to stumble and a rock that makes them fall" (Isa. 8:14). He cannot be ignored by those who come into contact with him. Some stumble and are broken by Him to repentance. Others fall and are crushed by the rock itself, that is, they are judged for their sin. Messiah is also "the stone the builders rejected" (Ps. 118:22; Matt. 21:42). But the one who believes in this Rock will not be ashamed (Isa. 28:16; 1 Pet. 2:6). During the wilderness sojourn, Moses struck the rock and water was provided for the thirsty Israelites (Exod. 17:6; Deut. 8:15; Ps. 78:15). Paul identified this rock with Christ (1 Cor. 10:4). The rock imagery of the Bible ultimately points to Jesus, the Rock of our salvation.

GOD OUR REFUGE

The image of God as our refuge is quite similar to God as our rock. In fact these images sometimes appear as parallel terms. In Psalm 62:7 David wrote that God "is my mighty rock, my refuge." The Hebrew root *hāsâ*, "to seek refuge," and the derived noun *mahseh*, "refuge," are used predominately in the psalms and other poetic literature. These words are used in a literal sense of taking shelter from a rainstorm (Isa. 4:6; 25:4) or refuge from danger in the hills (Ps. 104:18). But more frequently the words are used figuratively of seeking refuge in God.

The psalmists frequently identified Yahweh as a place of refuge. "O LORD my God, I take refuge in you" (7:1). "In the LORD I take refuge" (11:1). "In you my soul takes refuge" (57:1). "It is better to take refuge in the LORD than to trust in man" (118:8).

What did the psalmists mean by this imagery? Obviously God does not provide protection in the same physical way as defensive walls or a strong fortress. To take God as one's refuge means to "trust" in Him. This imagery is a poetic way of expressing confident trust in our powerful God who provides security for helpless, needy people. As the hills provided a safe refuge for those in danger (Josh. 2:22), so God is a "strong refuge" (Ps. 71:7). He acts as a "shield for all who take refuge in him" (2 Sam. 22:31).

Although a different Hebrew word is used for the cities of refuge (Numbers 35), one cannot help but see a link between them and God as a refuge. Six cities of refuge provided a place for an Israelite guilty of manslaughter. As long as the guilty one remained within the walls of the city, the blood avenger could not execute punishment. In a similar way Jesus Christ is a "refuge" for sinful, guilty people (Heb. 6:18). He is a sure and safe haven for those who put their trust in Him.

GOD OUR WARRIOR

Most people don't think of God in terms of military imagery. But since Israel was often under attack by foreign nations, God's people pictured their Lord as a mighty warrior who could both defend and vindicate them. Yahweh fought for His people not by sword and spear, but through divine miracles. After God defeated the Egyptians, drowning Pharaoh's army in the Red Sea, Moses and the people of Israel sang a song that included these words: "The LORD is a warrior; the LORD is his name. Pharaoh's chariots and his army he has hurled into the sea. The best of Pharaoh's officers are drowned in the Red Sea" (Exod. 15:3–4). The imagery of Yahweh as a warrior is so extensive and significant that a whole book has been written on the subject.[3] The Hebrew word translated "warrior" in this passage refers to one who has learned the art of war and has proven himself on the battlefield.

Advancing this theme of Yahweh as a warrior, Isaiah declared, "The LORD will march out like a mighty man, like a warrior he will stir up his zeal; with a shout he will raise the battle cry and will triumph over his enemies" (Isa. 42:13). And Zephaniah encouraged his people with the words, "The LORD your God is in your midst, a victorious warrior" (Zeph. 3:17, NASB). In these passages the Hebrew word translated "warrior" is an adjective meaning "strong" or "mighty." When used of an individual, it speaks of a strong or valiant man. When used of God, the term emphasizes His power to protect His people and defeat their enemies. Since "the LORD [is] mighty in battle" (Ps. 24:8), David declared, "May God arise, may his enemies be scatterred; may his foes flee before him" (68:1).

The imagery of the Lord as a mighty warrior will ultimately be fulfilled by the returning Messiah who "will go out and fight against those nations" gathered against Jerusalem (Zech. 14:3). John envisioned Jesus' return on a "white horse" (Rev. 19:11), the mount of a conquering warrior. It is noteworthy that the Roman leader Vespasian rode a white horse in his triumph over Judea.[4] In the Battle of Armageddon the Messiah the warrior will "strike down the nations" with a "sharp sword" and will "rule them with a rod of iron" (Rev. 19:15, NASB).

It is comforting to know that we have a strong Defender who is able to defeat the most powerful of supernatural foes—the Antichrist, the false prophet, and the devil (Rev. 19:20; 20:1–2, 10). Since He can give them what they deserve, no enemy can resist His blows. As Paul asked, "If God is for us, who can be against us?" (Rom. 8:31). No power can defeat us as we stand beside Jesus, our messianic Defender.

GOD OUR SHEPHERD

One of the most familiar images in Scripture is that of the shepherd. Since many of the Israelites were shepherds, we should not be surprised to find this imagery in the Bible. In fact, the shepherd metaphor was used throughout the ancient Near East as a designation for both divine and human rulers. In an ancient Sumerian hymn the god Enlil is addressed as the "faithful shepherd" of all living creatures. In the prologue of his famous law code the Babylonian king Hammurabi described himself as a shepherd appointed by Enlil for his people. And in the Old Testament the shepherd metaphor is applied to both the Lord (Gen. 49:24; Pss. 80:1; 95:7) and human leaders (78:70–72; Zech. 11:4–14).

The familiar twenty-third psalm begins with the words, "The LORD is my shepherd." Isaiah predicted the Messiah's shepherd-like ministry. "He tends his flock like a shepherd: He gathers the lambs in his arms, and carries them close to his heart; he gently leads those that have young" (Isa. 40:11). Using the shepherd imagery, Ezekiel indicted the national leaders, who were like false shepherds. They exploited the people instead of looking after their needs as a good shepherd should (Ezek. 34:2–4). Then Ezekiel predicted how Yahweh will become Israel's Shepherd. He will bring the scattered flock of Israel back to their land (34:13). He will "feed" his flock, "search for the lost and bring back the strays" and "bind up the injured and strengthen the weak" (34:14, 16).

The shepherd imagery has its ultimate fulfillment in Jesus, "the good shepherd" (John 10:11). He is the Good Shepherd because He cares for the sheep, provides for the sheep, and lays down His life for the sheep (10:12–15). The sheep know the voice of their Shepherd and follow where he leads them (10:2–4). He is also called the "great Shepherd" (Heb. 13:20) and the "Chief Shepherd" (1 Pet. 5:4). If you visit the land of Israel, you will see many shepherds with their flocks of sheep. You will see the shepherds calling their sheep with strange, guttural sounds. You will see the sheep respond and follow their shepherd. They know they can trust him to protect them and provide for their needs. And as believers we are members of God's flock, "the sheep of his pasture" (Ps. 100:3). Jesus is able to draw on all of His divine resources as the Good Shepherd in caring for and providing for His sheep.

GOD OUR HOVERING EAGLE

A picturesque but perhaps surprising image of God is that of an eagle. After the Exodus from Egypt God said to His people, "You yourselves have seen what I did to Egypt, and how I carried you on eagles' wings and brought you to myself" (Exod. 19:4). In a masterpiece of Hebrew poetry Moses likened God's relationship with Israel to an eagle caring for her young. "He cared for him . . . like an eagle that stirs up its nest, that hovers over its young, he spread his wings and caught them, He carried them on pinions" (Deut. 32:10–11).

David was fond of the imagery of God's wings. David prayed, "Hide me in the shadow of your wings" (Ps. 17:8). He acknowledged that God's wings provide refuge from danger: "I will take refuge in the shadow of your wings until the disaster has passed" (57:1; see also 61:4; 91:4). Knowing the security to be found in the shadow of God's wings is a source of joy for believers. David declared, "Because you are my help, I sing in the shadow of your wings" (63:7).

In a similar metaphor Jesus spoke with sadness about His rejection by the people of Jerusalem. "O Jerusalem, Jerusalem, you who kill the prophets and stone those sent to you, how often I have longed to gather your children together, as a hen gathers her chicks under her wings, but you were not willing" (Matt. 23:37). In rejecting the Messiah, the people of Israel rejected the protection provided under God's "wings." The destruction of Jerusalem by Titus and his Roman legions soon followed (23:38; 24:2).

As believers in Jesus Christ we can be grateful for the loving protection God gives us under His powerful wings. This is a great picture of our security in Him and of His care, protection from harm, and love.

GOD OUR SHIELD

Genesis 15:1 records God's comforting words to Abram, "Do not be afraid, Abram. I am your shield." The word translated "shield" *(māgēn)* derives from the verb *gānan,* "to defend or put a shield about." In ancient times warriors used two types of shields. The *māgēn* was the smaller and more common round shield carried by light infantry. The *ṣinnâ* was a much larger rectangular shield, like the one carried by Goliath's attendant (1 Sam. 17:7, 41), which could protect the whole body. The earliest shields were made out of wood or wicker and overlaid with leather. They were sometimes reinforced with bronze trim. The shield was basic to a soldier's defense. With it he could deflect the blows of the enemies' swords, spears, and arrows.

Since God is the One who protects His people, it should not be surprising that He is described figuratively as "a shield for all who take refuge in him" (Ps. 18:30). Moses reminded Israel that Yahweh is "your shield and helper" (Deut. 33:29). As a warrior David knew of the importance of a shield in personal defense on the battlefield. In a psalm that David wrote while he was fleeing from Absalom, he said, "You are a shield around me, O LORD" (Ps. 3:3). In another psalm he wrote, "My shield is God Most High, who saves the upright in heart" (7:10). Being shielded by God means salvation for His people (18:2). The people of Israel were exhorted to "trust in the LORD" for "he is their help and shield" (115:9–11). Knowing that God was His shield gave David confidence in the face of conflict. He wrote, "The LORD is my strength and my shield; my heart trusts in him, and I am helped" (28:7).

Although David most frequently used *māgēn* to describe God as the shield and protector of His people, he used *ṣinnâ* in Psalm 5:12 (see also 1 Kings 10:16; Pss. 35:2; 91:4). A group of soldiers could use these shields to provide a protective roof over their heads. Roman soldiers later mastered the art of moving through the battlefield enclosed in this manner. They called this approach a phalanx. And so God blesses the righteous person and surrounds him or her with His "favor as with a shield" (5:12). How encouraging to know that God shields and defends believers against the attacks by Satan, who uses clever "schemes" (2 Cor. 2:11; Eph. 6:11) to try to deceive and destroy us (1 Pet. 5:8).

GOD OUR REDEEMER

Eighteen times in the Old Testament God is referred to as Redeemer. Job may have been the first to use this term of God, when he said, "I know that my Redeemer lives" (Job 19:25). David the psalmist wrote, "May the words of my mouth and the meditation of my heart be pleasing in your sight, O LORD, my Rock and my Redeemer" (Ps. 19:14). Isaiah was fond of this imagery; he used it thirteen times. He wrote, "The Holy One of Israel is your Redeemer" (Isa. 54:5). We may be so familiar with this designation of God as our "Redeemer" that we don't realize it is actually a metaphor.

The word "Redeemer" comes from the word gā'al which means "to do the part of a kinsman and thus redeem his kin from difficulty or danger."[5] It suggests the various things a good and faithful person would do for a needy relative. The close relative ("near kinsman," NKJV) was responsible to repurchase a field that earlier had been sold in time of need, thus keeping the property in the family (Lev. 25:25). Also he was responsible to purchase and free a relative who had sold himself as a slave because of poverty (25:48–49). The relative was also to avenge the murder of a family member (Num. 35:16–19). The idea behind this system of execution is that the loss of life must be paid for by the life of the murderer. Each of these acts of "redemption" must be performed by a close relative.

Three things were required of a redeemer. First, since redemption was a family obligation, only a near relative had the right to redeem. Second, since redemption is costly, one must have the resources to redeem. Third, since redemption requires decisive action, one must have the resolve to redeem. The Book of Ruth describes a "kinsman-redeemer" who had the right and the resources to redeem the land of Naomi and Ruth but was unwilling to do so (Ruth 4:1–8).

When God is described as our Kinsman-Redeemer, the imagery points ultimately to Jesus Christ. Christ became our kinsman as He took on human flesh and entered into humanity by the virgin birth (Matt. 1:18; John 1:14). As our Kinsman-Redeemer, Christ had the resource of His own precious blood to pay the price of our redemption (1 Pet. 1:18–19). And He had the resolve to lay down His life for our redemption (Mark 10:45). Only Jesus Christ can provide "redemption [from sin] through his blood" (Eph. 1:7) and by His grace (Rom. 3:24). How blessed are God's people, knowing that in Him they have a strong Redeemer (Jer. 50:34).

GOD OUR HIDING PLACE

David prayed to the Lord, "You are my hiding place; you will protect me from trouble" (Ps. 32:7). This imagery appears again in Psalm 119:114, "Thou art my hiding place and my shield" (NASB). David expressed confidence that "in the day of trouble" Yahweh "will keep me safe in his dwelling; he will hide me in the shelter of his tabernacle" (27:5).

Malinta Tunnel is located on Corregidor Island in Manila Bay. This tunnel served as a weapon arsenal before World War II. But when the Japanese Imperial Army invaded the Philippines in 1941, Malinta Tunnel became an army hospital and the headquarters of General Douglas MacArthur. Later when Japanese warplanes were bombing Corregidor Island, this tunnel provided protection for the American and Filipino soldiers. Although deserted today, Malinta Tunnel remains a mute witness of the protection it offered soldiers through deadly bombardment. I hope none of us ever face a bombardment by warplanes. But often God's people experience the hostilities of an evil and unbelieving world. In the face of spiritual attack, believers have a sure hiding place in our God.

The only requirement for those seeking entrance into God's hiding place is an attitude of repentance and faith. Zephaniah instructed the people of his day to "seek righteousness" and "seek humility." Then he encouraged them, "Perhaps you will be sheltered on the day of the Lord's anger" (Zeph. 2:3).

God is a "hiding place" where His people can find safety and refuge in times of danger. He is the One we can go to when no one else knows or understands what we are going through. As our hiding place He can provide protection when people's assurances fail.

GOD OUR FOUNTAIN

If the Bible had been written in rainy Oregon rather than the land of Israel, the imagery of God as our fountain may not have appeared. But much of the land of Israel experiences marginal rainfall, and water there is very precious. During the summer months, when the sun is directly overhead, it is easy to become overheated and dehydrated. When I take students to Israel, I remind them to carry a water bottle on field trips and drink frequently.

In a dry land Yahweh is said to be the "fountain of Israel" (Ps. 68:26, NASB). David said to God, "For with you is the fountain of life" (36:9). By this he meant that God is a source of spiritual refreshment and life to those who trust Him.

When the Israelites entered the Hill Country after the conquest of Canaan, they discovered that many of the cities were built in close proximity to a natural spring. Ancient Jerusalem, for example, featured the ever-flowing Gihon Spring as its main water source. This was known as "living water" since in its continuous flow it was lifelike and life-giving. Such springs gave the Israelites a consistent supply of fresh, clear, cold water. But as the cities grew, so did their need for water. This need was met by cutting holes in the limestone rock and channelling rainwater into plastered cisterns for use during the six-months-a-year dry season. This rainwater was not as fresh and tasty as spring water, especially if there was sediment or algae in the cistern. But it was better than no water at all!

The Lord used this water imagery when he rebuked the Judeans in Jeremiah 2:13. "My people have committed two sins: They have forsaken me, the spring of living water, and have dug their own cisterns, broken cisterns that cannot hold water." Here we discover that people are thirsty for the truth of God, but they are looking for satisfaction in the wrong places. They are turning to broken, dusty "cisterns" when they could be drawing from the thirst-quenching Fountain of living water.

The imagery of God as a fountain of spiritual life and refreshment has its ultimate fulfillment in Jesus. He offered the Samaritan woman "living water" (John 4:10). Those who drink from Jacob's well will thirst again, but Jesus said, "Whoever drinks the water I give him will never thirst. Indeed, the water I give him will become in him a spring of water welling up to eternal life" (4:14). Only God can quench our spiritual thirst and give us eternal life.

That is why Jesus said of our spiritual need, "If anyone is thirsty, let him come to me and drink" (7:37). Interestingly the very last chapter of the Bible includes an invitation for people to have their spiritual thirst satisfied in Christ: "Whoever is thirsty, let him come; and whoever wishes, let him take the free gift of the water of life" (Rev. 22:17).

GOD OUR HUSBAND

Leo Perdue has pointed out that the marriage relationship is used as a "theological lens for understanding God and Israel."[6] God is depicted as "mother" (Num. 11:12; Deut. 32:18), who conceived and gave birth to Israel; as a "father" (Deut. 32:6; Mal. 2:10), who nurtured and loved His son Israel; and as a "husband," who took Israel for His wife (Jer. 2:2).

The imagery of God as husband is applied to Israel as a corporate unit. To Israel God declared, "For your Maker is your husband—the LORD Almighty is his name" (Isa. 54:5). The imagery of God as husband is introduced by Ezekiel in his account of Israel as an adulterous wife (Ezekiel 16). In the analogy Ezekiel told of how God found Israel as a neglected, abandoned child and took her to Himself. In Ezekiel's powerful analogy, when Israel matured, God entered into a marriage covenant with His people. "Later I passed by and when I looked at you and saw that you were old enough for love, I spread the corner of my garment over you and covered your nakedness. I gave you my solemn oath and entered into a covenant with you, declares the Sovereign LORD, and you became mine" (16:8).

The prophets were particularly fond of the imagery of God as husband of His people. In Jeremiah the marriage relationship serves as a motivation to repentance. " 'Return, faithless people,' declares the LORD, 'for I am your husband' " (Jer. 3:14). Jeremiah described how Israel broke the old covenant, a violation more shocking because "I was a husband to them" (31:32).

In a strong rebuke against an idolatrous people who had broken the covenant, the Lord declared, "Rebuke your mother [that is, Israel], rebuke her, for she is not my wife, and I am not her husband" (Hos. 2:2). But Hosea anticipated a day when God's marriage with Israel would be restored and renewed. "'In that day,' declares the LORD, 'you will call me "my husband"; . . . I will betroth you in faithfulness and you will acknowledge the LORD'" (2:16, 20).

The imagery of God as husband appears also in the New Testament, where Christ is presented as the Bridegroom or Husband of His people, the church (Eph. 5:23–32). In describing the anticipated second coming of Christ, John spoke of "the wedding [feast] of the Lamb" and the "marriage supper of the Lamb" (Rev. 19:7, 9). Also John envisioned the New Jerusalem, the eternal dwelling place of God's people, coming down out of heaven "prepared as a bride beautifully dressed for her husband" (21:2).

This imagery of God as a husband is very instructive. As husband God provides for and protects His people. As husband, God loves His people with an everlasting love. As husband, God shares intimacy with His people. As God's bride, His people are to be faithful to Him. We must never give our attention or affection to another; we should never allow anything to take God's place in our lives. As God's bride, we must keep ourselves pure in mind and body. We must submit to His leadership, knowing that His requirements are sourced in His deep and abiding love.

GOD OUR VINEDRESSER

The vine is a familiar symbol of Israel in the Psalms and the Prophets (Ps. 80:8–16; Jer. 5:10; 12:10; Ezek. 15:1–8; Hos. 10:1). God said to His people, "I had planted you like a choice vine of sound and reliable stock. How then did you turn against me into a corrupt, wild vine?" (Jer. 2:21). Isaiah wrote a parable describing how God prepared a field, planted a vineyard, and anticipated an abundant harvest. But the vineyard produced only worthless grapes (Isa. 5:1–2). God expected His vineyard—Israel and Judah—to produce the fruit of "justice" and "righteousness," but the harvest He reaped was "bloodshed" and "cries of distress" (5:7). So God resolved to destroy the worthless vineyard. His people could expect to encounter the covenant's cursings rather than its blessings.

The imagery of God as Vinedresser appears in Jesus' analogy of the vine and the branches. He said, "I am the true vine, and My Father is the vinedresser" (John 15:1, NASB). Jesus is the "true vine" in contrast to the degenerate vine—unbelieving Israel. The word "vinedresser" ("gardener," NIV; literally, "one who works the ground") refers to a farmer preparing the soil to raise a crop. Jesus then described two types of "branches" and two actions taken by the Vinedresser. He throws away the fruitless branches (15:6) and He trims clean (prunes) the branches that have fruit that they may bear even more grapes (15:2).

What can we learn about God through the imagery of the vinedresser? The most basic truth is that God is committed to growing fruit. There is no point in a farmer preparing the soil and planting the seed if he doesn't expect to produce a crop. God expects those who are united with Him by personal faith to produce spiritual fruit. Jesus said to His disciples, "I chose you . . . to go and bear fruit" (15:16).

We also learn from this passage that God is committed to increasing our "productivity." As stated, the fruitful branches are pruned so that they might bear more fruit (15:2). Growing grapes in my backyard has provided some insight into the need for pruning the vine. Each year in the fall old growth needs to be removed to prepare the way for new branches. In the spring, suckers need to be stripped away from the trunk and main branches. During the summer, grape clusters must be thinned and long, vigorous shoots pinched off. As the vinedresser cuts away what would hinder the productivity of the vine, so God the Father, through loving discipline (cleansing, purging, purifying), removes things from the lives of believers that do not contribute to their spiritual fruitfulness. The writer of Hebrews may have had this "pruning" in mind when he pointed out that God disciplines His children (Heb. 12:6).

Another lesson to be gleaned from imagery of God as Vinedresser is that the Lord is pleased when His people produce fruit. Jesus said, "This is to my Father's glory, that you bear much fruit" (John 15:8). We can't add to God's attributes. But we can glorify Him, contributing to the public display of His greatness and goodness by the way we live and the things we do. Jesus said, "Let your light shine before men, that they may see your good deeds and praise your Father in heaven" (Matt. 5:16).

For Further Study

Bullinger, E. W. *Figures of Speech Used in the Bible.* Reprint, Grand Rapids: Baker Book House, 1968.

Caird, G. B. *The Language and Imagery of the Bible.* Philadelphia: Westminster Press, 1980.

Ryken, Leland, James C. Wilhoit, and Tremper Longman, eds. *Dictionary of Biblical Imagery.* Downers Grove, Ill.: InterVarsity Press, 1998.

Zuck, Roy B. *Basic Bible Interpretation.* Wheaton, Ill.: Victor Books, 1991.

10

THE TRIUNITY OF GOD

May the grace of the Lord Jesus Christ, and the love of God, and the fellowship of the Holy Spirit be with you all.
—2 Corinthians 13:14

I RECENTLY ATTENDED a wedding for the son of one of my colleagues at Western Seminary. As the service began, the officiating minister informed the friends and loved ones that they were about to witness the inauguration of a covenant—a covenant of marriage. Vows would be exchanged, binding Bill and Julie together for life. But not only would the congregation witness the beginning of a covenant, the minister explained. Those gathered would also witness a miracle, for in the marriage union two people actually become one. As God said, "For this reason a man will leave his father and mother and be united to his wife, and they will become one flesh" (Gen. 2:24). Although Bill and Julie would retain their own individuality and personhood, in a mystical but real way they would be indissolubly united into one spiritual entity.

The mystery of the marriage union may serve to illustrate something of the Triunity of God. In their wedding cereemony Bill and Julie lit a unity candle signifying that the two were becoming one in marriage. In a similar but totally unique and distinctive way, God the Father, God the Son, and God the Holy Spirit are one in deity. They are three distinctive persons united together in one Godhead.

This chapter considers the doctrine of the Trinity, or triunity, addressing these questions: Is there a biblical basis for this doctrine? Have

Christians always been in agreement on the Trinity? What are the practical implications of this doctrine? How can an appreciation of the doctrine of the Trinity help us get to know God better?

THE BIBLICAL BASIS FOR GOD'S TRIUNITY

The word *Trinity*, which literally means "the state or character of being three," may leave the impression that Christians worship three Gods. Following Charles Ryrie, I prefer the word *triunity* since it expresses more concretely what we believe about God.[1] The Bible teaches that in the Godhead, there are three distinct and individual persons—Father, Son and Holy Spirit—a Trinity. But in a mystical and supernatural way the three are united in one—a Triunity.

Evidence for Oneness

The Bible states rather emphatically that there is only one true God. This is evidenced in the Shema, which is recited every Sabbath in Jewish synagogues. "Hear [$š^ema^c$], O Israel: The LORD our God, the LORD is one" (Deut. 6:4). This is a strong declaration of the oneness and uniqueness of God. This text is sometimes cited as evidence against the doctrine of the Trinity. Commenting on Deuteronomy 6:4 a Jewish commentator said, "The belief that God is made up of several personalities, such as the Christian belief in the Trinity, is a departure from the pure conception of the Unity of God."[2] However, theologians differ on whether the Hebrew word *'eḥād* refers to the unity of God, the uniqueness of God, or both.[3] Possibly *'eḥād* means unity in the sense of the three persons of the Godhead being one, because in Genesis 2:24 the same Hebrew word is used of Adam and Eve being "one," that is, two distinct persons seen as a unit. On the other hand, Wolf suggests that both the broad context of Deuteronomy and the immediate context of Deuteronomy 6:4 emphasize the fact the oneness of God and that Israel owed its exclusive loyalty to Him as the one unique God (5:9; 6:5).[4] With this in mind, the words "The LORD is one" may be translated "Yahweh alone!"

Among all the deities competing for the attention of the Israelites, including Asherah and Anath, Baal and Marduk, there is only one who truly merits worship—Yahweh alone!

The first of the Ten Commandments reminded the Israelites that they were to worship only the one true God (Exod. 20:3; Deut. 5:7). Having reminded the Israelites of God's work on their behalf, Moses said, "The LORD is God; besides him there is no other" (4:35). The New Testament is equally clear in affirming that "there is but one God" (1 Cor. 8:6; see also Eph. 4:4–6; James 2:19).

EVIDENCE FOR THREENESS

Among the world's great religions Christianity is the only one that embraces the doctrine of three divine persons in one Godhead. The deity of these three persons is clearly evidenced in Scripture.[5] First, the Father is called God (1 Cor. 8:6). Jesus recognized the Father as God. He said, "Do not work for food that spoils, but for food that endures to eteternal life, which the Son of Man will give you. On Him God the Father has placed His seal of approval" (John 6:27). Peter also referred to "God the Father" (1 Pet. 1:2).

Second, the Son is called God (Heb. 1:8). In Romans 9:5, Paul referred to "Christ, who is God over all, forever praised!" When doubting Thomas saw the resurrected Jesus, he declared, "My Lord and my God!" (John 20:28). Jesus' claims of omniscience (Matt. 9:4), omnipotence (28:18), and omnipresence (28:20) indicate that He is God. In John 8:58 He declared, "before Abraham was born, I am!" The words "I am" (Greek, *egō eimi*) are a clear reference to God the Father who identified Himself in Exodus 3:14 as "I am who I am." (See the discussion in the section "A Question about God's Name [Exod. 3:13–15]" in chapter 3.) The Jews who heard Jesus recognized this assertion of deity and picked up stones to execute Him for blasphemy (John 8:59). Jesus affirmed His equality with God in the words, "I and the Father are one" (10:30). Further proof of Christ's deity is evidenced by His miracles (20:30–31) and His power to forgive sins (Mark 2:1–12)—works only God can do.

Third, the Holy Spirit is called God. In Acts 5:3–4 we read of how Peter rebuked Ananias for his deception regarding a gift given to the church. "Ananias, how is it that Satan has so filled your heart that you have lied to the Holy Spirit and have kept for yourself some of the money?" Then Peter added, "You have not lied to men but to God." In other words, to lie to the Holy Spirit was the same as lying to God. The Holy Spirit possesses the attributes of God, including omniscience (1 Cor. 2:10), omnipotence (Job 33:4), and omnipresence (Ps. 139:7). Further proof of the deity of the Holy Spirit is seen in the works He performs, including regeneration (Titus 3:5), intercession (Rom. 8:26), and sanctification (2 Thess. 2:13).

Evidence for Triunity

The first evidence of God's Triunity in the New Testament is seen at the baptism of Jesus, when the Father, Son, and Holy Spirit were involved together (Matt. 3:13–17). When Jesus was baptized by John, the "Spirit of God" (v. 16) came on Him and God the Father spoke from heaven and said, "This is my Son, whom I love; with him I am well pleased" (3:17).

Jesus told His apostles to make disciples, baptizing these new believers "in the name of the Father and of the Son and of the Holy Spirit" (28:19). Three divine persons are identified—Father, Son, and Holy Spirit—but Jesus used the word "name" (singular) rather than "names" (plural). By doing so, Jesus was recognizing God's Triunity.

Paul's benediction in 2 Corinthians 13:14 adds support for the Triunity of God: "May the grace of the Lord Jesus Christ, and the love of God, and the fellowship of the Holy Spirit be with you all." Only three verses earlier Paul spoke of "the God of love and peace" (13:11). Paul believed in one singular God (1 Cor. 8:4), but he acknowledged that divine spiritual blessings come from God the Father, the Lord Jesus Christ, and the Holy Spirit.

Is God's Triunity only a New Testament doctrine, or do we find evidence for it in the Old Testament as well? The evidence is not as direct or distinctly stated, but it is there. Isaiah 48:16 is probably the clearest reference to the Trinity in the Old Testament. Here Isaiah recorded the words of the Messianic Servant: "Come near me and listen to this: 'From the first announcement I have not spoken in secret; at the time it happens, I am there.' And now the Sovereign Lord has sent me, with his Spirit." Notice the last line—"the Sovereign LORD" (God the Father), "me" (the Messiah), and "his Spirit" (the Holy Spirit). The three persons of the Godhead are closely associated in what appears to be a coequal relationship, a Triunity. In a similar passage Isaiah revealed that God the *Father* ("the Sovereign LORD") anointed the *Messiah* ("me") with His *Spirit* (61:1).

In another place Isaiah predicted the Messiah's birth and kingdom rule. "For to us a child is born, to us a son is given, and the government will be on his shoulders. And he will be called Wonderful Counselor, Mighty God, Everlasting Father, Prince of Peace" (9:6). By calling the Messiah "Mighty God," Isaiah was clearly affirming Christ's deity. When predicting the Messiah's birth in Bethlehem the prophet Micah wrote that His "goings forth are from of old, from everlasting" (Mic. 5:2, NKJV). This is evidence for the Messiah's preexistence and eternality.

Old Testament references to the Angel of the Lord also lend support to the concept of multiple persons in one Godhead. Jacob wrestled with a "man," an "angel" according to Hosea 12:4, who is later identified as God. Jacob named the place "Peniel" (literally, "face of God"), for he said, "I saw God face to face" (Gen. 32:30). The "man" Jacob wrestled with seems to have been the second person of the Godhead, Jesus Christ before His incarnation. In another place "a man of God," identified as "the angel of the LORD," appeared to an Israelite couple to announce the birth of Samson (Judg. 13:3). At the end of the encounter, Manoah, the husband, concluded, "We are doomed to die [for] we have seen God!" (13:22). Once again we see evidence that a "man" is recognized as deity. This is another reference to Christ, the second person of the Trinity, before His incarnation. These references to the Angel of the Lord support the view that there are at least two coequal divine persons.[5]

Many Christian theologians and commentators have seen evidence for God's Triunity in the plural word for God, *'Ĕlōhîm*. While the plural form of *'Ĕl* ("god") allows for and is consistent with the later revelation of the Triunity, it does not demand this interpretation. It is possible to understand the plural form *'Ĕlōhîm* as a plural of majesty that emphasizes the fullness of God's character and attributes. Our Jewish friends, for example, recognize the plural form but don't accept the Trinity doctrine. And yet the plural form allows for the Triunity, which is more explicitly stated in later revelation.

Considering the revelation of both Testaments, we conclude that there is strong biblical evidence for God's Triunity.[6] There is only one God, but in the unity of the Godhead there are three eternal and coequal Persons—Father, Son, and Holy Spirit.

Many attempts have been made to illustrate the doctrine of the Triunity. Some of these are helpful because they enable us to recognize things in nature that are three-in-one. An egg is three-in-one, with the shell, the white, and the yolk. The parts are distinct, but they all make up the one egg. Yet this illustration is inadequate because the parts of the egg do not possess the properties or "attributes" of each other. Ryrie uses the sun to illustrate God's Triunity.[7] There are three distinct aspects of the sun—the ball of exploding hydrogen gas, the light emanating from the burning gas, and the power or radiant energy which can heat the earth and make things grow. The sun itself is like the Father, the light is like the Son, and the energy is like the Holy Spirit. On earth we see the light of the sun, not the sun itself. Yet the light beamed to earth possesses the properties of the sun and reveals something of the nature of the sun. The energy of the sun possesses the qualities of the sun but yet is distinct from it. The sun, with its light and energy, may help some people get a handle on this complex doctrine of God's Triunity.

Ancient Christians used the following diagram to illustrate the divine Triunity. It helps visualize the idea that the persons of the Trinity are distinct, but they share in one Godhead.

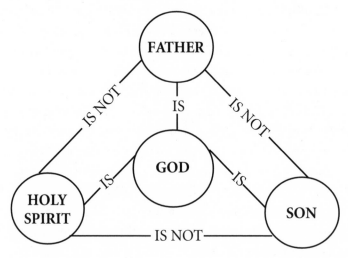

We must be careful with these illustrations since they are imperfect and inadequate to describe this great mystery of God. As believers, we must recognize that God's Triunity is a true biblical doctrine. But it is an aspect of God we will not fully comprehend this side of heaven. Even Paul acknowledged that "we know in part" (1 Cor. 13:9). Then he added these words, "Now we see but a poor reflection, as in a mirror; then we shall see face to face. Now I know in part; then I shall know fully, even as I am fully known" (13:12). In heaven we will understand this truth more clearly. But today we view the doctrine of God's Triunity from a distance, as with foggy binoculars. Bromiley's comment is helpful in this regard. A Christian "is not surprised if an element of mystery remains which defies ultimate analysis or understanding, for he is only a man and God is God."[8] Someday we may understand this doctrine better, but even then we may not fully comprehend it.

HAS THE CHURCH ALWAYS AGREED?

With a teaching as difficult as God's Triunity, it is not surprising to learn that this doctrine has been the subject of debate in church. The debate, of course, centered on the relationship of God the Father, God the Son, and God the Holy Spirit to one another.

The doctrine of the Trinity arose from the need for Christians to distinguish Jesus from God, yet to identify Him with God. Tertullian (around 160–220), North African apologist and theologian, was the first to use the term "Trinity" and to begin the formulation of this doctrine. But his view involved the subordination of the Son to the Father. Origen (around 185–254) took this a step further, arguing that the Son is subordinate to the Father in His essential nature, and that the Holy Spirit is subordinate to the Son.

In the second century Theodotus of Byzantium expounded the view that Jesus was a mere man on whom came the dynamic influence of the Holy Spirit at His baptism and was then called to be "the Son of God." This view came to be known as "Dynamic Monarchianism" because it affirmed the "sole sovereignty" (monarch) or primacy of God the Father, yet recognized the spiritual "dynamic" of the man Jesus.

Whereas Dynamic Monarchianism actually denied the doctrine of the Trinity, another form of Monarchianism sought to affirm it but did so by reducing the persons of the Godhead to different modes or manifestations of the one God. Modalistic Monarchianism was promoted by Sabellius (known to us by the writings of Tertullian), who was active in Rome during the early third century A.D. He taught that there is one God who can be variously designated as Father, Son, or Spirit. The modalistic solution to the mystery of the Trinity was to reduce God's "threeness" to different names, roles, or activities.

Confusion regarding the Godhead eventually paved the way for the teachings of Arius (around 250–336), a Greek presbyter of Alexandria, Egypt, who argued from logic that if the Father begot the Son, then there was a time when the Son did not exist. Arius and his followers denied the full deity of the Son by representing Him as the first creature of the Father, and the Holy Spirit as the first creature of the Son.

The confusion regarding the Trinity began to be resolved in the fourth century. In 325 the Council of Nicaea was called by the Emperor Constantine to deal with Arianism, which threatened the unity of the church. After listening to the charges against Arius, the three hundred bishops present sought to develop a formula that would express Christian orthodoxy. Their creed affirms that Jesus Christ is "the Son of God, begotten of the Father, only-begotten, that is of the substance *(ousia)* of the Father, God of God, Light of Light, true God of true God, begotten not made, of one substance *(homoousion)* with the Father." The formula emphasized that the Father and the Son are distinct in existence, though essentially one. The Council of Constantinople, summoned by the Roman emperor Theodsius I in 381, applied the key word *homoousia* ("same substance") to the Holy Spirit. By asserting that the Holy Spirit is the "same substance" with the Father, the full deity of the Holy Spirit was affirmed.

Unforunately the decisions of these early councils did not settle the issue of God's Triunity for Christians of all ages. Wrong teaching has a tendency to be repeated, and around 550 Johannes Askunages and Johannes Philiponus contended that there were three divine substances *(ousiai)* in the Trinity. They essentially argued that there were three Gods rather than three persons in the Godhead. Unitarians err in viewing Jesus Christ as a mere man and the Holy Spirit as only a power or influence. Jehovah's Witnesses and Mormons share a common heretical view in their denial of the deity of Christ.

PRACTICAL IMPLICATIONS OF GOD'S TRIUNITY

The doctrine of God's Triunity is not merely a matter for theologians to ponder. It has practical implications for understanding the works of God, our personal salvation, and the Christian life.

Triunity in Creation

The Bible begins with the words, "In the beginning God [ʾelōhîm] created the heavens and the earth" (Gen. 1:1). This is a general and introductory statement about creation. Further study indicates that the members of the Triunity played individual roles in this grand work. God the Father, "from whom all things came" (1 Cor. 8:6), planned and decreed creation (Acts 17:24–26). He is the sovereign Architect of creation who does "everything in conformity with the purpose of his will" (Eph. 1:11).

God the Son executed God's decree by doing the work of creation. John wrote, "Through him all things were made; without him nothing was made that has been made" (John 1:3). This is confirmed in Colossians 1:16, "All things were created by him and for him."

Also the Holy Spirit was active in creation. Genesis 1:2 records that "the Spirit of God was hovering over the waters." The Hebrew word translated "hovering" is used in Deuteronomy 32:11 of an eagle fluttering over its young in a supervising and protecting role. And so the Holy Spirit was active in creation, hovering over it, ensuring its safe and secure development.

Trinity in the Incarnation

The Trinity of God is also evident in the incarnation and life of Jesus Christ. The Bible states that God is spirit (John 4:24) and invisible (Col. 1:15). He has no physical, bodily form. But in order to present God to the world, "the Word became flesh and made his dwelling among us" (John 1:14). In the person of Jesus Christ, God took on humanity and came to live on the earth. The apostle John wrote, "No one has ever seen God, but God, the One and Only, who is at the Father's side, has made him known" (1:18). As the Word (*logos,* 1:1, 14), Christ shares deepest intimacy with God the Father and thus can reveal deep truths about the Father. Jesus, the divine Logos, makes known (*exegeomai,* "declares" [NKJV] or "explains" [NASB]) the character of God. Thus Paul wrote, "He [Jesus] is the image [*eikōn*] of the invisible God" (Col. 1:15). The word eikon was used in ancient times of the emperor's image on a coin. Most Romans had never seen the emperor, but they knew what he was like from the image on their coins. So it is with God. In the incarnation of Jesus Christ humankind was given a glimpse of God the Father. As Jesus said, "Anyone who has seen me has seen the Father" (John 14:9).

John used the words "the One and Only, who came from the Father" (1:14) to describe Jesus' relationship with God. The translation, "only begotten from the Father" (NASB) has led to confusion regarding the relationship between the Father and the Son within the Triunity. If the Son was "begotten," how could He exist from eternity as coequal with the Father? To solve this dilemma, theologians have argued that Jesus was "eternally begotten" and thus had no beginning. I believe there is a better solution.

There is some debate whether the Greek word translated "only begotten" (*monogenēs*) is derived from *gennaō* ("beget") or *genos* ("kind"). The prefix *mono* means "one." Jesus is either the "one-begotten" or the "one-kind." The word *monogenēs* is also used of Isaac (Heb. 11:17), who was not Abraham's only son (Gen. 16:15–16), but his "one-of-a-kind" son of promise. The weight of the linguistic evidence suggests that Jesus was the "unique" or "one-of-a-kind" Son of God.[9] The NIV rendering, "the One and Only" of John 1:14 (see also 3:16) captures this idea.

What part did the Holy Spirit have in Christ's incarnation? Matthew reported that the Spirit of God came upon Him at His baptism (Matt. 3:16). Peter pointed out the significance of this event in his sermon to Cornelius when He explained that "God anointed Jesus of Nazareth with the Holy Spirit and power" (Acts 10:38; see also Isa. 61:1). Jesus said He did His miraculous works "by the Spirit of God" (Matt. 12:28). All this suggests that Jesus carried on His incarnate ministry by the Holy Spirit's enabling power.

Triunity in Salvation

The Triunity of God is very apparent in biblical texts that discuss the believer's salvation. In the introduction to his first epistle Peter addressed those "who have been chosen according to the foreknowledge of God the Father, through the sanctifying work of the Spirit, for obedience to Jesus Christ and sprinkling by his blood" (1 Pet. 1:2). Here we see that each person of the Godhead plays a distinct role: the Father chooses, the Son redeems, and the Spirit sanctifies.

This differentiation of roles in the believer's salvation is also evident in Ephesians. God the Father "chose" and "predestined" us (Eph. 1:4–5). In the Son "we have redemption through His blood, the forgiveness of sins, in accordance with the riches of God's grace" (1:7). The Holy Spirit plays a significant role in convicting unbelievers "in regard to sin and righteousness and judgment" (John 16:8). When a person comes to Christ in faith, he is "marked in him with a seal, the promised Holy Spirit, who is a deposit guaranteeing our inheritance" (Eph. 1:13–14). In ancient times a seal was used as an identifying mark, indicating the rightful ownership of the object sealed. And so the sealing ministry of the Spirit marks believers as God's own possession, guaranteeing their security for eternity.

Triunity in Revelation

God's Triunity is magnificently displayed in the process of revealing divine truth. God is the source of divine revelation (2 Pet. 1:21; Rev. 1:1). Paul wrote that "All Scripture is inspired by God" (2 Tim. 3:16, NASB). The word "inspired" (*theopneustos*) literally means "God-breathed," as in the New International Version. All Scripture comes from God as the "outbreathing" of His divine truth and revelation. God the Son is the subject of God's revelation. Jesus made this clear when He told the disciples, "These are My words which I spoke to you while I was still with you, that all things which are written about Me in the Law of Moses and the Prophets and the Psalms must be fulfilled" (Luke 24:44, NASB). The "revelation of Jesus Christ" (Rev. 1:1) is the revelation *about* Jesus Christ. Jesus is the subject and central figure of all prophetic revelation.

The Holy Spirit also has a significant role in God's work of revelation. The Spirit is the active agent of God's revelation. Peter stated that as men wrote the Scriptures, they "spoke from God as they were carried along by the Holy Spirit" (2 Pet. 1:21). Regarding the Spirit, Jesus told the apostles, "He will guide you into all truth. He will not speak on His own; he will speak only what he hears, and he will tell you what is yet to come. He will bring glory to me by taking from what is mine and making it known to you" (John 16:13–14). What God revealed to the early apostles, He revealed "by his Spirit" (1 Cor. 2:10).

Triunity in Prayer

A practical application of the Triunity is evident in the biblical instruction on prayer. Although God is one divine essence, He is also three persons. Which of these persons should we address in our prayers?

In His Sermon on the Mount Jesus instructed the disciples to pray to the Father. "This, then, is how you should pray: 'Our Father in heaven, hallowed by your name'" (Matt. 6:9). Later, in His Upper Room discourse, Jesus taught the disciples to pray "in Jesus' name." He said, "I tell you the truth, my Father will give you whatever you ask in my name. Until now you have not asked for anything in my name. Ask and you will receive, and your joy will be complete" (John 16:23–24). Christian prayer involves requesting the Father on the basis of the Son's merits, influence, and reputation ("the name"). Of course, our prayers can also be addressed to Jesus, as seen in John 14:14: "You may ask me for anything in my name, and I will do it."

How does the Holy Spirit participate in our communication with God through prayer? Paul wrote that the Spirit helps us pray when we are weak or don't know how to pray as we should. My mother experienced this for several months after the sudden death of my fifteen-year-old brother. In difficult times like these, "The Spirit himself intercedes for us with groans that words cannot express. And he who searches our hearts knows the mind of the Spirit, because the Spirit intercedes for the saints in accordance with God's will" (Rom. 8:26–27). When we can't pray or don't know how to pray, God's Holy Spirit searches our hearts and takes our groanings before our caring, compassionate God.

Knowing God Better

A study of God's Triunity certainly helps us to know Him better. We have learned that God is one, not several. But He is also three divine persons—Father, Son, and Holy Spirit. While this seems to be a contradiction from the perspective of human reason, the contradiction is only apparent, not real. By faith we accept the grand mystery of God's Triunity as a biblical truth. The Father sent His Son to the earth that we might come to know God through the convicting and regenerating work of the Holy Spirit. Apart from this fundamental truth, we have no basis for knowing God, much less knowing Him better.

For Further Study

Fortman, E. J. *The Triune God: A Historical Study of the Doctrine of the Trinity.* Philadelphia: Westminster Press, 1972.

Warfield, B. B. "The Biblical Doctrine of the Trinity." In *Biblical and Theological Studies.* Philadelphia: Presbyterian and Reformed Publishing Co., 1952.

Witmer, John A. *Immanuel: Jesus Christ, Cornerstone of Our Faith.* Swindoll Leadership Library. Nashville: Word Publishing, 1998.

11

THE DECREE OF GOD

*In him we were also chosen, predestined according to the plan of him
who works out everything in conformity with the purpose of his will*
— *Ephesians 1:11*

I N 1994 I was granted a summer sabbatical from my teaching at Western Seminary. I chose to spend the time in Israel in order to enrich my own background as a Bible teacher. The summer included many activities, all of which had to be arranged beforehand. I planned to spend the first three weeks of the summer with a group of my students, introducing them to the land of the Bible. The next two weeks I would participate in an archaeological excavation at Bethsaida, near the Sea of Galilee. From there I planned to rent a car and travel to Tel-Aviv to meet my family. We would spend the next four weeks together visiting the biblical sites and archaeological excavations. I was looking forward to being the personal tour guide for my family! After my family returned home, I planned to spend a week doing archaeological research in Jerusalem, followed by two weeks excavating at Tell Jezreel.

Before leaving for my sabbatical, I wrote out a complete itinerary of the summer with dates and addresses of the places I would be staying. It was quite a comprehensive plan! And except for a few adjustments because of human error, I was able to carry out the planned itinerary.

Planning an entire summer of study and travel is a challenge. But the significance of such an accomplishment is infinitely diminished when compared with God's plan for eternity. Incredible as it may seem, God has a plan for this universe and all creatures within it. This plan begins in the infinite past and continues into the infinite future. This is a comprehensive and complete plan, designed to bring glory to God.

In this chapter we will get to know God better by studying His plan for the ages. We will discover how each one of us fits into God's plan. We will also discover that God's plan cannot be altered or frustrated as were some of my plans during my summer sabbatical. Let's discover what this plan for the ages entails and how it involves us.

GOD'S SOVEREIGN PLAN

The Bible reveals that God has a sovereign and comprehensive plan for His entire creation, a plan He established in eternity. This plan is referred to by theologians as God's decree. The Bible uses the word *decree* to refer to sovereign decisions or judgments made by earthly rulers. King Cyrus issued a decree regarding the rebuilding of the Jerusalem temple (Ezra 6:3). Later King Darius issued a decree confirming this decision (6:12). King Ahasuerus issued a decree authorizing the destruction of the Jews throughout Persia (Esth. 3:13). King Artaxerxes issued a decree granting Ezra the authority to enhance the temple ministry (Ezra 7:13). Each of these decrees was a kingly decision, issued by one who had the authority to carry it out.

Yet while an analogy can be made between God's decree and those enacted by human rulers, there stands an important difference. The decrees of human rulers are limited by the kings' power and their subjects' willingness to obey. Human plans change. What a king decrees may need to be modified. God's decree, on the other hand, is absolute, inviolable, and unchangeable. God's decree has the backing and support of His infinite power. Because He is God, what He decrees *will* be accomplished.

God's decree may be defined as "his eternal purpose, according to the counsel of his will, whereby, for his own glory, he has foreordained whatever comes to pass."[1] Or to put it more simply, God's decree is "his eternal decision rendering certain all things which shall come to pass."[2]

WHAT THE BIBLE TEACHES ABOUT GOD'S DECREE

Both the Old and New Testaments reveal that world history, including the events of our lives, is being carried out according to God's decree.

Old Testament Teaching

The psalmist wrote about "the decree of the LORD" regarding His messianic Son (Ps. 2:7). Referring to God's creation, the psalmist wrote, "He gave a decree that will never pass away" (148:6). According to the prophet Jeremiah, God has set even the boundaries of the sea by an eternal decree: "For I have placed the sand as a boundary for the sea, an eternal decree, so it cannot cross over it" (Jer. 5:22, NASB). Unlike human decisions God's decree is determined in eternity and applies for all time. Isaiah revealed that God planned "long ago" to use Assyrian King Sennacherib as His agent of judgment against Jerusalem (Isa. 37:26). The futility of opposing God's plan is evident in Isaiah's words, "For the LORD Almighty has purposed, and who can thwart him? His hand is stretched out, and who can turn it back?" (14:27).

The judgment that came on Nebuchadnezzar was according to "the decree [of] the Most High" (Dan. 4:24). Prophecy has its basis in God's decree. God told Daniel, "Seventy 'sevens' are decreed for your people and your holy city" (9:24). He then outlined the key events of that period, including the coming of the Messiah, His crucifixion, the devastation of Jerusalem, the events of the Tribulation, and the destruction of the Antichrist (9:24–27). Regarding the activities of the Antichrist, Daniel wrote, "He will be successful until the time of wrath is completed, for what has been determined [that is, 'decreed'] must take place" (11:36).

God's decree is evident in the well-known words of Ecclesiastes, "There is a time for everything, and a season for every activity under heaven: a time to be born and a time to die" (Eccles. 3:1–2). The point is not so much that there is an appropriate time for these events, but that there is a divinely ordained time. That is, everything fits into God's plan. Solomon wrote, "The LORD works out everything for his own ends—even the wicked for a day of disaster" (Prov. 16:4).

New Testament Teaching

The New Testament writings further our understanding of God's decree. Although the New Testament does not use the word *decree* of God's sovereign plan, other significant words are introduced. In the Gospels God's decree is revealed through the fulfillment of prophecy. This is particularly prominent in Matthew. The virgin birth of Jesus "took place to fulfill what the Lord had said through the prophet" (Matt. 1:22; see Isa. 7:14). Matthew pointed out that the place of His birth had been determined beforehand and was announced by the prophet Micah (Matt. 2:5–6; Mic. 5:2). The slaughter of the children at Bethlehem (Matt. 2:16–18), the ministry of John the Baptizer (3:1–3), the location of Christ's ministry in Galilee (4:12–16), and His miracles (8:16–17)—all these accomplished God's decree by fulfilling prophecy. In His Olivet Discourse Jesus spoke of the coming judgment on Jerusalem which must take place "in fulfillment of all that has been" (Luke 21:22). And His betrayal would take place "as it has been decreed" (22:22).

The apostles recognized God's decree in the events of the life of Christ. In His sermon on the Day of Pentecost, Peter testified that Jesus was delivered up and crucified "by God's set purpose and foreknowledge" (Acts 2:23). In their prayer the apostles recognized that God anointed Herod, Pontius Pilate, the Gentiles, and the Jewish people to do "what your power and will had decided beforehand should happen" (4:28).

In Paul's sermons and writings the doctrine of God's decree is presented most thoroughly. In his sermon to the Athenians, Paul acknowledged that God made every nation and "determined the times set for them and the exact places where they should live" (17:26). All of God's redemptive work is according to His divine plan in which He sent forth His Son at exactly the right time (Gal. 4:4). Israel's unbelief and rejection of their Messiah was anticipated by prophecy (Rom. 11:7–10; Ps. 69:22–23; Isa. 29:10), and Gentile inclusion in the plan of God was anticipated beforehand in God's covenant with Abraham (Gal. 3:8; Gen. 12:3). Believers in Christ are chosen "before the creation of the world" and are "predestined . . . to the praise of his glorious grace" (Eph. 1:4–6). "For those God foreknew he also predestined to be conformed to the likeness of his Son" (Rom. 8:29). In a rather all-encompassing statement Paul asserted that God does everything "after the counsel of His will" (Eph. 1:11, NASB). Elsewhere Paul acknowledged that "God causes all things to work together for good to those who love God, to those who are called according to His purpose" (Rom. 8:28, NASB).

ESSENTIAL CHARACTERISTICS OF GOD'S DECREE

What can be said about God's decree by way of a systematic summary? The following five points should be noted.

First, God's decree was fixed in eternity but is executed in time. As previously noted, Jeremiah used the word "everlasting" to describe God's decree (Jer. 5:22), and Paul wrote that believers were chosen by God "before the creation of the world" (Eph. 1:4). This phrase means "from all eternity"[3] and refers to the eternal past. Peter used this same phrase to refer to Jesus who was "chosen before the creation of the world." Then Peter added that "He was revealed in these last times for your sake" (1 Pet. 1:20). God's plan for Christ was fixed in eternity but was executed at a particular point in time. The same is true of the believers' calling and salvation: God called us "before the beginning of time" but "saved us" at a particular point in time (2 Tim. 1:9).

Second, God's decree is all-encompassing. One of the things I discovered during my 1994 summer sabbatical in Israel was that while my plan was comprehensive it was not all-encompassing. There were several important matters I had overlooked in making my plans. Not so with God's plans. According to Scripture nothing is left out of God's plan. When Paul wrote that God "works all things after the counsel of His will" (Eph. 1:11, NASB), he clearly meant that nothing is left out or left to chance. Nothing comes into our lives which has not part of God's plan.

Third, God's decree is a good and wise plan. Because God is good (Nah. 1:7), we can be confident that God works everything together "for the good" of His own (Rom. 8:28). Because God is wise (16:27), His plan weaves rather remote and seemingly unrelated events together into one harmonious whole. God's wisdom is evident in the crucifixion of Christ (1 Cor. 1:23–24) and in uniting believing Jews and Gentiles in one body in Christ (Eph. 3:6–10). Having reflected on the profound mystery of God's plan for the people of Israel (Romans 9–11), Paul concluded the discussion with a great statement of praise for God's wisdom in it all: "Oh, the depth of the riches of the wisdom and knowledge of God! How unsearchable his judgments, and his paths beyond tracing out! (11:33).

Fourth, God's decree is ultimately intended to bring Him glory. All that God creates and does is for the purpose of magnifying His attributes so that people praise Him. The physical universe was created to manifest His glory (Ps. 19:1), and humanity was created for His glory (Isa. 43:7). His election and predestination of believers is intended "to the praise of his glorious grace" (Eph. 1:4–6). Believers are instructed to live their lives in such a way that they bring glory to God (Matt. 5:16; 1 Cor. 10:31). Even using your spiritual gifts as believers is so that "in all things God may be glorified" (1 Pet. 4:11, NASB). John's vision of thousands and thousands of living creatures around the throne of God suggests that worship is intended for His glory. "Worthy is the Lamb, who was slain, to receive power and wealth and wisdom and strength and honor and glory and praise." (Rev. 5:12). God's plan for His creation is glorious and brings Him glory.

Fifth, God's decree does not annul human responsibility. Although God has a sovereign plan which will be accomplished, this does not do away with personal responsibility for one's actions. This is especially important as God's decree relates to sinful human actions. While God is sovereign over our actions, He cannot rightly be blamed for our actions. This truth is illustrated in the life of Joseph. After Joseph's father Jacob died, Joseph's brothers were fearful he would punish them for the wrong they had done against him. But Joseph responded, "You intended to harm me, but God intended it for good to accomplish what is now being done, the saving of many lives" (Gen. 50:20). Joseph's brothers did an evil thing when they sold their brother into slavery. But God used that sinful act to accomplish something good for Jacob's family. As a result of Joseph's being sold into slavery in Egypt, he was later able to provide for Jacob's family during a time of famine. Joseph's brothers bore responsibility for their wrongdoing. And yet God used those actions to accomplish something good.

Another illustration of this truth is the crucifixion of Jesus. In Acts 2:23

Peter explained that Jesus died "by God's set purpose and foreknowledge." What happened in the betrayal, trial, and crucifixion of Christ was the outworking of God's predetermined plan (4:27–28). But did God's sovereign plan annul the human responsibility of Judas, Pilate, and those who put Christ to death? No. Peter added that Jesus was nailed to a cross by "wicked men" (2:23). Klooster notes, "The crucifixion was part of God's eternal decree, and sinful human action was involved; but the guilt of such action is not minimized even when it functions as means to effectuate God's decree."[4] Jesus noted this important balance between divine sovereignty and human responsibility when He said, "The Son of Man will go as it has been decreed, but woe to that man who betrays him" (Luke 22:22).

Also God's decree does not absolve people of the responsibility for taking action. God will save those whom He has chosen. But this does not mean that we can neglect our responsibility to evangelize (Matt. 28:19–20; John 15:16). God will bring His chosen ones to faith in Himself, but this requires the witness of obedient Christians (Rom. 10:14). Again, God will save those whom He has chosen, but no one is saved apart from personal belief in Christ. Luke pointed out this truth when he wrote, "all who were appointed for eternal life believed" (Acts 13:48).

Sixth, God's decree is unchangeable. Since God is perfect (Matt. 5:48), His plan is perfect. He never needs to change His mind because of some unforseen circumstance or to work out His plan in a different way because someone isn't cooperating. God does not change (Mal. 3:6); with Him there is "no variation or shifting shadow" (James 1:17, NASB). "God is not a man, that he should lie, nor a son of man, that he should change his mind. Does he speak and then not act? Does he promise and not fulfill?" (Num. 23:19). However, do some verses suggest that God does change His mind? (For discussion of this question see the section "God Is Constant" in chapter 7.)

GOD'S DECREE AND PERSONAL SALVATION

One aspect of God's decree that is of special interest to believers is how God's plan relates to our personal salvation. Here we introduce some important biblical terms——predestination, election, and divine foreknowledge.

After considering what the Bible says about these matters, we will then make a theological statement about God's decree and personal salvation.

The Bible clearly teaches the concept of predestination. As He predestined the death of Christ (Acts 4:28), so God predestined the salvation of believers (Rom. 8:29–30; Eph. 1:5). But predestination extends beyond our salvation. Ephesians 1:11 indicates that God predestined not only our salvation, but also our entire lives! In keeping with His divine decree God has sovereignly determined whatever comes to pass. The word *predestined* translates the Greek *proorizō*, "to mark out boundaries beforehand."[5] Predestination involves God's choice (Eph. 1:4), is done in love (1:4), is according to His good pleasure (1:5), and ultimately glorifies God (1:14). How comforting to know that in His great love for us, God has "marked out the boundaries" of our lives in ways that ultimately glorify Him!

Another important word the Bible uses to relate God's decree to individual salvation is *elect*, from the Greek *eklektos*, which means "to be called out, picked out, or chosen from." This word is used of Christ, the chosen of God (Luke 23:35; 1 Pet. 2:4), of angels (1 Tim. 5:21), of Jewish believers during the Tribulation (Matt. 24:22, 24), and of the elect of the church (Rom. 8:33; 1 Pet. 1:1; 2:9). The verb form *eklegomai* ("to choose or select") is used of the apostles whom Christ chose (John 13:18; Acts 1:2) and of believers whom God chose (1 Cor. 1:27–28). The noun *eklogē* denotes a "selection," "election," or "choosing" and is used of Paul as a "chosen instrument" (Acts 9:15) and especially of the divine election of believers (Rom. 11:5, 7; 1 Thess. 1:4; 2 Pet. 1:10). Each of these important words conveys the concept of God's election. In relationship to the church, election is God's act of choosing those who will believe and be saved as members of the body of Christ.

The doctrine of election is one of the most difficult doctrines for believers to accept because it does not seem fair that God has chosen some and not others. Paul explained that as a potter, God has the right to "make out of the same lump of clay some pottery for noble purposes and some for common use" (Rom. 9:21). I never think of election without reminding myself that this doctrine must be understood in light of the fact that God is loving, sovereign, and just. While the biblical doctrine of election is difficult to understand and appreciate, it is comforting to know that it will not contradict any of these facts about God.

Another key word that must be properly understood when discussing God's decree and personal salvation is *foreknowledge*, a translation of *prognōsis*, derived from *pro* ("before") and *gnōsis* ("knowledge"). This word is used only of God in the Bible. Divine foreknowledge is one aspect of God's omniscience. Christ was executed, as already noted, according to "God's . . . foreknowledge" (Acts 2:23). Believers were "chosen according to the foreknowledge of God the Father" (1 Pet. 1:2). The verb form *proginōskō* ("to foreknow") is used in Romans 8:29 with reference to believers in Christ and in Romans 11:2 with reference to the remnant of Israel.

According to a popular interpretation of divine foreknowledge, God "knew beforehand" our response to the gospel and therefore chose believers based on this prior knowledge. However, a careful study of *proginōskō* does not support this view. *Ginōskō* means more than simply a knowledge of certain facts. It is used in the Bible of an intimate, personal knowledge, the kind of knowledge a man has of his wife. The biblical concept of divine foreknowledge in relation to individual salvation is more along the lines of being "forechosen." God preselected in a loving and intimate way those whom He would graciously call to Himself by personal faith. To suggest that "foreknowledge" refers merely to God's advance knowledge of human actions is refuted by His choice of Israel. If God foreknew the people of Israel because of His advanced knowledge of a favorable response, He was wrong! Israel rebelled against God and rejected their Messiah. God "foreknew" the people of Israel (Rom. 11:2) in the sense that He sovereignly chose them to be His own in spite of the unbelief that He knew would characterize that nation (10:21).

In his classic discussion on the election of Israel, Paul wrote that God "has mercy on whom he wants to have mercy" (9:18). The key question in this discussion is, "On what basis is God's mercy and grace extended?" There are three possible answers. First, God grants mercy based on His preknowledge of the decisions of those who will choose to believe in Christ. Second, God grants mercy based on merit and good deeds. Third, God grants mercy according to His sovereign choice for reasons known only to Him.

The first view, that God grants mercy based on preknowledge, gives human beings the ultimate say in their own destiny. According to this view God responds to a person's decision to believe. But this undermines God's absolute sovereignty and is refuted by a proper understanding of divine foreknowledge, which means, as noted, "forechoosing." When the Bible says that God "foreknew" us (Rom. 8:29), it means He actually "forechose" us in an intimate and personal way.

The second view, that God grants mercy based on good deeds, emphasizes the ability of human beings to earn their salvation. This view is clearly refuted by Scripture. In Romans 3:12, Paul alluded to the Book of Psalms to demonstrate that people are completely unable to achieve merit with God. "All have turned away, they have together become worthless; there is no one who does good, not even one" (Ps. 14:3; see also 53:3). The apostle emphasized in Galatians that people are not justified by the works of the Law (Gal. 2:16), and he wrote to the Ephesians that salvation is "the gift of God—not by works, so that no one can boast" (Eph. 2:8–9).

We are left with the third view, that God grants mercy on the basis of His sovereign choice for reasons known only to Him. According to this view only by God's sovereign intervention and gracious choice can individuals become "objects of his mercy, whom he prepared in advance for glory" (Rom. 9:23). This view has the strongest biblical support and reflects a proper understanding of the doctrines of predestination, foreknowledge, and election.

One further question must be answered in our consideration of God's decree as it relates to personal salvation. Is "double predestination" a biblical concept? Those who hold to the doctrine of election generally agree that as an exercise of His sovereignty, God chose certain individuals to believe and be saved. The question is whether in choosing some to believe, God also chose others to disbelieve and be condemned. The concept of God choosing some people to disbelieve and be condemned seems unfair and is contrary to God's mercy. The ultimate question for students of Scripture is whether this doctrine is biblical.

A number of biblical passages seem to support this doctrine, including Exodus 4:21; Proverbs 16:4; Isaiah 6:9–10; Romans 9:22; 1 Peter 2:8; and Jude 4. But we must be careful here. The Bible clearly teaches that

God is ultimately behind every action (Eph. 1:11). But while God stands behind the destiny of both the elect and the nonelect, He may not do so in exactly the same way. It is probably significant that when Paul used the participle *katērtismena* ("prepared") in referring to the nonelect in Romans 9:22, he did not specify God as the subject as he did when he wrote of the elect's destiny in 9:23. The difference is subtle, but significant. While God is sovereign over the destinies of both the elect and nonelect, He is not behind the destiny of the nonelect in the same way He is behind the destiny of the elect. The problem with double predestination is that it gives the idea that the two predestinations are of equal character, when this does not appear to be the case. This crucial difference is supported in Romans 6:23 where punishment is considered as "wages" earned, whereas eternal life is a "free gift."[6] In addition we need to remember that everyone deserves hell because of his or her sin, but that God decided to save some by His grace and to let the others go on their way. He did not predetermine or decide to send some spiritually neutral people to hell; instead He let them follow their own path of sin which, because of God's justice, results in their eternal condemnation. For more on this issue, see chapter 20, "Answers to Tough Questions about God."

GOD'S DECREE AND INDIVIDUAL FREE WILL

If God's decree is absolute and all-inclusive, what freedom of choice do we have as individuals? Do I have freedom of choice when it comes to the issues of my salvation, my marriage, and my career? Or has God worked it all out and I am simply a pawn in His powerful hand?

The key to answering this important question is to maintain a biblical balance. As noted, the Bible clearly teaches that God's decree is absolute and all-inclusive (Eph. 1:11). But the Bible also teaches that individuals bear responsibility for their actions (Luke 22:22). Divine sovereignty never cancels out human responsibility. If people must bear responsibility for their actions, then there must—by moral necessity—be freedom of choice. And the Bible clearly teaches this.

Jesus taught that no one knows the Father, "except the Son and those to whom the Son chooses to reveal him" (Matt. 11:27). Natural reason cannot lead people to place their faith in Christ. A knowledge of the Father comes only through the Son's divine will. But in the next verse Jesus said, "Come to me, all you who are weary and burdened, and I will give you rest" (11:28). While verse 27 emphasizes God's sovereignty, verse 28 recognizes the place for human response. People have the freedom to respond to Jesus' invitation, "Come to me." This delicate balance is also seen in John 6:37, "All that the Father gives me will come to me [God's sovereignty], and whoever comes to me [human decision] I will never drive away." This verse affirms the two great truths of divine sovereignty and human responsibility. Some tend to focus on one of these truths to the neglect of the other, but we must embrace these seemingly contradictory concepts with equal enthusiasm.

Human freedom to decide is evident in Jesus' words, "I am the gate; whoever enters through me will be saved. He will come in and go out, and find pasture" (10:9). A condition is pointed up in the words, "whoever enters through me." This involves a personal choice. Apart from such a decision, there is no salvation. The "whoever" in John 3:16 and the "all who received him" (1:12) acknowledge the place and importance of human freedom to choose. Klooster's comment is helpful, "Even though Adam's fall and Christ's crucifixion were included in God's decree, Scripture clearly indicates that the decree did not force the outcome. Humans acted freely but irresponsibly; they did precisely what God commanded them *not* to do."[7]

When discussing God's sovereignty and human freedom, it is important to recognize three different aspects of God's will. God's *sovereign* will is what God decrees to come to pass. It includes all things (Eph. 1:11) and is irresistible and immutable. God's *preceptive* will is what He prescribes or prefers. This aspect of the will of God includes His moral desires as revealed in His Word (Exod. 20:1–17). Third, God's *permissive* will refers to what the Lord permits even when it is not in conformity with His revealed or prescribed will. God may permit sin, though it is not in keeping with what He prefers.

What does it mean to have freedom of choice within God's divine decree? I suggest that this has to do with the absence of any conscious *constraint* or *compulsion* to act according to God's divine decree. When I made a decision to marry my college sweetheart, I was not consciously following God's divine decree. I simply made what I thought was a wise decision—one that was in keeping my own desires and had the approval of Nancy's and my parents. Only after the marriage could I look back and say, "This union was God's decree." God's decree makes our acts *certain*, but not in the sense of our being *compelled*.[8]

God's preceptive will is clearly revealed in His Word. His permissive will becomes known as people make decisions contrary to what He has revealed. God's sovereign will or divine decree is known to us mainly through history. Human freedom means we have the responsibility to act according to God's precepts and cannot use God's decree as an excuse for our sin.

THE PRACTICAL APPLICATION OF GOD'S DECREE

The doctrine of God's comprehensive and all-inclusive decree is not "armchair theology" reserved for a few saints who pride themselves in probing deeper. The truth of God's decree has very practical implications for believers.

Klooster noted that "Scriptural references to God's decree are generally set forth in concrete relation to historical situations for the purpose of promoting comfort, security, assurance, and trust."[9] For example, are you worried that the world is out of control? Psalm 33:10–11 provides reassurance: "The LORD foils the plans of the nations; he thwarts the purposes of the peoples. But the plans of the LORD stand firm forever, the purposes of his heart through all generations." We can entrust our lives and our destinies to the God who has the nations under His control.

Are you troubled by circumstances that seem to thwart your best laid plans? There is comfort in the words of Romans 8:28: "And we know that in all things God works for the good of those who love him, who have been called according to his purpose."

Do you feel rather ordinary and not very special? Remember that God chose you before the foundation of the world and predestined you to be adopted as His child (Eph. 1:4–5).

Are you wondering if your salvation can be lost? Paul answered that question in Romans 8:29–30 where he recounted a leak-proof succession of God's actions. "For those God foreknew he also predestined to be conformed to the likeness of his Son, that he might be the firstborn among many brothers. And those he predestined, he also called; those he called, he also justified; those he justified, he also glorified." We have the assurance that when God initiates a redemptive act, His decree guarantees that it will be brought to completion.

Believers may find great comfort in the truth that God is sovereignly controlling all things and is working out His good and perfect plan for this world and our lives.

For Further Study

Carson, D. A. *How Long, O Lord?* Grand Rapids: Baker Book House, 1990.

Packer, J. I. *Evangelism and the Sovereignty of God.* Downers Grove, Ill.: InterVarsity Press, 1961.

12

GOD AND THE PRESENCE OF EVIL

When times are good, be happy; but when times are bad, consider:
God has made the one as well as the other.

—Ecclesiastes 7:14

A LITTLE BOY approached Brian and Haley on a Sunday morning at Sunset Park Community Church. He looked past Brian's burn-scarred face to study what's left of his arms.

"Brian is healing good," the little boy said. "I can tell because his arms are growing back!"

In December 1995 a workplace fire burned 97 percent of Brian's body. Doctors and nurses at the burn center saved his life. But the fire robbed Brian of his vision, and infection cost him parts of each limb.[1]

At the time of the accident Brian was engaged to be married to his high-school sweetheart. Haley demonstrated what true love is all about when she went ahead with the marriage after Brian was released from the hospital, knowing that their life together would be much different from what they had planned. She will be the primary caregiver for her husband for the rest of his life.

Why did God allow Brian, a Christian man, to be so badly burned, deformed, and scarred? If God is good and sovereign, could He not have prevented this disaster?

You don't have to read beyond the front page of any newspaper to be confronted with the question of why God permits bad things to happen. Seven-year-old Patrick Meier was riding home on his new mountain bike when he was run over and killed by a recycling truck.[2] Patrick was returning home from a visit with his grandmother who lived a few blocks away. The truck driver told police he had missed a turn and was backing up to make the turn when the accident occurred. As the truck was backing, Patrick apparently tried to shoot behind the back of the truck. He didn't make it.

Why did God allow a happy second-grader to be struck and killed by a fifteen-ton truck? Couldn't He have prevented this disaster and spared the Meier family such sadness and suffering?

David Cornwall was a successful small-town physician. He had been involved in a bitter custody battle with his wife. The divorce threatened to take away the one thing that mattered most to him, his family. Taking his three young daughters for the day, Cornwall apparently gave the girls lethal doses of drugs, put them to bed, and then killed himself with carbon monoxide from car exhaust fumes.[3]

Why does God allow such bad things to happen? Why does a good God allow evil to run rampant in His creation? If God is sufficiently powerful to do all things, why doesn't He intervene to prevent good and godly people from suffering?

THE ISSUE OF THEODICY

A particular aspect of God's decree is the problem of evil. Did God include evil in His decree? If so, why? Why didn't He instead use His power to prevent evil and suffering? These questions relate to the subject of "theodicy" (from *theos*, "God," and *dikē*, "justice"), a term used to refer to attempts to justify the seemingly evil ways of God.[4]

The issue of theodicy is both logical and theological. The logical question is, "If God is good and He is all-powerful, why is there evil in the world?" Theologian Millard Erickson says this question is "the most difficult intellectual problem for the Christian faith."[5] If God is good, He would certainly want to eliminate evil. And if He is omnipotent, He is able to eliminate evil. Therefore some conclude that since evil exists in the world, either God is not good or He is not omnipotent.

In addition to the logical question, a theological issue is raised. What does God reveal in His Word about His sovereign purposes? What does Scripture say about the subject of evil in this world? According to John Feinberg, "A successful theodicy resolves the problem of evil . . . and demonstrates that God is all-powerful, all-loving, and just, despite evil's existence."[6] This chapter seeks to demonstrate through logic and Scripture that the presence of evil in the world does not negate His goodness or undermine His sovereignty. God certainly has the power to prevent sin and evil, but He is willing to allow them to accomplish a greater good.

FAULTY THEODICIES

Throughout the centuries theologians and philosophers have offered several answers to the question, Why does God allow evil?

God Can't Prevent All Evil

One solution to the problem of evil is to conclude that God cannot prevent all evil. The bad things that happen are not part of God's plan or decree. He wills "good" for people, but the existence of evil in the world limits the good that He can accomplish. According to this view God is doing the best that He can to make the world a pleasant place, but don't expect more than He is able to accomplish. This solution to the problem of evil is advocated by Rabbi Harold Kushner in his best-selling book, *When Bad Things Happen to Good People*.[7] Obviously, such a view compromises God's omnipotence, for if God is all-powerful, He can indeed deter evil.

God Won't Prevent All Evil

Some scholars have questioned whether God is really good, at least as we commonly understand that word. They argue that if God is truly in control of this world, He is not a good God. At least, He is not so good as to prevent evil. In support of this view it is observed that God commanded the people of Israel to slaughter the Canaanite people—men, women, and children. How can that be good? He gave Job and his family over to

Satan for untold suffering just to prove a theological point. How could a good God do that?

Philosopher Friedrich Nietzsche (1844–1900), famous for his "God is dead" view, similarly compromised the goodness of God when he suggested that God created both good and evil.[8] He is the god of falsehood, Nietzsche said, as well as of truth, of pain as well as pleasure.

Evil Is Not Reality

Some have sought to resolve the problem of evil by denying its reality. Christian Science dogma asserts that there is no reality except Mind or Spirit. Things that are evil—like sin, sickness, and death—are illusory. According to Christian Science's definitive book, *Science and Health, with Key to the Scriptures*, by Mary Baker Eddy,[9] salvation comes as people recognize that sin, sickness, and death are unreal.

GOD'S PLAN AND THE ENTRANCE OF EVIL

The problem with the three previously mentioned approaches to the issue of pain and evil is that they are not consistent with the clearly revealed teachings of the Word of God. These views are faulty in that they compromise God's goodness, deny God's sovereignty, or reject the reality of evil. A Christian theodicy must be consistent with the Scriptures. The place to begin our study is in Genesis, the book of beginnings. Here we discover that God's original plan to bless creation was disrupted by the entrance of sin.

God's Plan to Bless

Genesis 1–2 makes it clear that God's original plan for His creation was to make it a place for good and blessing. In the first chapter of Genesis the term "good" is used six times to describe what God did during the six days of creation. The word may refer to abstract goodness such as "desirability, pleasantness, and beauty," or moral goodness, as in "the good way." Quite clearly, God creates and desires what is "good." The word "blessed" occurs three times in the creation account. God blessed the creatures (1:22), man and woman (1:28), and the seventh day (2:3). The word "bless" (bārak) means "to endue with power for success, prosperity, and longevity." The repetition of the words "good" and "blessed" emphasizes an important theological truth: God's original plan for His creation was that it be a place for good and for blessing.

The Entrance of Sin and Evil

Sadly, God's plan for His creation was disrupted by the entrance of sin and evil. Genesis 3 tells the tragic story. Because we are made in the image of God, we possess the capacity to make moral decisions. But in contrast with God, who cannot sin, we can reject His will and violate His commands. As a result of Satan's influence, the first couple, Adam and Eve, chose evil instead of good. And their decision brought a terrible tragedy on all humanity. Paul commented, "death came to all men, because all sinned" (Rom. 5:12). As a result of Adam's sin, fellowship with God was broken and humankind became subject to spiritual and physical death.

The entrance of sin into God's good creation has brought great suffering upon humankind. While the whole animal kingdom was affected by the Fall (Rom. 8:20–22), the instrument of deception—the serpent—was "cursed" (Gen. 3:14). As a result of the Fall, Eve and her female descendants would experience increased pain in childbirth and frustration in their marriage relationship (3:16).[10] Further, the ground was cursed so that it would yield its fruits only after much hard work (3:17–18). Finally, life on earth would end in death—God's promised judgment for Adam's disobedience (3:19).[11]

While God created this world as a place for good and blessing, evil, through the sin of the first couple, was brought alongside the good. Life on this earth has never been the same since those days of innocence in Eden. Virtually all the natural and moral evil experienced by humanity comes as a result of the Fall. Because of the Fall people get cancer and die. Because of the Fall children are abused and victimized. Because of the Fall drunk drivers kill and maim thousands of innocent victims every year. All this is because of the entrance of sin and evil on this earth.

God's Plan to Reverse the Curse

It is encouraging to know that God has not given up His plan to make this earth a place of blessing. As we trace the workings of God from Genesis to Revelation, one great theme prevails: God has a plan to reverse the curse and replace it with His blessing. This plan involves the redemption of sinners, the reclamation of His kingdom authority, and the execution of judgment on Satan and his followers. The apostle John anticipated the day in which God's plan will be accomplished. In Revelation 22:3 he wrote, "No longer will there be any curse." One day, according to God's plan, this sin-marred creation will be brought back into conformity with His goodness and blessing—to the praise of His glory.

Preliminary Observations about God and Evil

First, it is clear that evil exists. Students of Scripture cannot deny the reality of evil which has come into this creation because of sin. Second, this evil is traced to Satan, who seduced Adam to disobey God, which brought the chaos of sin and evil on all creation. Third, God has a plan to deal with evil and to bring this creation back into conformity with His goodness and blessing. Evil is not out of control. God is dealing with it and will judge Satan and his followers at the appropriate time.

LEARNING FROM JOB

The Book of Job presents a classic study of the problem of pain and suffering. Here we read of the acute suffering of a very righteous man. We also see how he eventually triumphed over his tragedy. We can gain much insight into the problem of evil from Job's story. Here we can begin to build a theodicy that upholds both the goodness and sovereignty of God without compromise.

Job's Tragedy

The first verse of the book introduces Job as a righteous person: "In the land of Uz there lived a man whose name was Job. This man was blameless, and upright; he feared God and shunned evil." Even the Lord Himself testified to Job's unique moral and spiritual character (Job 1:8; 2:3). To understand the message of Job, we must recognize that Job's suffering did not result from sin in his life. Even in his calamity he did not sin (1:22), nor did he curse God, as Satan had predicted (2:5, 10).

The first two chapters of the book tell the reader why tragedy and suffering came on Job. As the story begins, the curtains of heaven are drawn back to reveal a drama of which Job was completely unaware. Among the angels of heaven appeared a visitor—our adversary, the devil—Satan himself. Like a proud parent, the Lord called Satan's attention to Job—a man of exemplary righteousness and godliness. But Satan was unimpressed. He explained that Job's good conduct was due to the benefits he had received from God. Satan reasoned that Job was good only because God was good to him.

Satan then challenged, "But stretch out your hand and strike everything he has, and he will surely curse you to your face" (1:11). To demonstrate the genuineness of Job's faith and spiritual character against Satan's challenge, God gave Satan permission to destroy Job's possessions. "Very well, then, everything he has is in your hands, but on the man himself do not lay a finger" (1:12). It is important to observe here that Satan did not have free access to Job or authority over his life. Only by God's permission was Satan was able to bring physical harm to Job.

Job was prospering and enjoying life when four staggering blows filled his world with sorrow. First, looters attacked and killed Job's workers, stealing his oxen and donkeys. Second, a fire from heaven, perhaps lightning, killed his sheep and servants. Third, three bands of raiders captured his camels, killing more of his servants. Fourth, a great wind blew down his oldest son's house, killing all ten of his children.

While Job lost all his children and property, he did not lose his faith. Job responded to this personal tragedy by worshiping God. Instead of cursing God, as Satan had predicted, Job blessed God. "The LORD gave and the LORD has taken away; may the name of the LORD be praised" (1:21). His response to the tragedies powerfully refuted Satan's theory that Job was good because God was good to him.

But Satan does not give up easily. When God pointed out Job's steadfast character in spite of personal loss, Satan argued that Job accepted these losses in order not to endanger his own life and health. With the genuineness of Job's piety still in question, God gave Satan permission to test Job again.

Satan's second assault took the form of physical suffering. Job was stricken with "painful sores from the soles of his feet to the top of his head" (2:7). Medical opinion differs in its diagnosis of Job's disease (2:7–8; 7:5, 14; 19:17; 30:17, 30). Whatever Job had, it wasn't pleasant! As was the custom of a mourner, he sat in a pile of ashes. Seeking relief from his affliction, he scraped his itching sores with a piece of broken pottery.

Job's Response

We can learn a great deal from Job's response to the tragedies which befell him. Distraught by the loss of her ten children, family property, and her husband's health, Job's wife suggested that Job renounce his faith: "Are you still holding on to your integrity? Curse God and die!" (2:9). This is exactly what Satan had hoped Job would do. But Job responded, "Shall we accept good from God, and not trouble?" (2:10). This is a key principle in developing a biblical theodicy. Job has recognized that nothing comes into the lives of God's people except by His sovereign design. God is sovereign over good as well as over adversity. Even the evil which Satan flung into Job's life came by God's permission.

Job's friends, Eliphaz, Bildad, and Zophar, were convinced that suffering is always punishment for sin. Since Job was suffering so severely, they concluded that he must have sinned greatly. Job responded to the repeated challenges of his friends by asserting his innocence, insisting that his suffering couldn't be attributed to some secret sin in his life.

When human insight into Job's tragedy was finally exhausted, God Himself addressed Job. We might have expected God to explain the reason behind Job's suffering and how his response to personal tragedy refuted Satan's false view of Job's spiritual life. But that did not happen. In fact, God did not even mention the problem of Job's suffering. Instead, God directed Job to His own greatness and power as Creator. In chapters 38–41, God showed Job that He controls the intricate details of all creation, mysteries that Job could only dimly understand. And so Job must trust

God to order the details of his life even though he could not fully understand His ways.

God has not seen fit to give mankind the reason for everything He does. But the Book of Job sets forth a God so great that no answer is needed. In the end Job matured in his relationship with God because he learned to live with unanswered questions. The mystery of God's ways was not a hindrance to Job's ongoing faith.

Job's Lessons

The Book of Job teaches some important lessons about God and the presence of evil. First, from Job's experience we see that God is absolutely sovereign over good and evil. Job's words to his wife, "Shall we accept good from God, and not trouble?" reflect Job's faith in this fundamental principle. The blessings Job enjoyed and the tragedies that befell him did not come by chance or accident. Both were in the plan of God (see Eccles. 7:14).

Second, God is not behind good and evil in exactly the same way. Satan spoke the truth when he spoke to God of Job, "You have blessed the work of his hands, so that his flocks and herds are spread throughout the land" (Job 1:10). Later we read that "the Lord made him prosper again and gave him twice as much as he had before" (42:10). On the other hand, when Job encountered evil, it came into his life through the agency of Satan. We read that "Satan afflicted Job with painful sores" all over his body (2:7). Satan, not God, was the active agent in bringing tragedy and suffering to Job's life. As D. A. Carson remarked, "It must be the case that God stands behind good and evil in somewhat different ways; that is, he stands behind good and evil *asymmetrically*. To put it bluntly, God stands behind evil in such a way that not even evil takes place outside the bounds of his sovereignty, yet the evil is not morally chargeable to him; it is always chargeable to secondary agents, to secondary causes."[12] Never in Scripture is God presented as an accomplice of evil in the same way as He is a promoter of good.

Third, from Job we see that evil occurs as a result of God's sovereign permission. Satan had to receive God's permission to wage his war on Job. God granted Satan permission to destroy Job's possessions and take the lives of His children, but He did not permit Satan to harm Job (1:12).

Later, God granted Satan further authority over Job, "Very well, then, he is in your hands; but you must spare his life" (2:6). We see here that Satan does not have complete freedom over evil. He operates only by God's permission and within certain limits.

Fourth, there is a mystery about suffering. Job never knew the reason for his suffering, and the same is often true for suffering saints today. There may be suffering in your life or mine which is beyond explanation. We wonder, "Why?" but often no answer is forthcoming. In these situations we must remember that God is in control and that we don't need to know "why?" if we know God. The sovereign Lord has not seen fit to give us reason for everything He does. But the Book of Job sets forth a God so great that no answer is needed! Our hope is not in improved circumstances or clearer answers to our "why" questions. Our hope is in God alone.

DIFFICULT TEXTS ON GOD AND EVIL

The Bible makes it abundantly clear that God is absolutely opposed to all that is evil. The prophets of the Lord were sent to the idol worshipers of Judah with the message, "Do not do this detestable thing that I hate" (Jer. 44:4). Speaking for God to His people, Zechariah declared, "Do not plot evil against your neighbor, and do not love to swear falsely. I hate all this" (Zech. 8:17). Proverbs 6:16–19 lists seven wicked actions which Yahweh hates. To "fear the LORD" means, among other things, to share God's attitude toward sin, hating sin as He hates it (8:13). James reminded his readers that they cannot blame God for their sins since God is not one who tempts or solicits evil (James 1:13).

In spite of these clear statements regarding God's aversion to sin and evil, several verses in the Bible seem to link God directly with evil. How do these fit in with our developing theology of God and evil?

1 Samuel 16:14

When the Spirit of the Lord departed from disobedient King Saul, "an evil spirit from the LORD tormented him" (16:14). A similar thing is recorded in 18:10, where we read that "an evil spirit from God" came upon

Saul (see also Judg. 9:23; 1 Sam. 19:9). Do not these verses suggest that God perpetrates evil?

The "evil spirit from the LORD" has been understood in various ways: (1) demonic possession as divine punishment, (2) demonic attack or influence, (3) a spirit of discontent created by God in the heart of Saul. Since Saul appears to have been a believer (10:6, 9), it is unlikely he would have been demon-possessed. The contrast between the "Spirit of the LORD" and the "evil spirit from the LORD" would rule out a "spirit of discontent" view. First Samuel 16:14 probably means that God sovereignly appointed a demon, one of Satan's emissaries (Matt. 12:24), to torment Saul. This may have been intended by God to drive Saul to his knees and encourage him to return to the Lord. The major lesson from this text is that God is sovereign over all spiritual powers—even Satan and his assistants. And God can use even demons for His divine purposes. As in the case of Job, the evil that came on Saul came through a demonic, secondary agency rather than directly from the hand of God.

1 Kings 21:21

Speaking for the Lord, Elijah declared to wicked King Ahab, "I am going to bring disaster [rāʾâ, 'evil,' NASB] on you" (1 Kings 21:21). In a strikingly similar text, God promised to bring "disaster" (rāʾâ) on the house of idolatrous king Jeroboam (14:10). The Hebrew word rāʾâ has a range of meanings. It can refer to evil, misery, distress, calamity, disaster, or mischief. It can also be used of ethical evil. While God could not be the instigator of ethical evil, He does judge wicked people with calamity and distress as discipline for their sins (Prov. 3:11–12; Heb. 12:5–11). The calamity that God brought on Ahab and Jeroboam constituted deserved judgment on unrepentant sin.

Proverbs 16:4

This proverb reads, "The LORD works out everything for his own ends—even the wicked for a day of disaster." The first part of the verse highlights the fact that God is the sovereign Creator and Controller of the universe.

There is nothing in this world that is the result of mere chance or happenstance. All that we see fits into God's divine design. The second part of the verse seeks to emphasize the sovereignty of God by declaring that not even the perpetrators of evil are free from His authority and jurisdiction.

The proverb is not saying that God planned that people should be wicked. On the contrary, Solomon wrote, "God made mankind upright, but men have gone in search of many schemes" (Eccles. 7:29). The wicked are not wicked apart from their decisions, actions, and accountability. And in His sovereignty God has planned a day when they will receive the judgment they deserve (see Rev. 20:11–15). God is sovereign over the wicked, but they are not free of responsibility for their actions.

Ecclesiastes 3:1–8

Solomon emphasized that all events in life have their place in God's divine plan. "There is an appointed time for everything" (Eccles. 3:1, NASB). The idea here is that there is a *divinely* appointed time for all of life's experiences (see Eph. 1:11). The list in Ecclesiastes 3:2–8 includes such troubling things as "a time to die," "a time to kill," "a time to hate," and "a time for war." Does this mean that God is the cause of war, death, and hatred?

No. This passage does not address the issue of the direct cause of these events. While God is sovereign over all of life's experiences, and no tragedy is encountered apart from His divine permission, there is nothing in this text to suggest that God is the cause of these evil and painful experiences, and therefore responsible for them.

Ecclesiastes 7:14

Offering inspired wisdom to cope with life's circumstances, Solomon declared, "When times are good, be happy; but when times are bad, consider: God has made the one as well as the other. Therefore, a man cannot discover anything about his future" (7:14). Once again, this verse is emphasizing the truth that nothing takes place by mere chance. In the day of prosperity, it is easy to rejoice and thank God. But when the struggles come—family tragedies, deaths, and personal loss—God is still on the throne! Life is not out of control. We may have confidence that God is working out His all-wise, sovereign, and comprehensive plan even when the blueprint includes adversity and affliction.

Amos 3:6

In a his announcement of God's coming judgment on Israel, Amos declared, "When disaster [rā'â] comes to a city, has not the LORD caused it?" (Amos 3:6). As in 1 Kings 14:10 and 21:21, the word rā'â can be used of deserved judgment on unrepentant sin. The calamity referred to in Amos's prophecy was the destruction of Samaria by the Assyrians in 722 B.C., a well-deserved judgment on the wicked Israelites (see 2 Kings 17:7–17). God wanted His people to know that this calamity did not occur by chance. It was divinely determined because of Israel's sin.

Isaiah 45:7

Highlighting the sovereignty of God over the rise and fall of nations, Isaiah spoke for God declaring, "I form the light and create darkness, I bring prosperity and create disaster [ra']; I, the LORD, do all these things" (Isa. 45:7). The word ra' is used in Scripture of injury, disaster, distress, and more specifically of unethical activity ("evil"). Since God is absolutely opposed to evil and repeatedly calls people to turn from evil, the term ra' must be understood in this context to refer not to moral evil but to natural disaster or deserved judgment. Within the context of this prophecy (45:1–7), God was saying that the conquest of Cyrus over foreign nations was due to His sovereign intervention (45:1–2).

Jeremiah 25:29

God declared through Jeremiah, "See, I am beginning to bring disaster on the city [Jerusalem] that bears my Name" (Jer. 25:29). In this and other similar texts (31:28, Mic. 4:6, Zech. 8:14), God is the subject of the verb rā'a', "to do evil, hurt, or bring calamity." Within these contexts, the infliction of pain or calamity is not due to some moral flaw in God's character

151

but is the just judgment on sinners who have not responded to His call for repentance. Since the punishment of evil is not the same as perpetrating evil, God has not committed an immoral act or violated His holiness when He "brings calamity" to the wicked.

MAINTAINING THE BALANCE

Being a careful theologian is a lot like riding a bike. You have to maintain your balance. If you fail to do so, you will fall off. In our study of God and the presence of evil we have discovered that the doctrines of God's sovereignty and human responsibility are mutually compatible. To maintain a biblical balance, we cannot lean more toward one of these doctrines than the other. Both are thoroughly biblical and must be held simultaneously.

While I agree with Millard Erickson's comment that "a total solution to the problem of evil is beyond human ability,"[13] we have made significant progress. We have discovered that while God is sovereign over both good and evil, He stands behind the two in somewhat different ways. God does not allow evil to escape the bounds of His sovereignty. While He permits evil, God can never be credited with evil. Yet by granting permission for evil, which is always chargeable to secondary agents, it is included in God's decree. Yet the biblical writers did not say that God merely permits good. Rather, God stands behind good in such a way that it not only takes place as part of His decree, but is always credited to Him.[14]

Ultimately we must conclude that in His infinite wisdom God recognized that greater glory would come to His name by permitting evil rather than disallowing it altogether. And so we live in a sin-marred world where there is pain, sickness, and death. The good news for the Christian is that our experience on this earth is but a minuscule part of eternity. One day God will judge all evil and remove the curse of sin. There will be no "mourning or crying or pain" (Rev. 21:4) in God's eternal kingdom. Paul wrote, "For our light and momentary troubles are achieving for us an eternal glory that far outwieghs them all. So we fix our eyes not on what is seen, but on what is unseen. For what is seen is temporary, but what is unseen is eternal" (2 Cor. 4:17–18). An eternal perspective on the evils we encounter in life will help believers achieve victory through Christ.

Remember Brian and Haley whom I introduced at the beginning of this chapter? How have they responded to the tragedy that so profoundly changed their lives? In spite of the struggles, Haley cherishes the lessons she is learning. "There's more to life than being beautiful or handsome or doing everything you want," she said. Brian, too, maintains a positive attitude. "Everyone's going to have struggles," he said. "I think of myself as a tool. God is using me to touch certain lives."

Perhaps God is allowing some evil in your life to build your Christian character through suffering (Rom. 5:3–4). Perhaps God will use the evil He has permitted in your life to encourage others and bring Him glory. Perhaps through your struggle the "work of God" (John 9:3) will be displayed.

For Further Study

Blocher, Henri. *Evil and the Cross*. Translated by David G. Preston. Downers Grove, Ill.: InterVarsity Press, 1990.

Carson, D. A. *How Long, O Lord?* Grand Rapids: Baker Book House, 1990.

Feinberg, John S. *The Many Faces of Evil*. Grand Rapids: Zondervan Publishing House, 1994.

Wenham, John. W. *The Enigma of Evil*. Grand Rapids: Zondervan Publishing House,1985.

Yancey, Philip. *Where Is God When It Hurts?* Grand Rapids: Zondervan Publishing House, 1977.

13
GOD'S PLAN FOR THE AGES

I am God, and there is none like me. I make known the end from the beginning, from ancient times, what is still to come.

—Isaiah 46:9–10

My SEMINARY TEACHING brings me into contact with many students. As we get acquainted in my office or over lunch, I usually bring up the question of the student's plans for the future. "What would you like to be doing," I ask, "after you complete your studies at seminary?" Or I ask, "What do you picture yourself doing four or five years from now?"

Many students in the thick of their studies have a hard time projecting their lives beyond graduation! But if I give them time, they usually have a fairly good idea of why they came to seminary and how they want to be serving the Lord in the future. I find that getting to know their plans helps me to get to know them.

I believe that this same principle applies as we are seeking to know God better. It is rather amazing to me how ignorant some Christians are of God's plans. In fact we are more interested in our own plans than in His! It should be the other way around. Our lives as believers are to bring Him glory (1 Cor. 10:31). It is very difficult to do that if we don't know God's plans. This chapter discusses God's plan for the ages, so that we can come to know Him better.

Many Christians suffer from what Richard Foster calls "biblical myopia."[1] They know a lot of Bible facts, but lack a world-view—a vision of the whole. Many believers have never been presented with a picture of

God's all-encompassing plan for the ages. As a result, they have difficulty seeing how everything that God is doing fits together.

As we look at the "big picture"—God's plan for the ages as revealed in Genesis through Revelation—we won't pause at every milepost along the way, but we will note major junctions and points of interest.

Knowing God's overall plan can help make us more aware of His *sovereignty*. And this gives us more of a sense of His perspective when we encounter some of the inevitable difficulties of life. When a child is sick, when a loved one dies, when a job is terminated, we are able to remain confident, being assured that God knows our future and is sovereign over it.

THE ETERNAL KINGDOM OF GOD

Scripture reveals that God possesses absolute authority and rules as King. The psalmist proclaimed, "The LORD is King for ever and ever!" (Ps. 10:16). Jeremiah declared, "But the LORD is the true God; he is the living God, the eternal King" (Jer. 10:10). David announced in Psalm 103:19, "The LORD has established his throne in heaven, and his kingdom rules over all." As King, God has authority ("a throne"), a realm ("the heavens"), and subjects ("all").

God's kingdom is timeless. As Creator, God has always possessed absolute sovereignty. His kingdom is also universal; God's sovereignty is unlimited in scope. He exercises His rule over *all* His creation.

God's rule on earth is often delegated to authorities who are raised up to officiate over His dominion. As Nebuchadnezzar had to learn, "The Most High is sovereign over the kingdoms of men and gives them to anyone he wishes and sets over them the lowliest of men" (Dan. 4:17).

THE FALSE KINGDOM OF SATAN

Sometime in antiquity, God's universal and eternal kingdom was challenged by an angel—a created being known as Satan or the devil. Scripture reveals very little about Satan's fall, but his sin constituted an act of rebellion against the sovereign authority of God (1 Tim. 3:6; Rev. 12:4).

At his fall Satan instituted a counterfeit kingdom to parallel God's kingdom and challenge His authority. Satan is a usurper, claiming kingship and seeking the exercise of his authority over an earthly kingdom. Paul referred to him as "the god of this age" (2 Cor. 4:4) and "the ruler of the kingdom of the air" (Eph. 2:2). During this present age, Satan exercises a *limited* power over God's sin-alienated creation.

To fill his kingdom with followers, Satan persuaded the first human couple—Adam and Eve—to join him in rebelling against God. The divine command was clear. "You must not eat from the tree of the knowledge of good and evil, for when you eat of it you will surely die" (Gen. 2:17). But Satan successfully carried out his scheme to bring about the fall of humanity.

Sin's effect on Adam and Eve was immediate and conclusive. For the first time, fellowship with God was broken and the human couple was separated from God by their sins. This constituted spiritual death. In addition, they and their posterity became subject to physical death. Paul summarized the consequences of sin in Romans 5:12: "Therefore, just as sin entered the world through one man, and death through sin, and in this way death came to all men, because all sinned."

Because of man's sin, God cursed the earth so that it would bear its fruit only after much hard work (Gen. 3:17–18). Thorns and thistles would increase the work and frustrate the labors of humankind. All creation presently struggles under the curse because of Adam's sin (Rom. 8:22).

GOD'S PLAN

God created a world He called "very good." But now God's kingdom authority has been challenged by Satan; man has fallen into sin; and the world, under Satan's sway, is in open rebellion against God. What a mess! In view of this situation God inaugurated a program to bring the sin-marred creation back into the blessings of His glorious reign.

As with a fine jewel with several facets, so God's program has several aspects—redemption, kingdom rule, and judgment. God has graciously determined to restore humankind, reestablish His kingdom authority, and deal justly with sin. All of this is ultimately designed to honor and glorify God. Most of biblical history and theology can be viewed as the outworking of one of these aspects of God's divine program. (a) *Redeem humankind.* Because of His infinite grace and sacrificial love, He chose to provide a way of deliverance from our fate of spiritual death. We call this God's redemptive program—a program to redeem fallen humanity. (b) *Reclaim His kingdom.* The sovereign God cannot let His kingly authority be successfully challenged. To do so would suggest that the King is not really sovereign. So God set about to reclaim His kingdom and to reassert His sovereign authority on this earth— the sphere in which it was challenged. (c) *Execute judgment.* Since God is holy, He cannot look on sin and rebellion with indifference. He must execute judgment on Satan and his followers, thus purging the earth of the effects of sin.

GOD'S REDEMPTIVE WORK

Because of His infinite love and grace, God provided a way of salvation for all who would believe in Jesus Christ.

The Noahic Covenant

God's promise to Noah after the Flood provides the crucial foundation for His redemptive work. God promised Noah there would never be an- other universal destruction of every living thing by flood (Gen. 8:21–22; 9:8–17). Even though wicked generations would arise after Noah's time, God would hold back the floodwaters of judgment until the time when sin would be dealt with fully and finally—at the cross of Christ. The Noahic Covenant graciously provided the necessary time for God to implement His redemptive plan.

Redemption Illustrated

The Old Testament sacrifices (Exodus 12 and Leviticus 1–7, 16) illustrated God's redemptive provision whereby an innocent victim dies on behalf of the guilty. We call these sacrifices "types" because they point ahead to a great truth. They anticipate the coming of a Substitute (Jesus Christ) who would deal with sin fully and finally.

The blood of animals could not ultimately atone for sins (Heb. 10:4). The sacrifices simply anticipated what Christ would finally accomplish. As Paul wrote, "in [God's] forbearance he had left the sins committed beforehand unpunished" (Rom. 3:25) until Christ's blood could satisfy God's holy wrath on sin.

God's Plan Expounded

God's provision of salvation for people in every era is by grace, through faith in God's promise, based on the blood of Christ. Paul stated this truth in Ephesians chapter 2. In verse 8 he wrote, "For it is by grace you have been saved, through faith." Then in verse 13 he added that the Ephesians who were formerly separated from God "have been brought near through the blood of Christ."

The words "by grace" mean that salvation is a divine gift, free and undeserved. This prevents boasting and means that God, rather than people, get the glory (2:8–9).

The words "through faith" indicate that the divine gift of salvation is appropriated individually by personal faith. Faith ("belief" or "trust") involves a complete reliance on God's provision of Christ's atonement.

The "blood" reminds us that because God is holy, He must judge our sin. But because He is gracious, God provided a substitute to die in the place of the guilty (Lev. 17:11; Heb. 9:22). The Old Testament sacrifices were insufficient by themselves to provide atonement (10:4). So God prepared the ultimate sacrifice—His own Son—to be the sacrificial Lamb who would take away the sins of the world (John 1:29; Acts 2:23).

Christ's Atonement Provided

Christ gave His life on the cross in order to satisfy God's holy wrath on sin (Rom. 3:25; 1 John 2:1–2). The most significant moment in redemptive history was when Jesus bore the sins which the Old-Covenant sacrifices only covered. As He bore the sins of everyone past, present, and future, He became "sin on our behalf" (2 Cor. 5:21, NASB). In the ultimate moment of His agony, Jesus cried out, "My God, my God, why have you forsaken me?" (Matt. 27:46). It was as if the Father had turned His back on His Son as Jesus bore the sins of humankind. Then Jesus declared, "It is finished" (John 19:30). The provision of redemption was complete.

The New Covenant Enacted

Christ's death for sins meant the end of the Old Covenant and the enactment of the New Covenant (Jer. 31:31–34; Ezek. 36:24–28; Heb. 8:6–13). The New Covenant provides regeneration and the forgiveness of sin through faith in Christ and His sacrificial atonement for sins (1 Cor. 11:25; Heb. 7:22; 8:6–13; 10:15–22). Virtually all the blessings we have in Christ are based on spiritual provisions of the New Covenant.

GOD'S KINGDOM WORK

From the time when God's sovereign rule over the universe was challenged by Satan, God has been working to reassert His sovereignty in the sphere where it was challenged. God's kingdom program involves a King who rules, a people who are ruled, and a sphere where this rule is recognized. Graeme Goldsworthy has concisely stated that: "the kingdom of God involves: (a) God's people (b) in God's place (c) under God's rule."[2]

God's kingdom work involves the demonstration and recognition of His divine authority on this earth, the place where His rule was challenged. It is in this facet of God's plan for the ages that many of the prophecies of Ezekiel come into focus. The messianic temple he envisioned (Ezekiel 40–48) will be operational during the future millennial kingdom. The kingdom of God is developed in several significant passages in the Bible.

The Kingdom Promised (Gen. 12:1–3)

With God's call of Abraham, He began to initiate some significant developments in the reestablishment of His kingdom authority on earth. These developments center on God's promises to Abraham in Genesis 12:1–3. These unconditional promises assured Abraham and His descendants of three things: a land, a nation, and a blessing.

First, Abraham's descendants are to have a land—the land of Israel. The dimensions of the land are given in Genesis 15:18 and Joshua 1:4. The *land* promise is further developed in Deuteronomy 30:1–10. Second, Abraham's descendants are to become a great nation. The *national* promises are developed in the Davidic Covenant (2 Sam. 7:12–16). Third, Abraham's descendants are to be blessed and be a blessing to others. The *blessing* promises are developed in the New Covenant (Jer. 31:31–34).

The Abrahamic Covenant contributes in a significant way toward the outworking of God's kingdom program. It guarantees Israel a permanent national existence, perpetual title to the land of Israel, material and spiritual blessings (through Christ), and that gentile nations will share in the blessings God has for Israel (Gal. 3:8–14).

The Kingdom Foreshadowed (2 Sam. 7:12–16)

During David's reign another significant development in God's kingdom program occurred. Second Samuel 7:12–16 records that God entered into an eternal, unconditional covenant with David, guaranteeing that in his line the theocratic kingdom would come to full realization and that one of David's descendants would reign over the kingdom forever.

In essence God promised David that his house, throne, and kingdom would be eternal (7:16). This means (a) David's line or dynasty will always be the royal line, (b) the right to rule will always belong to David's descendants, and (c) the right to a literal kingdom will never be taken away from David's posterity.

The Kingdom Presented (Matt. 4:17)

When the angel Gabriel told Mary she would be the mother of the Messiah, he linked the birth of Jesus with God's promise to David in 2 Samuel 7:12–16 (Luke 1:31–33). Gabriel made it clear that Jesus was destined to receive the throne of David, to reign over the house of Jacob forever, and to rule a kingdom that has no end—all in fulfillment of 2 Samuel 7:12–16.

Jesus presented the prophesied kingdom to Israel when He announced, "Repent, for the kingdom of heaven is near" (Matt. 4:17). This was an invitation to the Jews of His day to accept Him as King and enter into His kingdom. Jesus authenticated His offer of the kingdom by doing miracles, which exhibited the characteristics of what God's rule would be like when it is fully manifested (Isa. 35:5–6; Matt. 12:28).

The Kingdom Rejected (Matt. 12:22–32)

The Jews living at the time of the first century were anticipating the literal fulfillment of the kingdom promises which had been expounded by the prophets. Yet they had difficulty accepting the person of Christ. Expecting a powerful military deliverer, they rejected the humble Savior.

The most significant turning point in Christ's ministry was His rejection by the Jewish religious establishment. The Jewish leaders accused Jesus of casting out demons by the power of Satan (Matt. 12:22–24). In effect, they rejected His miracles and attributed these powerful works to Satan rather than to God's Spirit through whom Christ did His miracles. The decision of the Jewish leaders turned the people against Jesus and set the nation on the course of rejecting their Messiah. Because of the terrible consequences of this decision by the religious leaders, Jesus referred to their sin as one that "will not be forgiven" (12:31–32).

The Kingdom Culmination Delayed (Luke 19:11–27)

Since the kingdom was based on unconditional covenant promises, it could not be canceled, even by unbelief. So Christ's rule over Israel's land was delayed until such a time as there would be a more responsive generation.

In the parable of the ten pounds (Luke 19:11–27) Jesus revealed that since Israel would not accept her King, the kingdom was to be postponed and the rejecting generation judged (see 19:14, 27).

The Kingdom Realized (Rev. 20:4–6)

Revelation 11:15 indicates that the kingdom promises will be realized following the still-future events of a seven-year span of time called the Tribulation period. At the second advent of Christ the Jewish people will accept Him as their Messiah (Zech. 12:10–13:1). Then Jesus will set up His millennial government and rule the world for one thousand years (Rev. 20:4–6). This is the period when Ezekiel's prophesied temple will be the worship center of the whole world!

The Kingdom of God in the Present Age

Some theologians, equating the church with the kingdom, deny the existence of a future kingdom for Israel. Others, denying any relationship between the church and the kingdom, believe that the kingdom is entirely future. We would like to suggest that there is scriptural evidence for both positions. The kingdom of God is both present and future.

Following a literal interpretation of Scripture, a future kingdom cannot be denied (Matt. 26:29; Luke 19:11; 22:30). Yet there also seems to be a kingdom work going on in the present age (John 3:3; Col. 1:13; 4:11). While the church itself is not the kingdom, it is an important aspect of God's rule. Perhaps we could say that the church is the most visible and significant aspect of the kingdom of God as it is developing in the present age.

After recording Jesus' announcement, "The kingdom of God is near" (Mark 1:15; Matt. 4:17), Mark recorded a series of Jesus' miracles. The miracles, reflecting characteristics of the kingdom (Isa. 35:5–6), serve to validate His announcement. Jesus' miracles demonstrated that the future has broken into the present. When Jesus gave sight to the blind, healed the sick, caused the lame to walk, cleansed lepers, and liberated those with demons, He was providing a picture of what God's kingdom is all about.

The kingdom of God involves God's people, in God's place, under God's rule. Today the people of God are believers in Christ (whether Jew or Gentile). God's "place" is the body of Christ, the church. God's rule over His people is exercised through Christ and His undershepherds (church elders).

The present form of God's rule is in the church. But the rule of Christ as Israel's Messiah awaits the Millennium, when He will reign on David's throne over a literal kingdom on earth. In that future kingdom age, Jerusalem will serve as the world's worship center (Isa. 2:2–4, Mic. 4:1–2).

THE JUDGMENT WORK

God's work of judgment is both contemporary and future. It is presently and progressively taking place (John 3:18–19) and also has a prophetic culmination.

Judgment on Satan and His Angels

Jesus spoke of the "eternal fire prepared for the devil and his angels" (Matt. 25:41). The actual judgment on Satan commenced at the cross (John 12:31). His sphere of activities will be further restricted during the Tribulation (Rev. 12:9) and the Millennium (20:2). At the end of the thousand-year messianic kingdom Satan will be cast into the lake of fire where he will remain for eternity (20:10).

Judgment on Satan's Followers

Revelation 20:11–15 reveals that after the messianic kingdom the unsaved dead will be raised and judged. "If anyone's name was not found written in the book of life, he was thrown into the lake of fire" (20:15).

Purging of the Earth

Second Peter 3:10 reveals that this present earth—the sphere of Satan's rebellion against God—-will be purged by fire in preparation for the new heavens and the new earth (Rev. 21:1; Isa. 65:17–25). This purging will result in the removal of all the effects of sin and the Fall. Then will be fulfilled the words of John in Revelation 22:3, "No longer will there be any curse!"

The Bible begins with a curse because of sin. It concludes with the removal of the effect of sin and an end to the curse. In summary this is God's plan for the ages—to reverse the curse.

CONCLUSION

Believers today are living between the first and second advents of Christ under the provisions of the New Covenant. They are participating in a form of God's kingdom, but are yet awaiting its full consummation when Christ will establish His reign on the earth.

Understanding God's plan for the ages helps us know God better. We also find encouragement in knowing that God does have a plan! He knows the end from the beginning (Isa. 46:9–10). All of history and human existence is under His rule and design. In the face of uncertainty and misfortune, Christians can be sure that God is in control! As He rules the affairs of the nations, so He rules the affairs of our lives—according to His sovereign will.

For Further Study

McClain, Alva J. *The Greatness of the Kingdom*. Winona Lake, Ind.: BMH Books, 1974.

Pentecost, J. Dwight. *Things to Come*. Grand Rapids: Zondervan Publishing House, 1958.

Walvoord, John F. *End Times*. Swindoll Leadership Library. Nashville: Word Publishing, 1998.

14

BEING A FRIEND OF GOD

*Abraham believed God, and it was credited to him as righteousness,'
and he was called God's friend.*

—James 2:23

M Y FRIENDSHIP with Gary Classen began about ten years ago when
we discovered that we shared an interest in distance running. Since 1988
Gary and I have run about a dozen marathons together. We have partici-
pated together in six 195-mile "Hood to Coast" relays. We have eaten
countless meals together. I have slept at Gary's house and helped myself
to cereal from his kitchen cupboard at midnight.

Gary is the only person I know, besides my mother, who has read each
of the books I have written. Gary prays for me and encourages me. If
Gary came to me and asked to borrow a thousand dollars, I would respond without hesitation, "Can I write you a check, or would you prefer
cash?" That's what it means to share a friendship.

Only a few weeks after our family moved to Dallas, Texas, to begin
studies at Dallas Theological Seminary I began to realize what it meant to
be without a friend. Nancy, my wife, had just started working as a secre-
tary for the football coaches at Southern Methodist University. Just before
she left for work I went to get the car for her. But as I turned on the
ignition, there was silence. The battery was dead! Had this happened while
living back home in Portland, there would have been no problem. I knew
many friends there who were committed enough to get out of bed at a
moment's notice to help me start my car. But I was new in Dallas and had

not yet made any friends. There was no one I knew well enough to call on for help!

I began to panic. Nancy had to be at work in a few minutes. What was I going to do? About that time a young man stepped from the apartment across from ours. I immediately confronted him, explaining our situation. Fortunately he graciously brought his vehicle around, and we used cables to jump-start my car.

As Nancy drove off that morning, I determined that I would seek to develop some friendships in Dallas. I would get to know some people there who would share in a reciprocal and committed friendship. During our three years at Dallas, several deep and lasting friendships developed. There was Roger Raymer, my jogging partner, and Jim Amandus, a fellow-student and neighbor. I enjoyed a friendship with Duane Lindsey, the seminary registrar. I can't count the number of evenings Nancy and I spent in his home. We met Walter and Jean Mack at church and shared several Thanksgivings in their home. These people became my friends in Dallas. And though we have scattered to different states, they are still my friends today.

DEFINITION OF "FRIEND"

The New Testament uses the term "friend" (*philos*) in two ways. The normal usage of the word is illustrated in the story of the prodigal son. The self-righteous son complained to his father, "Look! All these years I've been slaving for you and never disobeyed your orders. Yet you never gave me even a young goat so I could celebrate with my friends" (Luke 15:29). The word *friends* is used here in the normal sense of special or trusted companions.

Also a technical use of the word *philos* was familiar to those living in the first-century Roman world. This use is found in John 19:12, where the Jews cried out to Pilate saying, "If you let this man go, you are no friend of Caesar." To be "a friend of Caesar" was the highest title and honor one could enjoy in relationship with the Roman government.[1] The implication of the statement made by the Jews was that Pilate was still a friend of Caesar, but that this relationship would be jeopardized if he released Jesus.

To be "a friend of Caesar" meant four things. First, it meant that the person knew the emperor intimately. "Friends of Caesar" would actually open the emperor's mail and carry on his correspondence. They knew him that well. Second, it meant that the friend was willing to go wherever the emperor sent him. "Friends of Caesar" were often sent to the provinces to do business for the emperor. There they would represent him and conduct his affairs. Third, "a friend of Caesar" retained the title even if the emperor died. "A friend of Caesar" remained a friend of the Roman Empire. Fourth, if the friend betrayed the emperor, he would lose his privileged status and this would mean his political doom.[2]

ILLUSTRATIONS OF THE TERM "FRIEND"

How did this relationship of being "a friend of Caesar" really work? Fortunately, we have several illustrations of the use of this term.

King Herod

The rule of King Herod, popularly remembered as "Herod the Great," can be divided into three main periods. From 37 to 25 B.C. Herod contended with his enemies and consolidated his kingdom. From 25 to 14 B.C. he engaged in a series of building projects, the most famous of which was the Jerusalem temple. Herod spent the last ten years of his life (14–4 B.C.) dealing with domestic troubles and searching for a worthy successor. During this third period Herod had some trouble with some foreign enemies, and with the Roman emperor Augustus Caesar!

Jewish historian Josephus recorded the story in *The Antiquities of the Jews* (16.271–91).

According to Josephus, Herod loaned sixty talents of silver to the Arabs, but they failed to repay the debt. Since Syllaeus, who ruled in the place of the Arabian king, refused payment, Herod invaded Arabia and collected the money by force. Meanwhile, Syllaeus had gone to Rome on business. When he received the report of Herod's punitive attack, he went straight to Augustus. He falsely accused Herod and, with tears in his eyes, gave the emperor a very distorted report of the incident. Having been persuaded by Syllaeus that Herod was to blame, Augustus wrote him an angry letter saying, "Whereas formerly he had treated him as a friend, he would now treat him as a subject" (16.290). Herod then sent representatives to Rome to explain the situation to Augustus. After some difficulty, Augustus was won over and Herod regained his status as "friend."

Pontius Pilate

It seems probable that Pontius Pilate received his appointment as prefect of Judea (A.D. 26–36) through Lucius Aelius Sejanus, commander of the Praetorian Guard. The Praetorian Guard was an elite group of nine thousand soldiers who guarded the imperial palace in Rome. They eventually became a powerful force, and the emperors had to court their favor to stay in office. When Tiberius, weary of public office, retired to the island of Capri, Sejanus was virtually in control of the government.

According to Philo, Sejanus wanted to exterminate the Jewish race (Philo, *De Legatione ad Gaium* 159–61). Apparently Pilate implemented Sejanus's anti-Jewish policy in Judea. Almost immediately after his arrival in Judea he introduced in Jerusalem Roman military standards with the image of the emperor. This outraged the Jews whose law forbids the making of images (Josephus, *The Antiquities of the Jews* 18.55). Pilate's disdain for the Jews is also seen by the fact that he seized funds from the temple treasury to construct an aqueduct in Jerusalem (Josephus, *The Jewish Wars* 2.175–77). Biblical evidence of Pilate's hostility against the Jews is found in Luke 13:1, where Luke referred to "the Galileans whose blood Pilate had mixed with their sacrifices."

One wonders how a prefect so insulting to the Jews could remain in office without Jewish protest and investigation by Rome. This was no problem so long as the anti-Semitic Sejanus was in control of the government in Rome. Any complaint sent by Jews to Tiberius would be intercepted by Sejanus!

In A.D. 29 the Senate voted that Sejanus's birthday be publicly observed. He had become so influential that senators and other high officials looked on him as if he were actually the emperor. Finally Tiberius discovered what was going on. Sejanus was tricked into appearing before the Senate, believing that Tiberius was going to grant him supreme authority over Roman civil affairs. Instead, a letter from Tiberius denounced Sejanus as a usurper. He was immediately taken from the Senate and executed on October 18, A.D. 31.[3]

Now we understand why Pilate responded as he did when the Jews at Jesus' trial cried out that he was no friend of Caesar's if he released Jesus (John 19:12). Before the execution of Sejanus, he could do as he pleased with the Jews, confident that reports of his hostilities would never reach the ears of the emperor. But now things were different. He no longer had his protector in Rome. He could not afford any trouble with Tiberius. Fearing an accusation of disloyalty and the resultant political doom, Pilate washed his hands of the case and let the Jews have their way. Even though he knew that Jesus had done nothing worthy of death, Pilate did not want to offend the Jews and risk losing his status as "a friend of Caesar."

APPLICATION OF THE TERM "FRIEND"

What does all this historical background have to do with being a "friend" of God? Quite clearly the term "friend" has a rich cultural and historical background. Being a friend in the biblical period often meant more than being someone's "buddy." Being someone's friend in the technical sense involves a relationship marked by knowledge, obedience, and commitment. A friend of God, then, is one who knows Him intimately and obeys Him willingly.

The Pattern of Abraham

Abraham is the only person in the Bible who is called a "friend of God." Facing the invasion of Judah by the Moabites and Ammonites, Jehoshaphat prayed, "O our God, did you not drive out the inhabitants of this land before your people Israel and give it forever to the descendants of Abraham your friend?" (2 Chron. 20:7). God Himself declared His friendship with Abraham when He referred to the Israelites as the "descendants of

Abraham my friend" (Isa. 41:8). In his discussion on the relationship of faith and works, James quoted Genesis 15:6, "Abram believed the LORD, and he credited it to him as righteousness." Then James added, Abraham was "called God's friend" (James 2:23).

What do we know about Abraham's relationship with God? First, he obeyed God willingly. When God instructed him to take Isaac—his only son, the son of promise—and offer him as a burnt offering, Abraham didn't raise objections or suggest any alternatives. He simply arose early in the morning, took Isaac, and started on the journey to the place God had told him (Gen. 22:3). His obedience was exemplary.

Second, Abraham knew God intimately. Abraham had learned of God's power to make and keep great promises. God had promised that Abraham's descendants would be as numerous as the stars in the sky (15:5). How could God now command him to sacrifice Isaac? Though Abraham did not know how God would accomplish this miracle, by faith he told his servants, "Stay here with the donkey while I and the boy go over there. We will worship and then we will come back to you" (22:5). Abraham knew that the God who could bring life to Sarah's barren womb could, if necessary, resurrect Isaac from the dead! This is clear from the comment by the writer of Hebrews, "By faith Abraham, when God tested him, offered Isaac as a sacrifice. He who had received the promises was about to sacrifice his one and only son, even though God had said to him, 'It is through Isaac that your offspring will be reckoned.' Abraham reasoned that God could raise the dead, and figuratively speaking, he did receive Isaac back from death" (Heb. 11:17–19).

Abraham's example provides believers with a pattern for knowing God intimately and obeying God willingly. I believe the order is significant. You are less inclined to obey someone you don't know. But if you *know* the person who gives you orders and you have confidence in his or her power, wisdom, and loving concern, you will be willing to obey that person's most challenging demands.

The Potential for Believers

On the last night He spent with the disciples before His crucifixion, Jesus instructed them on many important topics. His Upper Room discourse

(John 13–16) contains teaching on prayer, heaven, the Holy Spirit, peace, persecution, and witnessing. But one of the most significant lessons of this discourse is on the subject of friendship.

In John 15:14–15 Jesus addressed His disciples as His "friends": "You are my friends if you do what I command. I no longer call you servants, because a servant does not know his master's business. Instead, I have called you friends, for everything that I learned from my father I have made known to you." I believe that we find in this passage the technical use of the term "friend" (*philos*). Once again, we see that two things characterize a "friend" of Christ.

Obeying God willingly. First, a friend of Christ is one who obeys Him willingly. As Jesus said, we are His friends if we obey His commands (John 15:14). The friendship spoken of by Jesus is not merely a casual, "good-buddy" relationship. The relationship He is referring to involves commitment and obedience. Jesus added the condition, "if you do what I command." The test of a disciple's true friendship with Christ is his obedience to Jesus' commands.

Interestingly many Christians find excuses for not obeying Christ. We argue, "That is cultural and doesn't apply to me." We say, "That commandment doesn't make sense to me, so I should not have to obey it." One Christian who was contemplating a clear violation of God's Word said, "I know what the Bible teaches, but I am sure that God will forgive me." Other Christians are not so flagrant in their disobedience. They simply neglect the responsibilities of being a disciple because they are so busy with other things in life.

But for those who want to be God's friend, obedience makes a difference. Obedience is the distinguishing characteristic of those who share a friendship with Christ. Jesus also said that our love for Him is measured by our obedience to His Word. "If you love me, you will obey what I command" (John 14:15). The present tense is used in both verbs and could be rendered, "If you keep on loving Me, you will keep on obeying what I command." Continued love for Christ serves as a preventive against disobedience and guarantees a continued friendship with Him.

The apostle Paul would qualify as a "friend" of Christ. At the end of his life he was able to write, "I have fought the good fight, I have finished the race, I have kept the faith" (2 Tim. 4:7). Paul was obedient to the faith and honored God by his consistent obedience throughout life. Two things, I believe, helped Paul be obedient. First, he had a deep and abiding love for Christ (John 14:15; Phil. 1:21). Second, he had a humble attitude toward himself (Acts 20:24). Paul did not consider his life his own, pursuing his own goals and doing his own thing. Rather, Paul saw himself as expendable—a life to be spent in serving and living for God. Like John the Baptizer, Paul viewed himself not as the central figure but as a humble servant commissioned to communicate the gospel of grace.

Garcia Iuiguez was a Cuban patriot and an outstanding military leader who suffered wounds, imprisonment, and separation from his family during his thirty-year struggle for Cuban independence from Spain (1868–1898). While Garcia was hiding out in the jungles of Cuba, it became urgently necessary for him to be contacted by the rebel leaders not yet in hiding. The problem was that they didn't know where Garcia was or how to reach him.

Three seasoned soldiers were selected as candidates to take the message to Garcia. They were individually and privately interviewed regarding their fitness for the task. Then each was asked the question, "Are you ready to take the message to Garcia?"

The first soldier responded that he was willing but would need time to plan and prepare for the assignment. The second soldier said he was willing, but would need to recruit others to assist in the mission. When the third soldier was asked, "Are you ready to take the message to Garcia?" he took a deep breath, paused, and then answered, "I am ready." It is this kind of readiness to serve and obey that truly delights God's heart!

Knowing God intimately. Knowing God intimately is the second characteristic of one who is a friend of Christ. As we noted in John 15:15, Jesus calls us friends because we are no longer servants. A slave's relationship to his master involves duty and obligation. But this is not a friendship, for the slave is expected to obey his master even if he does not understand or agree with the command. In contrast to one's dealing with servants, Jesus has shared intimately with His friends. He kept nothing from them that they could bear (16:12). He revealed to the disciples "all things" that the Father made known to Him.

To be a friend of Christ means more than simply knowing certain facts about Him. You can know God's attributes and not know Him personally. But to be a friend of Christ means that you have a growing, vital, dynamic relationship which is cultivated by the study of God's Word and prayer.

I believe that most people are much like Martha in the account recorded in Luke 10:38–42. While traveling through Judea, Jesus and His disciples visited the home of Mary and Martha in Bethany. Martha welcomed Jesus and immediately began preparing a meal for the guests. Mary, on the other hand, seated herself at Jesus' feet, eagerly listening to His every word. With all that had to be done, and Mary not helping, it wasn't long before Martha had worked herself up into a fret. She interrupted Jesus to say, "Lord, don't you care that my sister has left me to do the work by myself? Tell her to help me!" (10:40).

Jesus responded, "Martha, Martha . . . you are worried and upset about many things, but only one thing is needed. Mary has chosen what is better, and it will not be taken away from her" (10:41–42). Martha was focused on preparing a meal, an important but temporal need. Mary, on the other hand, recognized the priority of growing in her knowledge of the Master. She realized that fellowship with God is sometimes more important than serving His people.

Many of us are much like Martha. We are busily going about our ministries. We teach Sunday school, serve on church committees, and assist as youth sponsors. We never miss a church workday, a prayer meeting, or a church social. We are teaching our kids about God, writing to our missionaries, and giving generously to support the ministries of the church. We are so worn out by ministry that we don't have the energy to invest in our own spiritual growth and development. And all the time Jesus is saying, "I'm available, My child. I'd love for you to sit with me and visit for a while. It would be great if we could have some time alone. I would like for you to get to know me better."

Paul was a mature believer, a seasoned saint, when he wrote from a Roman prison that he wanted to know Christ better. "What is more, I consider everything a loss compared to the surpassing greatness of knowing Christ Jesus my Lord, for whose sake I have lost all things. I consider them rubbish, that I may gain Christ. . . . I want to know Christ and the power of his resurrection and the fellowship of sharing in his sufferings, becoming like him in his death" (Phil. 3:8, 10). When Paul wrote these words, he knew a lot about God. But he still longed to *know Him better*!

As a father, one of my great desires in life is to develop a deep and personal relationship with my children—John, Elisabeth, Laura, and David. I want to know them—their hopes, their dreams, and their longings. And I want them to know me. I want them to know what motivates me, what challenges me, what concerns me. I believe that God has a similar desire for His people. He knows them, as a shepherd knows his flock (John 10:14). And He wants them to know Him.

ARE YOU GOD'S FRIEND?

In this chapter we have discovered that a friend of God is one who *knows* Him intimately and *obeys* Him willingly. A friend of God is characterized by uncompromising obedience to Christ and a growing knowledge of Christ.

Are you God's acquaintance, or His friend?

For Further Study

Curtis, Brent, and John Eldredge. *The Sacred Romance*. Nashville: Thomas Nelson Publishers, 1997.

Needham, David. *Close to His Majesty*. Portland, Oreg.: Multnomah Press, 1987.

15

BELIEVING IN GOD

*And without faith it is impossible to please God, because anyone who
comes to him must believe that he exists, and that he rewards those
who earnestly seek him.*

—Hebrews 11:6

WHAT DOES IT MEAN to "believe" in God? This is an extremely
important question. When the Philippian jailer asked the question, "Men,
what must I do to be saved?" Paul and Silas responded, "Believe in the
Lord Jesus, and you will be saved" (Acts 16:31). Believing in the Lord
Jesus results in one's personal salvation. Disbelief, on the other hand, leaves
one unsaved and under God's judgment (John 3:18, 36; 5:24). Since "belief" or "unbelief" determines one's eternal destiny, it is imperative that
we learn what the Bible means when it invites people to "believe" in God.

I vividly recall my first encounter with the concept and consequences
of belief. It was an Easter Sunday morning at the First Baptist Church of
Eugene, Oregon. I was sitting in the balcony with my parents and my six-
year-old brother. I was just ten at the time, but I was old enough to pay
attention to the sermon and benefit from it. Dr. Vance Webster was preaching on the resurrection of Jesus and emphasizing that people needed to
receive the benefits of His death for their sins.

Although I had not committed any flagrant sins, I knew that pestering
the baby-sitter and lying to my little brother were enough to send me to
hell. Dr. Webster emphasized that there was only one way of salvation
and that was through Jesus Christ. At that moment I knew that I wanted
to become a Christian. I was already "believing" in Jesus, but I wanted to

make sure that I was doing it right. I spoke to my mother after the church service, and she directed me to the pastor. Sitting in his office I professed my faith in Christ. I don't remember the details of our conversation, but Dr. Webster was satisfied that I was a genuine "believer" and he baptized me several Sundays later. More than forty years have passed since my baptism, and I am still learning about what it means to "believe."

BELIEF IN THE OLD TESTAMENT

The Old Testament concept of faith is revealed in the Hebrew verb *'āman*, "to confirm, support, or uphold." The basic idea is firmness or certainty. One form of *'āman* gives expression to an unalterable fact on which future generations could rely, despite contrary circumstances or misfortune. This form of the verb is used of "the faithful God" (Deut. 7:9). In the causative form the verb means "to cause to be certain" or "to be certain about." This is translated in our English Bibles by the word "believe." The background of the word indicates that biblical faith involves "a certainty, in contrast with modern concepts of faith as something possible, hopefully true, but not certain."[1]

The first Old Testament occurrence of this word is in Genesis 15:6, which states that "Abram believed in the LORD, and he credited it to him as righteousness." God had just promised Abraham, an elderly man with a barren wife, that his descendants would be as numerous as the stars. In spite of the physical hindrances to the fulfillment of this promise, Abraham trusted God. He regarded God's word as dependable and sure, "and for that belief God credited him with righteousness."[2] Because Abraham accepted God's word as true and reliable, God declared him righteous, and therefore acceptable. Paul's use of Genesis 15:6 in Romans 4:3, 9, 22 and Galatians 3:6 demonstrates that this Old Testament verse is foundational for our understanding of what it means to "believe" God.

The word *'āman* is used in Exodus 14:31 where Moses reported that as a result of their miraculous crossing of the Red Sea, the Israelites "believed in the LORD and in His servant Moses" (NASB). The miracle confirmed the fact that the Lord can be trusted to protect and deliver His own. And by faith the Israelites followed Moses, their leader, into the desert of Sinai.

But their faith was fickle. As a result of their refusal to follow Caleb and Joshua into the Promised Land, God questioned Moses, "How long will they refuse to believe in me, in spite of all the miraculous signs I have performed among them?" (Num. 14:11). God had revealed His power to deliver, but the people did not follow through with faith and obedience.

In the Book of Psalms we see that the Israelites were rebuked because "they did not believe in God or trust in his deliverance" (Ps. 78:22). The word translated "trust" is the Hebrew word *bātaḥ*, which expresses the sense of well-being and security that results from having someone on whom to rely. It is used here as a near synonym to "believe." In Psalm 106 the psalmist recounted the history of Israel's rebellion against the Lord. The Israelites "despised the pleasant land; they did not believe his promise" (106:24). Instead, they "grumbled in their tents and did not obey the LORD" (106:25). The point here is that they did not act in obedience to what God had revealed.

The word *'āman* appears again in Isaiah 43:10, which speaks of Israel's responsibility as a witness to the nations. The purpose of this ministry, God declared, is so that future generations "may know and believe me, and understand that I am he." Here "belief" is linked with the concept of knowing God and recognizing that He is the one true God. Jonah 3:5 reports that the people of Nineveh "believed God." It is noteworthy that their belief was accompanied by actions reflecting repentance. They called a fast, put on sackcloth, summoned people to prayer, and urged others to turn from their wicked ways and violence (3:5–8).

Clearly "belief" in the Hebrew Bible involves more than wishful thinking. Biblical faith is an attitude of certainty that reflects confidence in God and His Word. In the Old Testament, people of faith knew that God is dependable, and they took action on the basis of that unseen reality.

BELIEF IN THE NEW TESTAMENT

While the Old Testament provides a foundation for an understanding of what it means to "believe" in God, the New Testament brings the concept into clearer focus. The key Greek word is *pisteuō*, "to believe" or "to be convinced of something." In religious contexts the word is used of "faith" or "trust" in God. The person who trusts God is convinced of His existence, that His revelations are true, and that He has the power to help in time of need. Jesus Christ is the object of this kind of biblical faith.

The word *pisteuō* appears in the Synoptic Gospels twenty-eight times. Before giving sight to the blind men at Jericho Jesus asked them, "Do you believe that I am able to do this?" (Matt. 9:28). In response to their affirmative answers Jesus touched their eyes and said, "According to your faith will it be done to you" (9:29). Announcing that the kingdom of God was at hand, Jesus told His listeners to "repent and believe the good news" (Mark 1:15). When Jairus was told that his daughter had died, Jesus said, "Don't be afraid; just believe [literally, 'keep on believing']" (5:36). Zacharias was judged because he "did not believe" Gabriel's announcement about the birth of his son, John the Baptizer (Luke 1:20).

The Gospel of John contains ninety-eight occurrences of *pisteuō* and provides keen insight into what it means to believe. The purpose of John the Baptizer's witness was "so that through him all men might believe" (John 1:7). In 1:12 those who "received him" are identified with those who "believed in His name." Believing in Jesus means "receiving" Him or welcoming Him into one's life. In 3:36 the one who "believes in the Son has eternal life" as a present possession. But the one who "does not obey the Son shall not see life." To disbelieve Christ is to disobey Him. And logically, to believe in Christ is to obey Him. As I have noted elsewhere, "This verse clearly indicates that belief is not a matter of passive opinion, but decisive and obedient action."[3]

The nature of biblical belief is emphasized in John's Gospel by the use of the present participle *pisteuōn* ("believing"), which is used in many of the passages dealing with belief (3:15–16, 18, 36; 6:35, 47, etc.). The present tense emphasizes the ongoing nature of the action. In each of these verses salvation results from "believing," not merely from "belief." The apostle John was interested in ongoing, continual believing. John would be more likely to ask the question, "Are you believing?" rather than "Did you believe?" When Jesus spoke to His perplexed and troubled disciples, He used the present imperative, "Keep on believing in God; keep on believing in me" (14:1).[4]

The Book of Acts makes it clear that belief in Jesus Christ, God's Son, is the means of salvation (Acts 8:37; 16:31). Paul wrote in Romans that the righteousness of God through faith in Jesus Christ is available "to all who believe" without distinction (Rom. 3:22). The righteousness of God and salvation from sin are received by those who believe (10:9–10), and belief in the name of the Son of God results in "eternal life" (1 John 5:13).

In the New Testament, belief never refers to a mere intellectual assent to a proposition. *Pisteuō* always involves a personal response. Believing in Christ means we acknowledge Him as God's Son and Messiah and trust His person and work in securing our personal salvation. Believing in Christ means that we rely on Jesus alone to bring us safely through life to heaven.

My favorite illustration of what it means to believe is the true story of Ann Seward, a resident of Portland, Oregon. She was asked to costar with high-wire artist Philippe Petit at the opening of the Portland Center for the Performing Arts. Intrigued by the opportunity, she responded, "I'd like to meet this man and see if I trust him." Her stage would be on an eighty-foot wire between the new theater building and the Arlene Schnitzer Concert Hall. On August 31, 1987, the ninety-one-pound Seward placed her life in the hands of the high-wire artist and was carried on his back while he performed high above the street.[5] She said that her performance had a lesson for those who witnessed it. "I think that one of the most beautiful things about the performance was that it took a lot of trust—absolute trust—to do that," she said. "I think in the world that is a very profound issue. . . . Here it is—I'm putting my life in someone else's hands and trusting the whole crowd not to do anything to distract him."

Many of those who witnessed the performance "believed" that Petit could successfully complete the performance with someone on his back. But their belief was merely intellectual and did not feature the absolute trust and total commitment exhibited by Ann Seward. She expressed her belief by placing her very life in the hands of the artist. This is the kind of "belief" referred to in the words of Paul, "Believe in the Lord Jesus, and you will be saved" (Acts 16:31). This belief is not merely head knowledge; it is the response of a heart to the person of Christ saying, "I trust Your redeeming work to deliver me from sin and carry me safely to heaven."

PROGRESS OF BELIEF

The New Testament, especially the Gospel of John, gives convincing evidence for the progressive nature of belief. This is seen in the nobleman of Capernaum who appealed for his son's healing on the basis of what he had heard about Christ's miracles. He believed the word of Jesus (John 4:50), and that belief was confirmed and strengthened by the miracle that led him to place his faith in Christ (4:53). The progress of belief is seen in the healed blind man who believed Jesus to be "a prophet" (9:17), "from God" (9:33), and the "Son of Man" (9:35).

The clearest evidence of the progress of belief is seen in the disciples. Nathanael believed in Jesus as Son of God and King of Israel when Christ revealed His omniscience before him (1:50). The disciples are said to have believed in Christ after the miracle at Cana (2:11). After Jesus' resurrection the disciples believed the Scriptures and Christ's words concerning His death (2:22). Their belief, conditioned on particular circumstances, is seen in 6:69; 16:30; and 17:8. Christ allowed Lazarus to die so that the disciples might "believe" (11:15). After the resurrection John entered the empty tomb and "believed" (20:8).

Belief among the disciples was initiated by the testimony of John (1:35–41). That belief was confirmed as they saw the miracles—the insignia of His deity (2:11; 6:69). The belief of the disciples was consummated by the resurrection and resurrection appearances of Christ (2:22; 20:8, 25–29). Merrill Tenney summarizes the concept of the progress of belief in John.

> The growth of belief depicted in the Gospel of John thus moves from an initial acceptance of the testimony of another to a personal knowledge marked by loyalty, service, and worship; from assumption of the historicity and integrity of Jesus to a personal trust in Him; from an outward profession to an inward reality; from attending to His teachings to acknowledging His lordship over life. Full belief may not be attained instantly; yet the incipient and tentative belief is not to be despised. The groping inquiry of Nicodemus, the wistful outreach of the woman of Samaria, the untaught earnestness of the blind man, the erratic commitments of Peter, the blunt incredulity yet outspoken loyalty of Thomas, were reshaped by Christ into a living faith that conducted the power of God.[6]

The progressive nature of belief is evidenced in Hebrews 11:6, "And without faith it is impossible to please God, because anyone who comes to him must believe that he exists and that he rewards those who earnestly seek him." The first step of belief is seen in the words "believe that he exists." This has to do with belief in the existence of God. One can come to this stage of faith through the witness of creation. Paul pointed out that God has made His existence known to humanity through His creation. "For since the creation of the world God's invisible qualities—his eternal power and divine nature—have been clearly seen, being understood from what has been made, so that men are without excuse" (Rom. 1:20). Cornelius was in this first stage of belief before Peter visited him (Acts 10:1–2). Cornelius believed in God. He was even a man of prayer and piety, but he was not a believer in Christ (11:13–14).

Belief in God is important, but it is only the first step. Many people believe in God but have not taken the second step of accepting Jesus Christ as their Savior. This second stage of faith is reflected in the words of Hebrews 11:6, "he rewards those who earnestly seek him." As people respond to the revelation of God's existence and seek Him by faith, God provides special revelation through His Word and by His Spirit to enable a person to have faith in Jesus Christ. Cornelius advanced to this next stage of belief as a result of Peter's message concerning Jesus (Acts 11:24–28). Biblical faith, then, is a dynamic, progressive, growing trust in God and in His divine Son.

BELIEF OF UNBELIEF

In the progress of belief there is a stage that falls short of genuine belief resulting in salvation. This is first seen in John 2:23, where many at the Passover "believed" as a result of Christ's signs, yet He did not "believe" (trust) them (2:23–25). Jesus discerned that their faith was superficial, based only on the miracles they had seen. Later during the Feast of Tabernacles many of the people "believed in Him" but apparently not as Messiah (7:31, NASB). Jesus spoke to the Jews "who had believed him" (8:31) and accused them of seeking to kill Him (8:40). He later accused the same Jews of unbelief (8:45–46).

A prominent example of the "belief of unbelief" in the Book of Acts is Simon, a practitioner of the magic arts in the city of Samaria (Acts 8:9–10). Simon "believed" and was baptized (8:13), but the account that follows raises serious doubt over the genuineness of his faith. When Simon saw that the Spirit was bestowed through the laying on of the apostles' hands, he offered money to buy the power and authority the apostles possessed (8:18–19). Peter rebuked him with strong words, "May your money perish with you, because you thought you could buy the gift of God with money! You have no part or share in this ministry, because your heart is not right before God. Repent of this wickedness and pray to the Lord. Perhaps he will forgive you for having such a thought in your heart. For I see that you are full of bitterness and captive to sin" (8:20–23).

The absence of any evidence of repentance or willingness to pray leads me to suspect that while Simon believed something about Jesus and went through the ritual of baptism, his belief was not genuine saving faith. Simon seems to have remained an unrepentant and unregenerate man in spite of his initial response and religious behavior.

Tenney refers to this kind of belief which falls short of genuine faith as "superficial."[7] Morris calls it "transitory belief" which is not saving faith.[8] It is based merely on outward profession. The problem with this belief is its object. It seems to have been based primarily on miracles and was not rooted in a clear understanding of the person of Christ as Messiah and Son of God. Many were inclined to believe something about Jesus but were unwilling to yield their allegiance to Him, trusting Him as their personal Sin-Bearer.

We see this today, don't we? My Muslim friend believes in Jesus in the sense that he believes that Jesus is a prophet. But he says the greater prophet is Mohammed, who received God's final revelation in the Koran. My Mormon friend believes in Jesus in the sense that he believes that Jesus is a man who became a god, and that we have the potential to do the same. His faith is founded on the Book of Mormon and other Mormon writings. Those of the Baha'i faith believe in Jesus in the sense that they believe that Jesus is one of many ways to God. They believe various religious traditions, practiced by sincere people, will lead them to God.

Tragically many people are convinced that it doesn't really matter what you believe, so long as you are sincere. This reminds me of a Peanuts cartoon in which Charlie Brown is returning from a disastrous baseball game. The caption read, "174 to nothing! How could we lose when we were so sincere?" The reality is, Charlie Brown, that it takes more than sincerity to win the game of life. Many people are sincere about their beliefs, but they are sincerely wrong!

BELIEVING IN JESUS

The key to a biblical faith is its content. What should we believe about Jesus? The answer is found in John 20:30–31: "Jesus did many other miraculous signs in the presence of his disciples, which are not recorded in this book. But these are written that you may believe that Jesus is the Christ, the Son of God, and that by believing you may have life in his name."

John wrote his Gospel to encourage his readers to believe. But he wanted to make sure they believed the right thing! First, he wanted them to believe that Jesus is "the Christ." The word *christos*, properly translated "Anointed One," is a title, not a personal name. It refers to God's promised "Messiah" anticipated by the Old Testament prophets (Isa. 7:14; 9:6–7; Mic. 5:2). This is the One who bore our sins on the cross, died a criminal's death, and rose again. The miracles of John's Gospel are designed to show that Jesus is indeed the Messiah—the promised One of God who fulfills Old Testament prophecy.

Second, John wanted his readers to believe that Jesus is "the Son of God." This phrase emphasizes His deity. In John's Gospel Jesus calls God His Father over one hundred times, and He appealed to His miracles to prove this claim (John 5:36; 10:25, 38; 14:11). Even Christ's enemies understood His claim to deity (5:18), though they rejected Him.

Believing in Jesus involves personally trusting in Jesus, God's divine Messiah, welcoming Him into your life, and relying on His redemptive work. Those who truly believe in Jesus are not merely standing around expressing intellectual agreement that Jesus can save. Like Ann Seward trusting in the high-wire artist, they place themselves in the Savior's care, trusting that He will carry them safely from this world to heaven. They install no safety net "in case something goes wrong." They cling to no backup system should Jesus fail. Instead they respond with obedient faith, stepping out onto the highwire of life with nothing to keep them from eternal destruction except Jesus Christ.

Those who take this step of faith experience a spiritual birth (John 3:5–8) and enter into the family of God as His beloved children (1:12). Their sins are forgiven, and they are cleansed from their former way of life (Titus 3:5; 1 John 2:12). On the basis of their faith they are "justified" or declared righteous (Rom. 5:1) and can rightly be called "saints" (2 Cor. 1:1). Their names are written in the Lamb's book of life (Rev. 21:27) and their eternal life is guaranteed by Christ (John 10:28). What blessings are ours in Christ, graciously made available to all who simply receive the gift by faith!

For Further Study

Connolly, John R. *Dimensions of Belief and Unbelief.* Lanham, Md.: University Press, 1980.

Helm, Paul. *The Varieties of Belief.* London: George Allen and Unwin, 1973.

16

RESPONDING TO GOD

Anyone who listens to the word but does not do what it says is like a man who looks at his face in a mirror, and, after looking at himself, goes away and immediately forgets what he looks like.

—James 1:23–24

WATCHING TELEVISED EVENTS of the 1998 Winter Olympics reminded me of my experience as a ski racer for the South Eugene High School. For three winters during high school I lived, ate, and breathed ski racing. Coach Tom Means put our team into shape running the hills around Eugene. Even before the snow was falling in the mountains, we were running up and down grassy hillsides practicing our turns and strengthening our muscles. When winter came, our ski team trained at Willamette Pass Ski Area on the weekends. We would set up a course of bamboo poles on the snow-covered slopes and practice our starts, turns, and other racing skills. "Hit those gates high and follow the fall line," Coach Means would shout, as we raced against the clock. Time and time again we would ski the course, trying to trim a second or two off our best time.

I practiced with the ski team on weekends, ran with the ski team during the weekdays, watched films of famous ski racers after practice, and read *Skiing* magazine when I should have been studying for my classes. My interest in skiing was not merely an intellectual endeavor. The knowledge, skills, and training were all in preparation to race! And race we did! I have the trophies and medals to prove that the hard work and discipline were well rewarded. Having "lettered" on the ski team, I wore my purple-and-white letterman's jacket with pride. And although none of my team members became Olympic racers, we did take first place at the state championship meet my senior year!

As my training for ski racing was not an end in itself, neither should be our study of God. Studying about God is intended not merely to stimulate our intellects and satisfy our curiosity. It is to help us win the race of life! Getting to know God better calls for action on the part of His people. God fully intended for us to respond to His self-revelation. Believers showed response with worship, love, fear, obedience, and service.

RESPONDING IN WORSHIP

Worship should be a believer's first and foremost response to God. Speaking to Moses about His attributes, the Lord said He is "the compassionate and gracious God, slow to anger, abounding in love and faithfulness" (Exod. 34:6). How did Moses respond to these wonderful truths about God? Did he immediately grab a tablet of stone and say, "Let me write that down"? Or, "Wow, that will make a great sermon!" Not at all! When God revealed Himself, "Moses bowed to the ground at once and worshiped" (34:8). Ezekiel responded in a similar way when he was confronted with a vision of God's glory. He wrote, "When I saw it, I fell facedown" (Ezek. 1:28).

A Definition of Worship

The word *worship* comes from the Anglo-Saxon *weorthscipe*, which became *worthship*, and eventually *worship*. The background of these English terms suggests that worship involves "attributing worth" to God. *Šāhâ*, the Hebrew word for worship, literally means "to bow down, to prostrate oneself." The act of bowing is intended to reflect one's acknowledgment of God's worth. *Proskyneō*, the term used most frequently in the New Testament to denote worship, literally means "to kiss toward." It reflects the ancient custom of kissing the earth as a means of honoring deities.

Ronald Allen and Gordon Borror offer a concise definition of worship: "Worship is an active response to God whereby we declare His worth."[1] They add, "Worship is not simply a mood; it is a response. Worship is not just a feeling; it is a declaration."[2] God's worth may be declared or acknowledged in many different ways—through song, thanksgiving, praise, prayer, or the reading of Scripture. Because worship is not a matter of mere outward form but of inward attitude, it can take place in a public worship service or in the privacy of one's home.

The scriptural concept of worship is illuminated by Jesus' conversation with the Samaritan woman. In her attempt to sidestep the issue of her sin, the woman raised a hotly debated theological question. While Samaritans regarded Mount Gerizim as the rightful place of worship, the Jews held that God was to be worshiped only on the temple mount in Jerusalem. Instead of engaging in this theological controversy, Jesus told the woman that true worship should focus on a person rather than a place. He said, "Yet a time is coming and has now come when the true worshipers will worship the Father in spirit and truth, for they are the kind of worshipers the Father seeks. God is spirit, and his worshipers must worship in spirit and in truth" (John 4:23–24). What is meant by the words "in spirit and in truth"?

To worship God "in spirit" is to worship after the pattern of God's essential nature. Since God is spirit, worship must be bound up with spiritual realities, not physical formalities. The Old Testament prophets condemned religious externalism that was devoid of spiritual reality (Hos. 6:6; Mic. 6:6–8). Worship has more to do with the state of the heart than the state of the art. God is not interested in our words unless they express the genuine attitude of our hearts.

To worship "in truth" means to worship the true God—the God of the Bible. It also suggests we should value God not because of what He provides but simply because of who He is. We live in a society that is very utilitarian. We use things. We use people. We seem to want to use God also. We may sometimes worship God not for His own sake, but because we want something from Him. To worship "in truth" means to worship honestly, genuinely, and from the heart. It means to exalt God for who He is, not for what He gives.

Activities of Worship

Scripture records specific invitations or commands to worship. The imperative of worship appears frequently in the Book of Psalms: "Worship the LORD in the splendor of his holiness" (Ps. 29:2). "Come, let us bow down in worship, let us kneel before the LORD our Maker (95:6). "Exalt the LORD our God and worship at his holy mountain" (99:9). "Let us go to his dwelling place; let us worship at his footstool" (132:7). The imperative form of the verb emphasizes the fact that worship is an activity, not just a topic for theological discussion.

Psalm 100 is an invitation to worship. It suggests a core of activities that are central to the worship experience. The first activity mentioned is singing. In Psalm 100:2 believers are exhorted, "Worship the LORD with gladness; come before him with joyful songs." Singing is a musical response to God whereby we declare His worth through song. The only thing the psalmist mentioned about the quality of our singing is that it should be "joyful." Many Christians, myself included, cannot sing parts or carry a melody. But we can sing with sincerity, enthusiasm, and joy in our hearts. Our song may not impress people who are musically trained, but God is pleased when we joyfully sing His praises in sincerity and truth.

The second activity of worship mentioned in Psalm 100 is thanksgiving. Worshipers are invited to "enter his gates with thanksgiving" (100:4). The "gates" refer to the temple entrances. When the Israelites came into the temple area to celebrate the feasts and to worship God, they were to come with "thanksgiving" on their lips. The word translated "thanksgiving" (*tôdâ*) literally refers to a "public confession." In the context of worship it refers to the public acknowledgement of God's character and worth. In ancient Israel, when a worshiper presented a thank offering in the temple, a public declaration would be made as to why the offering was being given (1 Sam. 1:26–28). The worshiper would declare what God had done to elicit this worship. God's gracious benefits would be recited and His attributes declared.

Although believers today are not involved in temple ritual, the writer of Hebrews insisted that sacrifices of thanksgiving are still appropriate. "Through Jesus, therefore, let us continually offer to God a sacrifice of praise—the fruit of lips that confess his name" (Heb. 13:15).

A third form of worship mentioned in Psalm 100 is praise. "Enter his gates with thanksgiving and his courts with praise" (100:4). Praise is an essential and integral aspect of worship. The Hebrew title of the Psalms is literally, "Book of Praises." The Hebrew word translated "praise" (*tᵉhillâ*) is from a verb *hālal* that refers to a verbal and public boasting. Allen has pointed out that in the mind of the psalmist there was no thought of "quiet, personal praise."[3] Biblical praise is always vocal and public in nature. Themes of rejoicing, singing, and celebration are often associated with biblical praise. It is clear that biblical praise is an enthusiastic and joyful public declaration of the greatness and goodness of God.

My daughter, Elisabeth, recently completed her first 26.2 mile Portland Marathon, placing tenth in her age division. On the same day, my daughter Laura took first place in her division in the Five Miler. I was so proud of my daughters! For the next week my seminary students and colleagues permitted me to engage in a bit of enthusiastic boasting about their accomplishments. Now if we can permit such exulting in human accomplishments, how much more appropriate is it for believers to boast in the great things accomplished by God! As the psalmist declared, "Praise him for his acts of power" (150:2).

The fourth activity mentioned in Psalm 100 is blessing God's name. "Give thanks to Him; bless His name" (100:4, NASB). The word "bless" may be derived from the Hebrew word for "knee," suggesting a posture of humility before the one being worshiped (95:6). We bless God's name when we bow our knee before His authority and obey His will. Further insight into what it means to "bless" the Lord is seen in Psalm 103:2, where David wrote, "Bless the LORD, O my soul, and forget none of His benefits" (NASB). David then recited many of God's gracious benefits (103:3–5). To bless the Lord is to remember, and not forget, His mighty, saving deeds.

Psalm 100 does not provide an exhaustive list of worship activities. Those who worship in spirit and truth must allow for spontaneity and creativity in the forms of worship. Worship may include the use of drama, audiovisual media, and group activity. Christians can maintain a freshness in worship by using creative activities along with the more traditional forms to "declare the worth" of our great God.[4]

RESPONDING WITH LOVE

One day when Jesus was teaching in the temple, a Jewish lawyer—an expert in the Mosaic Law—asked Him, "Teacher, which is the greatest commandment in the Law?" (Matt. 22:36). The Pharisees had reduced the Law to 613 commandments—365 negative commands and 248 positive ones. Since it was difficult to know and observe them all, most people had a priority list, and Jesus was asked, "Which do you consider number one?" Jesus responded by quoting Deuteronomy 6:5, "Love the Lord your God with all your heart and with all your soul and with all your mind" (Matt. 22:37). Then He added, "This is the first and greatest commandment" (22:38).

Responding to God means responding with love. Love is normally thought of as a spontaneous emotional response rather than religious obligation. Yet the Hebrew verb used in Deuteronomy 6:5 (*'āhab*) is also used to describe the love of a father for his son (Gen. 22:2), a slave for his master (Exod. 21:5), a husband for his wife (1 Sam. 1:5), a neighbor for a neighbor (Lev. 19:18). In each case there is an implication of duty or obligation. J. W. McKay has argued rather convincingly that the love referred to in Deuteronomy 6:5 should be understood in the context of the father-son relationship. In this case God is the Father (who teaches and disciplines), and Israel is the son (who learns and obeys).[5] In this context "love" is not a sentimental emotion; it is filial love and obedience that the son offers to his father. When *'āhab* is used of a person's love for God in Deuteronomy, it is virtually synonymous with obedience (Deut. 11:1, 18–22; 13:4–5). The fact that love for God is to be expressed in willing and joyful obedience to His commands is developed in 6:6–9. Love and obedience must be understood as paired concepts. And so Jesus said, "If you love me, you will obey what I command" (John 14:15).

The command to love God is elaborated in Deuteronomy 6:5 by the words, "with all your heart and with all your soul and with all your strength." This phrase is used to describe the unprecedented manner in which King Josiah "turned to the LORD . . . with all his heart and with all his soul and with all his strength" (2 Kings 23:25). McBride has observed that three parts (heart, soul, might) "reinforce the absolute singularity of personal devotion to God. Thus *kebab* [heart] denotes the intention or will of the whole man; *nepesh* [soul] means the whole self, a unity of flesh, will, and vitality; and *me'od* [might] accents the superlative degree of total commitment to Yahweh."[6] This is all-encompassing love for God.

The New Testament writers struggled with how to express the meaning of *meʾōd*, "strength, or abundance." Matthew rendered it "mind" (Matt. 22:37) while Mark and Luke used the words "mind" and "strength" (Mark 12:30; Luke 10:27). The basic idea is that our love for God should be "exceedingly abundant" or "to the highest degree."

While God's love can be commanded, we should not regard this as merely an obligation or duty. When we consider all God does for us and how He constantly watches over us, we feel obliged to love Him as one would any other benefactor. But the more we understand God's true nature, the more we love Him for who He is and for no other reason. As a husband, I have a moral obligation to love my wife (Eph. 5:25–28). But my relationship with Nancy is not built on moral obligation only. As I have gotten to know her over the years as a friend, lover, travel companion, mother of our children, prayer partner, and colaborer for Christ, I have grown to love Nancy for the person she is rather than because of any obligation or duty. And so it is with God as we get to know Him better.

RESPONDING WITH FEAR

God's people are repeatedly commanded to respond to God with "fear." Shortly before his death, Joshua told the Israelites, "Now fear the LORD and serve him with all faithfulness" (Josh. 24:14). Samuel repeated these words in his charge to Israel (1 Sam. 12:24). David commanded, "Fear the LORD, you his saints" (Ps. 34:9). Solomon passed on this message in Proverbs (3:7; 24:21) and Ecclesiastes (5:7; 12:13).

This theme is also present in the New Testament. Paul was motivated by fear of the Lord (2 Cor. 5:11; 7:1), and he described unbelievers as having "no fear of God before their eyes" (Rom. 3:18). Peter commanded his readers to "fear God" (1 Pet. 2:17). John recorded the warning of an apocalyptic angel, "Fear God and give him glory, because the hour of his judgment has come" (Rev. 14:7).

Most people are not very interested in "fearing God." It doesn't sound very relational and may seem a bit too scary for the average Christian. The problem is that we have not understood what this command means. Nor have we appreciated the benefit of fearing the Lord.

Should "the fear of God" be likened to the dread we sense during the hours before a major surgery? Is it like the trembling we feel after narrowly avoiding a collision? Are Christians to tremble in terror before their awesome, holy God?

There certainly is a place for this kind of apprehension or dread in relationship to God's eternal judgment of unbelievers or His discipline of disobedient Christians. But "the fear of the Lord," is not the same as being afraid. In Psalm 112:1 we read, "Blessed is the man who fears the LORD, who finds great delight in his command." The word "blessed" can be translated "happy." So one who fears God is described as in a state of joy, not terror.

Several verses in the Bible provide insight into the concept of fearing the Lord. Fearing God is equated in Proverbs 2:5 with knowing God: "Then you will understand the fear of the LORD and find the knowledge of God." In the Hebrew poetry of this proverb, the phrases "fear of the LORD" and "knowledge of God" are synonymous. This means that the concepts are virtual equivalents. To know God is to fear God. If we truly know God and appreciate His attributes, we can't help but have a healthy respect for Him.

As a seminary professor I am accountable to our academic dean. I have an appreciation for his position and I respect him as a person. I don't tremble when I pass him in the hall or when I sit with him in the faculty lunchroom. Yet I do recognize that he holds me accountable for the quality of my classroom instruction. I want to know and meet his standards. In the same way, fearing the Lord means knowing Him—knowing His character, His standards, His commandments—and responding to Him in light of who He is.

Job 28:28 associates the fear of God with departing from evil: "The fear of the Lord—that is wisdom, and to shun evil is understanding." In Psalm 111:10 fearing God is related to keeping His commands: "The fear of the LORD is the beginning of wisdom; all who follow his precepts have good understanding." A Christian will practice the fear of the Lord by departing from evil and obeying God's commandments.

I thought I was doing pretty well in living out the fear of the Lord until I came to Proverbs 8:13, "To fear the LORD is to hate evil." Rather than hate evil, I find that I have often been entertained by evil! Many of our television programs and newscasts feature illicit sex, murder, theft, and various forms of violence. I remember recently watching a newscast that provided very titillating details about the illicit relationship of a well-known public figure. Too often we respond to these programs with unnecessary interest and attention. We are not sharing God's attitude toward evil. We are not hating what He hates. Instead, we love it and waste much time seeking further information about the evil God hates.

The one who truly fears God is not standing around with trembling hands and knocking knees. Instead, the one who fears God seeks to obey Him and strives to do His will. As Allen wrote, "The fear of Yahweh is not a terror before him, but a positive response to His majesty and glory, a readiness to worship and serve Him, a recognition of who He is and who man is before Him."[7]

Is it possible to "fear God" and also love Him? While fear and love seem to be rather opposite responses, it is clear from the Bible that God expects His people to do both. This is evident from the words of Moses: "And now, O Israel, what does the LORD your God ask of you but to fear the LORD your God, to walk in all his ways [and], to love him" (Deut. 10:12). Fearing God and loving Him are not mutually exclusive concepts. As children respect their parents whom they love, so God's people must both love and fear Him.

RESPONDING WITH OBEDIENCE

I have always appreciated the accuracy and simplicity of the refrain of the old hymn written by John H. Sammis (1846–1919), "Trust and obey, for there's no other way to be happy in Jesus, but to trust and obey." Trusting and obeying God is really the "bottom line" for joyful Christian living. Knowing that God is holy, sovereign, good, and loving leads believers to respond to Him in trustful obedience.

The command to "obey" God is repeated throughout Scripture. God commanded the Israelites at Mount Sinai to "obey me fully and keep my covenant" (Exod. 19:5). The Hebrew word translated "obey" has the meaning "to hear," but is frequently extended to refer to *effective* hearing or listening. The word means "to listen, pay attention, understand, and obey."

Before entering Canaan, the second generation of Israelites were commanded to "obey the LORD God" (Deut. 27:10). Obeying the Lord is linked with observing His commandments (30:8). The priority of obedience is emphasized in Samuel's words to disobedient Saul: "Does the LORD delight in burnt offerings and sacrifices as much as in obeying the voice of the LORD? To obey is better than sacrifice, and to heed is better than the fat of rams" (1 Sam. 15:22). This point is highlighted by the prophets as well (Jer. 7:22–23).

Obedience is not just an obligation of the Israelites under the Mosaic Covenant. It is a New Covenant obligation as well. As already noted, Jesus said, "If you love me, you will obey what I command" (John 14:15). Faced with a conflict between civil and moral duty, the apostles exclaimed, "We must obey God rather than men!" (Acts 5:29). Paul pointed out the principle that "you are slaves to the one whom you obey—whether you are slaves to sin, which leads to death, or to obedience, which leads to righteousness" (Rom. 6:16). Although the Roman believers had been "slaves to sin," they now "wholeheartedly obeyed" the truth of the gospel (6:17). Having been "set free from sin" through faith in the redemptive work of Christ, they were now "slaves to righteousness" (6:18).

Under God's covenant with Israel, obedience was the condition for blessing. God said, "All these blessings will come upon you and accompany you if you obey the LORD your God" (Deut. 28:2). Disobedience to the covenant stipulations would result in judgment instead of blessing. "However, if you do not obey the LORD your God and do not carefully follow all his commands and decrees I am giving you today, all these curses will come upon you and overtake you" (28:15). The theme of God's blessing on obedience and judgment on disobedience is one that can be traced through the history of God's dealings with Israel. Israel did not *earn* God's blessing through obedience. Rather, their obedience simply maintained their covenant relationship with God, the Source of all blessing.

Under the New Covenant, spiritual blessings are secured for all believers through the redemptive work of Christ. Paul wrote that God "has blessed us in the heavenly realms with every spiritual blessing in Christ" (Eph. 1:3). Christians obey God, not to get a blessing, but because they have already been blessed! Our obedience to Christ is an expression of our love and appreciation for all that He has done for us (John 14:15).

But what about those times when I just don't "feel" like obeying God? At times, I would rather go my own way and do my own things. And our world today provides ample opportunity and encouragement for such behavior. Disobedience does not mean the loss of my salvation or the removal of spiritual blessings that have been secured for me through Christ. But disobedience means that I will be confronted with many unnecessary and avoidable problems as the consequences of my sin. Disobedience means that my fellowship with God will not be as sweet and enjoyable because of my guilty conscience. Disobedience means that I can expect God's chastening and correction as He disciplines me for my good.

Satan likes to deceive us into believing that the pathway of disobedience will be more fun, more satisfying, more exciting than walking in the light with God. This is a big lie. The very opposite is true. God wants the very best for His children. And His commandments are given, not to take away life's joys, but to enhance them.

I have a Ford van which I enjoy driving. To keep it in good condition I change the oil every three thousand miles. The owner's manual says that I should put in six and a half quarts of oil when I change the oil and oil filter. Now what would happen if I decided to ignore the owner's manual and "do it my own way"? If I decided to save a few dollars and put in two quarts of oil instead of six and a half, my engine would overheat, the piston rings would wear, and before long the engine would not work. The instructions in the owner's manual are not intended to take away my freedom or joy of life. Rather, the instructions are intended to help me enjoy driving my van by avoiding unnecessary problems. And so it is with God's Word. The Creator knows the very best way to live and how to help us get the most out of life. The instructions and commandments of His Word are for our own good. Solomon said, "I know that it will go better with God-fearing men" (Eccles. 8:12). God's commandments are for our good (Deut. 10:13). No wonder the psalmist exclaimed, "I will never forget your precepts, for by them you have renewed my life" (Ps. 119:93, literal translation).

RESPONDING WITH SERVICE

Before crossing the Jordan River into Canaan, Moses instructed God's people to fear the Lord, to walk in all His ways, to love Him, and to serve Him wholeheartedly (Deut. 10:12). When Joshua gathered the tribes at Shechem to recommit themselves to God's covenant, he reminded them of their obligation to fear the Lord and to serve Him (Josh. 24:14). The Israelites agreed to this commitment, saying, "We too will serve the LORD, because he is our God" (24:18). Samuel and the prophets who followed him continued to remind the people of their obligation to serve the Lord, not the false gods like Baal and Asherah (1 Sam. 12:20). The psalmist insisted that such service should be rendered "with gladness" (Ps. 100:2).

Jesus called for single-mindedness in our service toward God. He spoke of the fact that no one can serve two masters. To love one is to hate the other. "You cannot serve both God and Money" (Matt. 6:24). In his defense before Felix, the Roman governor, Paul testified, "I do serve the God of our fathers" (Acts 24:14, NASB). Paul was pleased that the Thessalonian believers had realized that faith and service go together, for they had "turned to God from idols to serve the living and true God" (1 Thess. 1:9). To the Colossians he wrote, "It is the Lord Christ you are serving" (Col. 3:24). Serving God is not merely a temporal experience limited to our life on earth. The apostle John revealed that in the eternal state when creation is redeemed from the curse and God reigns over all, "His servants will serve him" (Rev. 22:3).

What does it mean to serve God and how do we go about doing it? Serving God means recognizing the lordship of Jesus Christ in every area of our lives and responding to Him in obedience. Responding to Him in obedience may involve using my spiritual gifts to edify and encourage the body of Christ (1 Pet. 4:10). It may mean leading others in worship (Rev. 19:5–6). For those who are called to serve as elders, serving God will include the study of God's Word and prayer (Acts 6:4). We can serve God through our financial resources to support the work of His church (1 Cor. 16:1–2; 2 Cor. 9:8–12). Believers can serve God through the work of evangelism, discipleship, and church planting (Matt. 28:19–20; 2 Tim. 4:5), or through teaching Sunday school and Bible studies (2 Tim. 2:2; Titus 2:3).

A major lesson of the foot washing in the Upper Room was that believers can serve God by serving each other (John 13:14–15). There Jesus reminded His followers of their status as slaves in the service of Christ, their Master (13:16). If the Master serves, how much more ought the slaves to serve? When a cathedral in Europe was bombed in World War II, a statue of Christ was damaged. Its hands were blown off. The statue has not been restored. It stands there today with its hand missing, but underneath is an inscription, "Christ has no hands but yours." By serving others you serve Christ and meet the needs of His people.

There are so many ways to serve God. It doesn't have to be through a formal position or elected church office. I recently became acquainted with Gladys Gassoway, who is confined to her home for health reasons. But she has a significant ministry for God and His people in spite of her confinement. Gladys sings to people over the telephone! Each week she calls over one hundred people who have requested her ministry and sings one of the great hymns of the faith over the phone. Her call includes a brief visit and a word of prayer. Gladys Gassoway is serving God by encouraging others with songs that lift up His marvelous name.

RESPONDING TO GOD'S LOVE

I have always enjoyed sending valentine cards. So each year a few days before February 14, I purchase a package of children's valentine cards to send to the ladies on the staff at Western Seminary. It has given me joy to brighten their day a bit on Valentine's Day. Some have even responded by sending a valentine in return! Last year I returned to my office after delivering my valentines to find a pile of valentines and heart-shaped confetti in my mail box! I was surprised and overwhelmed. The staff women who had received my cards over the years wanted me to know of their appreciation. Although I wasn't seeking it, my cards led them to respond.

The apostle John wrote, "We love because he first loved us" (1 John 4:19). God's great love elicits a response from our hearts. As we are getting to know Him better, let's not fail to respond to our great God!

For Further Reading

Allen, Ronald, and Gordon Borror. *Worship: Rediscovering the Missing Jewel*. Portland, Oreg.: Multnomah Press, 1982.

Blackaby, Henry T., and Claude V. King. *Experiencing God*. Nashville: Broadman & Holman Publishers, 1994.

Laney, J. Carl. *Everything I Know about Success I Learned from the Bible*. Grand Rapids: Kregel Publications, 1996.

Watkins, William D. *The Busy Christian's Guide to Experiencing God More*. Ann Arbor, Mich.: Servant Publications, 1997.

17

DEALING WITH YOUR DOUBTS

Then the eleven disciples went to Galilee, to the mountain where Jesus had told them to go. When they saw him, they worshiped him; but some doubted.

—Matthew 28:16–17

CHRISTIANS ARE USUALLY EMBARRASSED to admit that they have doubts about what they believe. Nobody wants to be known as a "doubting Thomas." But it is only natural for Christians to have some questions, hesitations, and even doubts. After all, they are called to accept so much by faith. Mathematicians work on the basis of their proven formulas. Physicists work on the basis of certain natural laws of science. But Christians are called on to believe in an invisible God and accept an ancient book as His inspired Word. And their eternal destiny rests on whether this is true.

Have you ever doubted God's existence? Have you ever wondered if your prayers are really being heard? Would life be any different for you if you were not a Christian? Have you ever wondered if there is a heaven beyond the grave or if death is the end of it all?

If you have never had such questions, even for a fleeting moment, it may be that you have never encountered a testing that has cut you off at the kneecaps and left you wondering, "What's behind it all?" Or it may be that you have had some doubts, but have been too fearful to admit them. You may have thought to yourself, "What would people say if they knew that I had some doubts about my faith? They might even think that I'm not a Christian!"

Well, I must admit I have had doubts. I have been a Christian for about forty years. I spent seven years studying about God in seminary. I have pastored churches and preached hundreds of sermons. As a seminary professor I have repeatedly taught through the whole Bible, Genesis through Revelation. In spite of this training and Christian experience, there are times when I have wondered if I have not been caught up in one big mistake. These thoughts have usually crept into my mind when I'm weary from ministry, dealing with a perplexing matter, or have encountered an inexplicable tragedy in someone else's life.

Rather than be embarrassed by our doubts, we can be encouraged to know that we stand in good company. When the eleven disciples met with Jesus in Galilee after His resurrection, some among that famous group weren't sure it was "for real." The apostle Matthew, an eyewitness of the encounter, later wrote, "And when they saw him, they worshiped him; but some were doubtful" (Matt. 28:17, NASB). The reference here is to some of the apostles—those who had been with Jesus for three years and had witnessed His miracles and His resurrection. Yet some of these *apostles* were doubtful!

If you have ever struggled with doubts raised by perplexing issues in your life, then this chapter is especially for you. I would like to help you learn how to face your doubts honestly and to seek God's answers.

DEFINING DOUBT

What is this experience or emotion called *doubt*? Often we think of doubt as the antithesis of faith, as if the two were the opposite sides of a coin. But the antithesis of faith is unbelief. The person experiencing doubt is somewhere between belief and unbelief. The doubter wants to believe but is struggling with the rational basis for this belief.

Os Guinness points out that our English word *doubt* can be traced to an Aryan root meaning "two." So to believe is to be "in one mind" about accepting something as true; to disbelieve is to be in "in one mind" about rejecting it. To doubt is to waver between the two, to believe and disbelieve at once so as to be "in two minds."[1] Gary Habermas, author of one of the most thorough studies of the subject, has defined Christian doubt as "a lack of certainty concerning the teachings of Christianity or one's personal relation to them."[2]

While doubt always involves some wavering between two opinions, not all doubt is the same.[3] *Factual* doubts usually spring from questions regarding the foundations of one's faith. Is the Bible true? Did Jesus really rise from the dead? Is there a biblical basis for heaven? *Emotional* doubts are usually the result of psychological conditions such as anxiety or depression. Sometimes these conditions are the result of medical problems, childhood experiences, or lack of proper nutrition and rest. *Volitional* doubts often result when a Christian wishes to grow in his or her faith but experiences uncertainty because of repeated failures. Some uncertainty or doubt results from repeated but unsuccessful attempts to practice the principles of Christianity.

Doubting is not unique to Christian experience. A mountain climber may have doubts about how secure are the rope and pitons used to ascend a sheer cliff. A sky diver may have some doubts before leaping into empty space with only a parachute for protection. Parents may entertain some worries or doubts before sending their first child off to college. It is clear that doubt is a human problem, not just a Christian problem. C. S. Lewis's personal comment is instructive in this regard. "Now that I am a Christian I do have moods in which the whole thing looks very improbable; but when I was an atheist I had moods in which Christianity looked terribly probable."[4] Doubt is common to human experience—among believers and unbelievers alike.

HABAKKUK, THE PERPLEXED PROPHET

If you have ever grappled with doubt, you will be able to identify with Habakkuk, the perplexed prophet. The book which bears his name has an appeal to the honest doubter. Unlike other prophetic books, Habakkuk does not address Israel, Judah, or their enemies. Instead, it contains the record of Habakkuk's personal perplexity and prayer. The prophetic record of Habakkuk is set in the form of a dialogue between the prophet and God. Here we learn how a deeply spiritual prophet faced his doubts and brought them before his God.

Habakkuk lived and ministered in the Southern Kingdom of Judah around 600 B.C. during one of the darkest periods of Israel's history. Babylon had recently thrown off the Assyrian yoke and was becoming a powerful empire, bent on dominating the Near East. Hoping to maintain a balance of power in that part of the world, Neco, Egypt's pharaoh, marched north to help Assyria hold back the Babylonian advance. Judah's king Josiah calculated that any nation that wanted to help Assyria was his enemy. So he tried to stop Pharaoh Neco's advance at Megiddo, but was killed in the attempt (2 Kings 23:29). After the death of Josiah, the spiritual conditions within Judah rapidly deteriorated. Wickedness, injustice, and total disregard of the Law characterized the moral attitudes and actions of the people.

Perplexity over Judah's Unpunished Iniquity (Hab. 1:2–4)

The first thing that troubled Habakkuk was the fact of Judah's unpunished iniquity. Habakkuk wondered, "Why does evil triumph? Why doesn't God intervene?" He asked God, "Why do you make me look at injustice? Why do you tolerate wrong? Destruction and violence are before me; there is strife, and conflict abounds" (1:3). It seemed to Habakkuk that God was totally indifferent toward Judah's wickedness, violence, and strife. He wondered how a holy God could look on this sin with such seeming complacency. Habakkuk pointed out to God that as a result of sin ("Therefore"), "the law is paralyzed" (1:4). The Hebrew word translated "paralyzed" literally means "chilled" to the point of being numb. In Habakkuk's day justice was either "never upheld" or came out "perverted."

In addition to God's seeming indifference toward the persistent sin of His people, Habakkuk was troubled by unanswered prayer. He had prayed that God would deal with the nation's sin, but with no result. "How long, O LORD, must I call for help, but you do not listen? Or cry out to you, 'Violence!' but you do not save?" (1:2). The words "How long" indicate that Habakkuk had waited patiently for God's answer, but none came.

God's Answer: The Chaldean Judgment (Hab. 1:5–11)

In time, God answered Habakkuk's prayer and relieved his perplexity. Far from being unconcerned with Judah's sinful condition, God was raising up a nation to serve as His agent of judgment. An unbelievable catastrophe was about to occur! God revealed to Habakkuk, "Look at the nations and watch—and be utterly amazed. For I am going to do something in your days that you would not believe, even if you were told. I am raising up the Babylonians, that ruthless and impetuous people, who sweep across the whole earth" (1:5–6). Judah's sinful rebellion had not gone unnoticed. The delay in judgment was not an indication that sin didn't matter. Judgment was coming on Judah!

Perplexity over God's Use of a Wicked Instrument (Hab. 1:12–17)

God's answer to Habakkuk's first question was no doubt greatly appreciated, but it resulted in further perplexity! Now Habakkuk was perplexed over God's use of such a wicked instrument to judge His people. Habakkuk questioned, "O Lord, are you not from everlasting?" (1:12). The Babylonians treated the God of Israel with contempt. Their idolatry, immorality, and wicked atrocities against subject peoples were an affront to God's holiness. The wicked Chaldeans made the Judeans appear righteous by comparison! How, then, could a holy God tolerate the use of such an evil nation? It seemed so inconsistent with God's own holiness. Habakkuk said, "Your eyes are too pure to look on evil; you cannot tolerate wrong. Why then do you tolerate the treacherous?" (1:13). It seemed to Habakkuk that God's use of the Chaldeans indicated that He approved of their sinful ways. How could that be? Is God not so holy after all?

God's Solution: The Principle of Divine Recompense (Hab. 2:2–4)

Habakkuk had raised a serious question regarding God's holiness. His doubts were real. If God were to use the wicked Chaldeans, maybe He wasn't as holy as Habakkuk had previously thought. But Habakkuk was a humble and teachable doubter, and he took his concerns to God. He said,

"I will stand at my watch and station myself on the ramparts; I will look to see what he will say to me" (2:1).

In time God responded to Habakkuk's prayer and resolved his perplexity. God's answer to Habakkuk is found in the principle revealed in 2:4, "See, he is puffed up; his desires are not upright—but the righteous will live by his faith." The one who is "puffed up" refers to the Chaldeans whose arrogance Habakkuk had noted (1:10–11). The righteous in Israel are now set in contrast with the proud Chaldeans. God was saying to Habakkuk that the upright person ("the righteous") living in reliance on God will be preserved ("will live"), whereas the proud and wicked will perish. By way of application, the wicked Chaldeans would be held accountable for their actions. They may have enjoyed temporary ascendancy, but they would be judged for their actions. God's holiness has not been compromised by the use of such a wicked instrument, because the wicked instrument is indeed accountable (see Zech. 2:8).

LESSONS FROM HABAKKUK

The example of the prophet Habakkuk encourages us by showing that there is nothing wrong about having doubts about God and His ways. Many fine Christians have gone through a period of doubt. Peter experienced doubt when he was walking toward Jesus on the Sea of Galilee (Matt. 14:30–31). Thomas had his doubts about Jesus' resurrection (John 20:24–25). Other unnamed individuals among the apostles had their bouts with doubt (Matt. 28:17). Christians should not feel guilty, ashamed, or inferior to others when they encounter doubt.

The example of Habakkuk demonstrates that there is nothing wrong with expressing our doubts to the Lord in prayer. Habakkuk raised the question, "How can a just God allow evil to triumph without His intervention or judgment?" (see Hab. 1:2–4). He also wondered, "How can a holy God employ such a wicked agent as the Chaldeans?" (see 1:12–13). Behind Habakkuk's questions lay serious doubts: "Maybe God is not just. Maybe God can't do anything about evil. Maybe God isn't as holy as I thought."

The prophet Habakkuk also illustrates how to express our doubts humbly. In the midst of his perplexity and doubts, Habakkuk didn't turn his back on God. Instead, he turned to the Lord in prayer, and waited for Him to answer (2:1). Habakkuk knew where to turn when faced with doubt. Some people make the mistake of taking their doubts to others who are doubting or have denied the Lord. This usually results in more confusion than clarity on the issues of faith. Like King Hezekiah, when faced with Sennacherib's threats, we must spread out our concerns before the Lord (2 Kings 19:14).

Also we learn from Habakkuk that we must be willing to listen when God speaks. Habakkuk wrote, "Then the LORD replied" (Hab. 2:2). The prophet's doubts were resolved by a direct revelation from God. God answered Habakkuk's questions by confirming that He is indeed holy, sovereign, and just. As Habakkuk's doubts were eased through God's revelation, so the doubts of many Christians have been resolved by reading His Word. The Bible confronts and refutes our doubts with God's life-changing truth.

SUGGESTIONS FOR DEALING WITH DOUBT

An ability to deal with one's doubts can make the difference between success and failure in facing life's challenges. When Goliath approached the Israelite camp, the soldiers all thought, "He's so big, we'll never be able to kill him!" When David saw the giant, he thought, "He's so big, I can't miss!" The ability to deal with our doubts provides Christians with exciting opportunities to accomplish great things for God. Here are nine practical, scripturally based suggestions for dealing with your doubts.

• *Recognize that in many situations, doubt can be a positive virtue.*

Proverbs condemns the naive or gullible person who "believes anything" (Prov. 14:15). Critical thinking is necessary to avoid error and falsehood, even when we are thinking about God. Satan is in the business of deception (Rev. 12:9), and Paul recognized the possibility that even Christians might be deceived (Rom. 16:18; Gal. 6:7). In some situations there may be good reason for doubt. A wise person will recognize valid reasons for doubt and avoid being deceived. Doubt is often an incentive to search for truth. Around 1600 an Italian astronomer named Galileo entertained some doubts about an established church doctrine that said the earth is the center of the solar system. He suspected, and eventually proved, that the earth revolves around the sun, not vice versa. Galileo's doubt enabled him to avoid a commonly held error and led to the discovery of new truth.

• *Recognize that an element of faith may be embedded in honest doubt.*
Gamaliel Bailey (1807–1859), an American journalist, wrote, "He who never doubted, never half believed."[6] Doubt is not disbelief. Rather, doubt is the struggle of one who "half believes," but has questions regarding the validity of that belief. This positive element of faith in our times of doubt must be recognized and appreciated. Careful research and study will enable a doubter to distinguish between valid and invalid reasons for doubt. This can result in a more solid basis for one's faith or the abandonment of falsehood and error.

• *Recognize that doubts are sometimes due to unruly emotions that in turn can result from physical, mental, or spiritual weariness.*
Elijah experienced a wave of doubt shortly after his encounter with the prophets of Baal on Mount Carmel. Although he had been instrumental in the spiritual victory recorded in 1 Kings 18, in the next chapter we find the once-courageous Elijah running from Jezebel! Out in the wilderness under a juniper tree, Elijah prayed to the Lord, "Take my life; I am no better than my ancestors" (1 Kings 19:4). Elijah did not believe he was going to be any more successful in doing away with Baal worship than the prophets who preceded him. What Elijah needed at the time was food and rest. And that is exactly what the Lord provided for him in the wilderness (19:5–7). After a time of rest and refreshment Elijah found the faith and courage to continue his ministry.

• *Bring your doubts honestly before the Lord.*
As a father, I am pleased when my children share their concerns with me. I am encouraged they that trust me with what weighs heavily on their hearts. I am happy to help bear their burdens and bring their concerns

before the Lord in prayer. Similarly, God is pleased when His children entrust Him with their cares. Peter encouraged believers to cast all their anxiety on Him, "because he cares for you" (1 Pet. 5:7).

• *Make no major decisions while wrestling with doubt.*

James points out that the person who is plagued with doubts is "double-minded" and "unstable in all he does" (James 1:8). Such a person is in no condition to make any major decisions. Don't quit your ministry, leave your church, or reject your faith while wavering between belief and un-belief. Maintain your course and delay any life changes while you are dealing with doubt.

• *Seek solutions from God's Word.*

Although you may not *feel* like reading God's Word when you are strug-gling with doubts, it is one of the best things you can do. This is why it is important to maintain the discipline of regular devotions and Bible read-ing even when there is a chill in your spiritual life. The psalmist wrote, "Your word is a lamp to my feet and a light for my path" (Ps. 119:105). As we read and study the Word of God, its light will disperse darkness. Through His Word God will speak to your heart, answer your questions, and dispel your doubts. I know this is true, because I have often experi-enced it in my own life. In addition to the Word of God, there are several helpful books that can help you deal with doubt. These are listed at the end of this chapter. Other books address specific area of doubts, such as the resurrection of Jesus or the inspiration of Scripture.

• *Focus on God Himself rather than your doubts and confusion.*

When Jesus invited Peter to come to Him on the Sea of Galilee, Peter stepped out of the boat by faith (Matt. 14:29). Much to the astonishment of the other disciples, Peter walked on the water toward Jesus. But then something happened. "When he saw the wind, he was afraid" (14:30). Peter's problem is that he became distracted by the dark waters lapping at his feet and got his eyes off of Jesus. Peter suddenly became aware of his dangerous situation. He focused on his problems rather than on the per-son of Christ, and his doubts overcame his faith. Beginning to sink, he cried out saying, "Lord, save me!" Peter knew where to turn in a time of need, and he got his eyes back on Jesus where they belonged. Hebrews 12:1–2 encourages believers in the race of life to have their eyes focused on Jesus, "the author and perfecter of our faith." Such a focus stabilizes wavering faith, enabling believers to "run with perseverance" the race of the Christian life (12:1).

- *Be ready to hear and accept God's answer to your doubts.*

I am impressed with Habakkuk's example of readiness to respond to God (Hab. 2:1). And when the answer came, Habakkuk embraced it. No doubt it was troubling to hear that God would judge Judah through the attack of the Chaldeans. He was familiar with the horrors of siege warfare and knew that great suffering awaited the people of Judah. But he accepted God's answer and actually rejoiced in the Lord (3:18). By faith he knew God would not lead His people into a trial without providing the divine enablement to endure it (3:19).

- *Keep in perspective the central issues of our faith.*

Not all doubt will be resolved this side of heaven. As Richard Wolff observed, "Neither Christianity nor God's revelation were designed to remove all ambiguity from the human situation."[7] Living by faith means living with unanswered questions. But there is a solid foundation of central truth on which life can be built. When struggling over issues of our faith as Christians, it is important to remember that the theology of the Bible can be boiled down to one central truth. The songwriter said it so well when he wrote, "Jesus loves me, this I know, for the Bible tells me so." If you can embrace that with all your heart, then you are a believer, not a doubter. If you stay in the Word and communicate with Him through prayer, God will bring you through your periods of doubt and strengthen your faith.

DON'T LINGER IN DOUBTING CASTLE

In John Bunyan's classic allegory, *Pilgrim's Progress*, we read of how Christian and his companion Hopeful left the King's Highway and were captured by Giant Despair.[8] Accusing them of trespassing on his land, Giant Despair took them to the grim stone fortress known as Doubting Castle. There he forced them into a stinking dungeon.

The next morning the giant entered the dungeon and began to abuse the prisoners. He beat them until they were almost senseless. All day and night Christian and Hopeful groaned in agony. The next morning the giant again visited the dungeon and advised the prisoners that since they would never escape, they should end their lives by stabbing, hanging, or poisoning themselves.

After the giant's departure Christian became so morbidly depressed that he suggested that they might as well obey the giant and put an end to their misery. Hopeful, however, pointed out that killing themselves would be tantamount to committing murder, an act forbidden by their Prince. Besides, he said, we may yet escape.

The next day Giant Despair took the pilgrims to the palace courtyard and showed them the bones of former pilgrims whom he had killed. After forcing them to look at these gruesome remains, the giant took them back to the dungeon, pummeling them every step of the way. That night the prisoners could not sleep. At midnight they began to pray and continued in this attitude until dawn. Then Christian suddenly exclaimed, "What a fool I've been! All this time I have had the means of escape right here with me!" He put a hand inside his coat pocket and pulled out a bright object. It was the key of promise!

"Let's try it now," suggested Hopeful eagerly.

With beating hearts the pilgrims approached the door of the dungeon and tried the bright key in the lock. It turned easily. They pushed the door ajar and stepped out. They crept up the stairs to the outer door and tried the key again. Once more, it turned smoothly. Soon they had fled Doubting Castle and regained the safety of the King's Highway.

Is there hope for those who doubt? Yes! Our hope is firmly grounded in the character of our promise-keeping God! What promises may we look to when we face periods of doubt?

"Never will I leave you; never will I forsake you" (Heb. 13:5).

Nothing "will be able to separate us from the love of God that is in Christ Jesus our Lord" (Rom. 8:39).

"And my God will meet all your needs according to his glorious riches in Christ Jesus" (Phil. 4:19).

"Seek first his kingdom and his righteousness, and all these things will be given to you as well" (Matt. 6:33).

Our hope as believers rests in God, who is ever faithful and always keeps His promises. How long will we linger in the dungeon of Doubting Castle being pummeled by Giant Despair? Lay hold of the key of promise and return to the King's Highway!

For Further Study

Davidson, Robert. *Courage to Doubt*. London: SCM Press, 1983.

Guinness, Os. *In Two Minds: The Dilemma of Doubt and How to Resolve It*. Downers Grove, Ill.: InterVarsity Press, 1976.

Habermas, Gary R. *Dealing with Doubt*. Chicago: Moody Press, 1990.

McGrath, Alister E. *The Sunnier Side of Doubt*. Grand Rapids: Zondervan Publishing House, 1990.

18

KNOWING THE WILL OF GOD

Be joyful always; pray continually, give thanks in all circum-
stances, for this is God's will for you in Christ Jesus.
—1 Thessalonians 5:16–18

ONE IMPORTANT ASPECT of knowing God better is finding His
will for your life. If God loves you and has a wonderful plan for your life,
how do you discover that plan? Should you look to signs, circumstances,
or some inner leading by God's Spirit?

In the spring of 1977 I had an important decision to make regarding
my career. I was finishing up work on my doctoral studies at Dallas Seminary and anticipated the oral defense of my dissertation sometime during
the summer. After seven years of seminary, I would be free to begin a full-
time ministry in the fall. But what ministry would that be?

I had been in contact with Western Seminary regarding a teaching
position in biblical literature. This was an exciting possibility since I had
pursued a Master's degree at Western and was familiar with the school.
Western was also located in Portland, Oregon, the hometown of my wife,
Nancy. She liked the idea of being closer to her family. But while I was
waiting to hear from Western, I was approached by a church in Texas that
was looking for a pastor. I love to preach, so I wondered if this would be a
better choice for me.

I was on the horns of a dilemma. Two wonderful opportunities were
before me, and I did not know which to choose. Before I share with you
how I made my decision, I would like to put the subject of God's will in

biblical perspective. How do God's people come to know His will? What scriptural principles are there to guide us as we seek to make wise decisions about the course of our lives?

GOD'S WILL AND SIGNS

A friend was struggling with marital difficulties and wondered what to do. In the extremity of his need he went for a walk one night and asked God for a sign—a falling star to indicate God's will. He prayed, "God, if I should divorce her, show me a shooting star." He waited. But no star fell. Then he prayed, "God, if you want me to remain with her, show me a shooting star." Again, no star fell. Finally, he said, "Well, I guess this means that you want me to stay the way I am for a while." Then amazingly, a brilliant shooting star illuminated the sky.

I am happy to report that that marriage survived the crisis and remains strong today. But what about the sign? Did God reveal His will through the shooting star?

Many Christians who seek signs as an indicator for God's will justify their actions on the basis of Gideon's use of the fleece. A student recently told me that he had "put out a fleece" to determine if it was God's will for him to attend seminary. Does the story of Gideon provide a biblical precedent for seeking signs from God?

The story of Gideon is set in the period of the judges when there was no king in Israel and "everyone did as he saw fit" (Judg. 21:25). During this time of rampant idolatry and apostasy, God raised up foreign oppressors to discipline His people and drive them back to Himself. One of these oppressors was the Midianites, a nomadic desert people east of the land of Israel. In the time of Gideon the Midianites were raiding Israelite settlements and stealing their grain and flocks. When the Israelites finally came to their senses, they cried out to God in repentance and the Lord raised up Gideon to deliver His people from the Midianite menace.

Judges 6:14 records the commission God gave Gideon: "Go in the strength you have and save Israel out of Midian's hand. Am I not sending you?" When Gideon questioned his ability and cited his inexperience, God gave him a clear promise, "I will be with you, and you will strike down all the Midianites together" (6:16). It sounded almost too good to be true. Gideon wanted to make sure he wasn't being deceived by some person or spirit. So he asked God for a sign. "If now I have found favor in your eyes, give me a sign that it is really you talking to me" (6:17). In answer to Gideon's request, God caused fire to spring up from the rock, consuming the meat and bread Gideon had offered. This miracle verified that it was God who had spoken to Gideon and it authenticated his call.

God had commanded Gideon to go, promised him victory, and He authenticated His commissioning by a miraculous sign. But Gideon wasn't so sure. And so he asked God for another miracle, the sign of the fleece. Gideon said to God, "If you will save Israel by my hand as you have promised—look, I will place a wool fleece on the threshing floor. If there is dew only on the fleece and all the ground is dry, then I will know that you will save Israel by my hand as you said" (6:36–37). God graciously responded and gave Gideon the sign he requested. The next morning, the fleece was wet from dew, but the ground around it was dry. Significantly, this miracle occurred in the Valley of Jezreel (7:1), a region noted for its heavy dew fall. For the fleece to be wet and the ground to be dry would be truly unusual—a clear sign from God.

Still wrestling with doubts, Gideon asked God for another sign. "Do not be angry with me. Let me make just one more request. Allow me one more test with the fleece. This time make the fleece dry and the ground covered with dew" (6:39). Once again, God gave Gideon the sign he asked for. In the morning the fleece was dry but the ground was wet with dew.

Many people have followed Gideon's example in casting out a fleece. For example, "Lord, if you want me to go to seminary next semester, put the money in my campus mailbox by the end of next week." We must determine whether Gideon's example provides a valid way for believers to discover God's will. On one hand, the Bible does not condemn Gideon for doing as he did. However, some doubts about the appropriateness of Gideon's actions can be raised. First, God's directive had already been given (6:14). Second, victory over the Midianites had been promised (6:16). Third, Gideon did not keep his word. When God gave him the sign, he did not believe, but asked for one more miracle (6:37, 39). God had promised Gideon victory over the Midianites. But Gideon was testing God to find out if He really meant it.

Why, then, did God honor Gideon's repeated requests even though the command had been given and victory promised? I can only suggest that God meets us where we are. Gideon's faith was weak, and God graciously responded to meet his need. But I doubt that God intended for Gideon to serve as an example for us to follow when seeking to know His will. God's will was clearly revealed to Gideon; he just didn't believe it. In addition to the problem of Gideon's unbelief, he was making inappropriate demands on God. He was saying, "God, do this for me and do it in this particular way." Should the creature make such a demand on the Creator? What if God wants to provide for the student's education through a paycheck rather than an anonymous gift? Who are we to make demands on God, asking for a particular sign of His will? Such action is tantamount to testing God (Deut. 6:16) and should have no place in the life of a believer.

GOD'S WILL AND BIBLICAL IMPERATIVES

Most frequently when we think of God's will for our lives, we think of questions like the following: What does God want me to be? Does God want me to marry? If so, whom? Where does God want me to serve? It is rather interesting, and significant I think, that when the Bible addresses the subject of God's will, it is not in relationship with these issues of life. It seems that God is more concerned about our personal conduct, holiness, and lifestyle than whom we marry, where we attend college, and what vocation we should pursue. This is not to say that these issues are unimportant. But from God's perspective, the issues of conduct and morality take priority.

So, what is God's will for your life? He commands us to know it. Paul wrote, "Therefore do not be foolish, but understand what the Lord's will is" (Eph. 5:17). John revealed the destiny of those who do it: "The man who does the will of God lives forever" (1 John 2:17). Let's consider some specific examples of God's revealed will for our lives.

Personal Sanctification (1 Thess. 4:3)

Paul wrote the Thessalonian believers, "It is God's will that you should be sanctified: that you should avoid sexual immorality" (1 Thess. 4:3). God's revealed will for you is your personal sanctification. That this is a priority is evidenced by the fact that God addresses this issue specifically, but does not speak in His Word about colleges or careers. I believe God is saying, "Your personal sanctification takes precedence over all other important issues in your life." We cannot grow in our relationship with God unless we take this issue seriously.

To "sanctify" means "to set apart." The context of the passage indicates that God wants us to be separated from sin and set apart for the Savior. This means that God wants us to live holy lives. In the following verses (4:3–7), Paul clarified the meaning of sanctification in terms of moral purity. He said a believer should "avoid sexual immorality," "control his own body in a way that is holy and honorable," and not "wrong his brother." The mention of controlling one's own body may refer to premarital chastity during courtship and contracting of marriage. Defrauding one's brother refers in this context to indulging in a sexual privilege which is properly reserved for another. All of these instructions are designed to direct us from impurity (4:7) so that we might live sanctified, holy lives.

Do you wonder if it is God's will for you to have a sexual relationship with your fiancée before marriage? These verses tell us clearly that such behavior is contrary to God's will. It is strange how people who are involved in sexual immorality spend time trying to determine God's will for their career. If God were to respond verbally, perhaps He might say, "Career? Choose any career! It doesn't matter. What matters to Me is that you live a holy life! My will for you is your personal sanctification. Everything else is secondary."

Thanksgiving, Rejoicing, and Prayer (1 Thess 5:16–18)

In 1 Thessalonians 5:16–18 Paul made another clear statement about God's will. "Be joyful always; pray continually; give thanks in all circumstances, for this is God's will for you in Christ Jesus." The pronoun "this" refers to the trio of responsibilities just given to the readers. The present imperatives indicate that believers are to "keep on being joyful," "keep on praying," and "keep on giving thanks." This is clearly God's revealed will.

Is it God's will for Christian people to be prayerless grumblers, complaining about their circumstances? Absolutely not! Knowing this truth will make a difference in how you live your life. I have a Christian acquaintance who has made complaining an art form. I am never around this person more than a few minutes before the complaints arise—complaints about work, health, salary, and the church. If you are a perpetual complainer who is seeking God's will regarding a decision in life, God's message from 1 Thessalonians 5:16–18 is that you get back on focus. His will is that you keep on rejoicing, keep on praying, and keep on giving thanks, regardless of the troublesome circumstances.

Submission to Those in Authority (1 Pet. 2:13–15)

The expression, "the will of God," appears again in 1 Peter 2:15, NASB. In his discussion on submission to civil authority, Peter wrote, "Submit yourselves for the Lord's sake to every authority instituted among men: whether to the king, as the supreme authority, or to governors, who are sent by him to punish those who do wrong and to commend those who do right. For it is God's will that by doing good you should silence the ignorant talk of foolish men" (2:13–15). It is God's will that we submit to civil authority. The word "submit" *(hypotassō)* is a military term meaning "to arrange under or put in subjection." In the form in which it appears here the verb means "subject oneself." Believers are to place themselves under the authority of their civil government. Peter said nothing about certain forms of government. His teaching applies to both democracies and dictatorships, worthy and worldly rulers alike. In fact Peter wrote this instruction to people living under the dictatorship of the wicked emperor Nero!

Should a Christian fudge a little on an expense report to gain a tax advantage? First Peter 2:13–15 provides the biblical basis for answering no. Refusing to pay the tax due would not reflect an attitude of submission to one's government. Should a Christian break the speed limit in order to get to church on time? Again 1 Peter 2:13–15 provides a biblical basis for answering no. Breaking traffic laws is not consistent with God's clearly revealed will that we submit ourselves to civil authorities.

Biblical Imperatives

The imperatives (commands) of Scripture also reveal God's will for His people. It is never God's will for us to lie (Eph. 4:25), steal (4:28), or indulge in bitterness, anger, or slander (4:31). It is always God's will for us to be kind to each other and forgive each other (4:32). Is it His will for us to tell an off-color story? God says no (5:4). Is it God's will for us to get drunk? God says no (5:18). Is it God's will for us to abuse our spouses or children? God says, "Absolutely not" (5:28; 6:4).

I am not suggesting that our relationship with God should be reduced to a list of "do's" and "don'ts." This is certainly not the spirit of Christianity. The Bible teaches that we are saved by grace, through faith, apart from any good works. However, for those who are rightly related to God through faith, the imperatives of the Bible provide a trustworthy resource for discovering His clearly revealed will. There is no better way for Christians to know God's will than through His living Word. It is foolish for Christians to seek God's will for a career and ignore His clearly revealed will for their personal lives.

GOD'S WILL AND THE "GRAY" AREAS

Some issues are tougher to decide. How do you make decisions on matters which the Bible does not specifically approve or condemn? What is God's will regarding such matters as genetic manipulation, surrogate motherhood, and test-tube babies?

The big question facing Christians in the first century A.D. was whether to eat meat that had been offered to idols (1 Cor. 8:1). If offered at a private sacrifice, the meat could be served at a banquet or dinner party. If offered as a public sacrifice, the meat could be sold in the market—usually at a discounted price! Should a Christian buy and eat meat that had been offered to heathen gods? When invited to a friend's home, should a Christian eat meat which has been offered to an idol?

The questions confronting Christians today are different but are no less serious. Although opinions may vary on the issues not specifically addressed by Scripture, God has not left us without guidelines for determining His will in the so-called gray areas. And these principles are just as applicable to the concerns of today as they were for the issues of the first century. The following questions are designed to help Christians make ethical and God-honoring decisions about questionable issues.[1]

- *Is this activity forbidden in the Word of God?* In Psalm 119:9 we read, "How can a young man keep his way pure? By living according to your word." Don't be fooled into thinking that some activity is questionable because of the complicated circumstances or situation. Stealing and murder, for example, are always wrong. Overlooking divinely revealed biblical imperatives leads to sin and spiritual disaster.

- *Is this activity forbidden by the civil authorities?* Civil government is a divinely ordained authority to which Christians are to submit (Rom. 13:1–2; 1 Pet. 2:13–14). Christians are to obey the civil law as they would the commandments of Christ. The only exception to this guideline is a situation in which the civil law is contrary to God's commands (Acts 5:29).

- *Does this activity have a good appearance?* Peter told believers that they should live "good lives among the pagans" (1 Pet. 2:12). If the activity makes the believer appear to be compromising his standards, it is better to abstain. It is like deciding whether a shirt should go into the laundry. If it is doubtful, it is probably dirty. This is often true of activities that are thought to be in the "gray areas."

- *Is this activity commended by my conscience?* Paul pointed out in Romans 2:14–15 that even unbelievers have a moral conscience that reflects God's law written on their hearts. Paul served God "with a clear conscience" (2 Tim. 1:3) and advised believers to do likewise

(Rom. 14:23; 1 Tim. 1:19; 3:9). Christians should take care to avoid activities they could not participate in with a clear conscience.

- *Is this activity profitable or useful?* Some believers at Corinth were apparently trying to use their Christian freedom to justify their participation in questionable activities. Paul responded, " 'Everything is permissible for me'—but not everything is beneficial" (1 Cor. 6:12). Just because it is not prohibited does not mean that it is a worthy pursuit. Before spending an evening in front of the television, ask yourself, "Will this activity enhance my life and Christian experience?"

- *Will this activity enslave or control me?* Paul gave the Corinthians another guideline in 1 Corinthians 6:12: " 'Everything is permissible for me'—but I will not be mastered by anything." Some activities which seem rather innocent can be habit forming. Before participating, ask yourself, "Could this activity become a habit?" Christians should steer clear of anything that might hinder or encumber the "race" God has set before us (Heb. 12:1).

- *Will this activity harm my body?* Paul wrote, "Do you not know that your body is a temple of the Holy Spirit, who is in you, whom you have received from God? You are not your own" (1 Cor. 6:19). Our physical body is a temple in which the Holy Spirit dwells! God revealed the implication of this truth in verse 20. "You were bought at a price. Therefore honor God in your body." What is God's will regarding substances that will harm my body? If they would harm my body, they hinder my ability to glorify God. So anything that harms our bodies should be avoided.

- *Will this activity cause another Christian to stumble?* In 1 Corinthians 8:13 Paul offered another helpful guideline for those seeking God's will. "Therefore, if what I eat causes my brother to fall into sin, I will never eat meat again, so that I will not cause him to fall." Paul considered it a sacred responsibility to exercise loving concern for those less mature than himself. He did not want to do anything that would hinder faith or spiritual growth of another person. Causing another Christian to eat something while that person doubts whether he should do so is like tripping him up (Rom. 14:23). Paul affirmed our Christian liberty (Gal. 5:1), but that liberty must be regulated by love and self-restraint. It is not God's will for us to do anything that might lead a weaker brother or sister into sin.

• *Will this activity glorify God?* Paul submitted every decision and activity to the question of the glory of God. He exhorted the Corinthians to do the same. "So whether you eat or drink or whatever you do, do it all for the glory of God" (1 Cor. 10:31). When seeking God's will regarding a matter, believers should ask, "Will my participation in this activity manifest God's presence in my life and exalt His reputation in the sight of others?"

• *Is this what I would want to be doing when Christ comes?* The anticipation of Christ's return for the church is an incentive to proper conduct: "Everyone who has this hope in him purifies himself, just as he is pure" (1 John 3:3). We should want to be looking our best when Jesus comes. Keeping this thought before us can help us decide whether some "gray-area" activity is in accord with God's will.

It is encouraging to know that even when God has not revealed His will through a biblical imperative, He has given us many biblical principles, which are sufficient to help us determine His will in life's questionable areas.

MAKING WISE DECISIONS

Bruce Waltke has rightly pointed out that the New Testament gives no command to "find God's will."[2] Nor does the New Testament give any specific instructions or formula for finding His will. Instead, through His inspired Word, God has given us specific commands that express His will for our lives. Beyond that, God calls us to live wisely and to make God-honoring decisions. Garry Friesen calls this method of decision-making "the way of wisdom."[3] In the areas where the Bible gives no command or principle, believers are responsible to decide a course of action. When we decide wisely, we please God and are following His will.

What factors does God use in helping His people make wise and God-honoring decisions about personal areas of life? What factors did I consider when making my decision to join the faculty of Western Seminary?

Circumstances

God often uses circumstances in our lives to open doors of opportunity for His people. Joseph's circumstances in prison gave him an opportunity to interpret a cupbearer's dream (Gen. 40:9–19). Later the cupbearer, who had been restored to royal service, told Pharaoh of Joseph's ability. As a result of these circumstances, Joseph was called out of prison to serve in Pharaoh's court. The point here is that God often uses the circumstances in our lives to provide opportunities of ministry. In my own case God used the circumstances of my previous studies at Western Seminary and my familiarity with the dean to open up the possibility of serving on that faculty.

But the opportunities alone don't necessarily constitute a calling from God. While Paul was traveling through the Galatian region on his second missionary journey, he saw opportunities to minister in Asia and Bithynia, but was forbidden by God to go there. We must be wise and discerning, never putting circumstances above God's Word. Circumstances may open doors we would be wise not to enter. On the other hand, God can use circumstances to move us along a good and wise way.

Common Sense

God has given each human a beautiful, mysterious, complex organ—the human brain. Our brains enable us to make decisions about what we eat, where we go, what we do with our time, how we spend our money, and what kind of people we will be. God has given each of us a capacity for decision-making. And I believe that He expects us to use our brain and make decisions. As Waltke wrote, "God expects us to use our decision-making capabilities to make choices."[4] Paul had this principle in mind when he wrote, "Be very careful, then, how you live—not as unwise but as wise" (Eph. 5:15). Similarly, Paul wrote the Corinthians, "Brothers, stop thinking like children. In regard to evil be infants, but in your thinking be adults" (1 Cor. 14:20). This instruction was given in the context of making wise decisions regarding the use of one's spiritual gifts.

In using common sense in decision-making, it is helpful to see the "pros" and "cons" of each course of action. Sometimes I will use a piece of paper folded down the center to reflect on the advantages and disadvantages of a decision. I used this procedure when trying to decide whether to pursue a pastoral opportunity or return to Portland to teach. Both opportunities had a long list of pros. But I found fewer cons in the teaching column. Based on common sense and the use of my reasoning, seminary teaching seemed like the better choice.

Wise Counsel

The Bible repeatedly commends the wisdom of seeking wise counsel. "Let the wise listen and add to their learning, and let the discerning get guidance" (Prov. 1:5). "The way of a fool seems right to him, but a wise man listens to advice" (12:15). "Plans fail for lack of counsel, but with many advisers they succeed" (15:22). "Listen to advice and accept instruction, and in the end you will be wise" (19:20). "For waging war you need guidance, and for victory many advisers" (24:6).

I have often benefited from wise counsel when making important decisions. In fact I never make a significant life decision without receiving counsel. Sometimes the wise counsel of my wife, Nancy, has helped me avoid making a rash or foolish decision. I like to consult my dad, a seasoned businessman, when making financial decisions. For spiritual decisions, I go to a trusted friend, pastor, or faculty colleague. Often a counselor will help me see issues I may have missed because of my emotional involvement in the matter at hand. Before making my decision to move to Portland, I consulted my pastor at Scofield Memorial Church. Dr. Neil Ashcraft graciously spent an hour with me and helped me see some issues I had overlooked. With his counsel I was able to come to a wise decision regarding my immediate future.

Personal Desire

Some people make such a complicated thing out of decision-making. They are fearful they will "miss God's will." My fears in the process of making decisions have been put to rest by discovering that God works His will through my will. In Psalm 37:3–4 David declared, "Trust in the LORD and do good. . . . Delight yourself in the LORD and he will give you the desires of your heart."

Knowing that our desires can be skewed by sin, David mentioned several prerequisites necessary before relying on the desires of your heart. First, we must be people of faith who "trust in the LORD." Second, we must obey God's commandments ("do good"). Third, we must "delight" ourselves in God and a growing relationship with Him. If you are living a life that is in touch with God by His Spirit and through His Word, God will place His desires in your heart. Thus when He gives you your heart's desires, they will be none other than His desires for you!

The Scriptures include examples of God working through the desires of good and godly people (2 Sam. 23:5; Rom. 1:11; 15:20). Waltke points out several things to keep in mind as you ponder the desires of your heart.[5] First, are your desires correlated with Scripture? If your desire is inconsistent with what God has revealed, then your desire is sinful and should be disregarded. Second, are your desires correlated to presenting your body as a living sacrifice? If not, your desire may be personal and selfish. Third, are your desires correlated with faith? That is, can you fulfill this desire as an expression of your faith in God? "Whatever is not from faith is sin" (Rom. 14:23, NASB). Fourth, do your desires correlate with prayer? When we communicate with God through prayer, sharing our hearts with Him, He will shape our character and our desires to a greater conformity to His will.

When I was trying to decide what I wanted to do after seminary graduation, God led me through my desires. What I really wanted to do was to get back to the Northwest, where our parents lived, and to teach the Bible at Western Seminary. I believe God gave me this desire as I delighted in Him and honored Him through obedience and faithfulness in my life.

Dependence on God

One of the dangers of decision-making is leaving God out of the process. While God expects us to make decisions, this must always be done with an attitude of submission and dependence on Him. James, the half-brother of our Lord, addressed this issue in his epistle. He wrote, "Now listen, you who say, 'Today or tomorrow we will go to this or that city, spend a year there, carry on in business and make money.' Why, you do not even know what will happen tomorrow. What is your life? You are a mist that appears for a little while and then vanishes. Instead, you ought to say, 'If it is the Lord's will, we will live and do this or that'" (James 4:13–15).

James was not condemning intelligent planning and decision-making. Rather, he was rebuking arrogant planning that disregards God. We must make our decisions prayerfully, with an attitude of submission to His will. This is evidenced by the apostle Paul in his travel plans. Before leaving Ephesus, he said, "I will come back if it is God's will" (Acts 18:21). He wrote to the Corinthians saying, "But I will come to you very soon, if the Lord is willing" (1 Cor. 4:19). It seems that Paul left room in the process of decision-making for God to intervene and redirect him through circumstances, wise counsel, or the Spirit's leading (see Acts 16:6–7; Rom. 1:10; 15:32; 1 Cor. 16:7).

Proverbs 3:5–6 is often cited as a proof text for divine guidance. "Trust in the LORD with all your heart and lean not on your own understanding; in all your ways acknowledge [literally, 'know'] him, and he will make your paths straight." These verses are not so much about divine guidance as they are about depending on the Lord. In making decisions we must rely on God and what He has revealed in His Word rather than on our own fallible understanding. Those who truly trust in God will not go outside the bounds of His will. As we get to know Him better, placing our lives under His authority and living by His wisdom, God will clear away the obstacles, enabling us to reach our goals on a smooth, straight path.

We need to submit our plans to the Lord, for Him to intervene, correct, or redirect us, if necessary. Depending on God, we need to remain open to His leading. We should identify with the sentiments of Paul's companions who said, "The Lord's will be done" (Acts 21:14).

For Further Study

Friesen, Garry. *Decision Making and the Will of God*. Portland, Oreg.: Multnomah Press, 1980.

Howard, J. Grant. *Knowing God's Will and Doing It!* Grand Rapids: Zondervan Publishing House, 1976.

Robinson, Haddon. *Decision-Making by the Book*. Wheaton, Ill.: Victor Books, 1991.

Waltke, Bruce. *Finding the Will of God: A Pagan Notion?* Gresham, Oreg.: Vision House, 1995.

Smith, M. Blaine. *Knowing God's Will: Biblical Principles of Guidance*. Downers Grove, Ill.: InterVarsity Press, 1979.

19
COMMUNICATING WITH GOD

And pray in the Spirit on all occasions with all kinds of prayers and requests. With this in mind, be alert and always keep on praying for all the saints.

—Ephesians 6:18

A RELATIONSHIP CANNOT BE SUSTAINED over a long period without communication. Separation without communication tends to leave a friendship rather cold and sterile. Interest and affections fade when friends fail to maintain a regular exchange of news and information. Sadly, some of the people I was closest to during my student days have grown distant. Of course, it is understandable. We are busy people and are separated by thousands of miles. Our families and ministries place overwhelming demands on our time, relegating the friendships of former years to the status of a Christmas-card mailing list.

Even separation from children or a spouse diminishes the relationship over time if the relationship is not nourished by regular communication. Several years ago I was engaged in a ministry overseas which required a six-week separation from my family. Although I wrote postcards and letters to my family, I didn't receive a single reply. In my loneliness and weariness from ministry, I became a bit resentful that my family had not communicated with me. Our relationship as a family was weakened by a lack of communication. When I returned home, I learned that my family had indeed written me. But the mail failed to reach me as I traveled from place to place. The letters eventually reached me—when they were forwarded to my home!

If communication is important to the maintenance of friendships and family relationships, it must be important in developing our relationship with God. How can we know God better if we don't talk to Him and listen when He speaks to us? Communicating with God is an important key to maintaining a healthy and vital relationship with God.

GOD COMMUNICATES THROUGH HIS WORD

The Bible is a unique book. It was written over a period of fifteen hundred years by about forty authors. The literature of the Bible includes history, legal codes, prophecies, proverbs, parables, songs, praise, and letters. The Bible tells the past history of humanity and God's future plans for His creation. It tells us about God and reveals how we can know Him better. The Scriptures reveal God's plan for redemption, His kingdom program, and the future judgment on sin and Satan. Through the Bible, God has communicated with humanity, disclosing what we need to know to live life abundantly forever.

Someone has likened the Bible to a love letter. When Nancy and I became engaged to be married, she was traveling as a representative for her sorority. This meant that we were separated for the nine months leading up to our wedding. During that time we spoke with each other once a week by phone and wrote letters. Yes, they were love letters. I told Nancy about what was going on in my life as a seminary student. But I also told her of my love for her and wrote about our future plans together. Whenever I received mail from Nancy, I would take it to my dormitory room and spend some time alone reading the letter.

I did not read Nancy's letter and then toss it in the trash. I read the letter and then read it again. Then I put the letter in my desk to read again. I wanted to reflect on every word, every expression, every nuance. As I read Nancy's letters again and again, I felt close to her even though she was far away. My memories of her were rekindled and refreshed through reading her letters.

We should read the Bible as God's letter, expressing His love, concern, and plans for us. If you want to know God better, you can't leave His letter in the mailbox unopened and unread. You must read it, reread it, and study it.

WHAT GOD'S COMMUNICATION IS LIKE

What are some of the things we know about God's love letter, the Bible? First, it is *true*. Jesus said, "Sanctify them by the truth; your word is truth" (John 17:17). The "truth" to which Jesus referred is the "word" or revelation He received from the Father and made known to the disciples (17:8, 14). Although Jesus was not referring to the Bible itself, His statement, "Your word is truth," reflects His high view of the integrity of God's revelation. The Bible is given to us from the God "who does not lie" (Titus 1:2; see also Heb. 6:18). As such, the Word of God is the very essence of divine truth.

Second, the Bible is *divinely inspired*. Paul wrote Timothy, "All Scripture is God-breathed and is useful for teaching, rebuking, correcting and training in righteousness" (2 Tim. 3:16). The Greek word rendered "God-breathed" is *theopneustos*, from two words, *theos* ("God") and *pneō* ("to breathe"). This means that the Scriptures are the breathing out of God's message for us. This term is applied to all of Scripture, not just part of it. All Scripture, in the original manuscripts, shares this supernatural quality of being divinely inspired.

Third, because God's Word is divinely inspired, it is both *inerrant and infallible*. The term *inerrancy* refers to the accuracy of the biblical record. As a divinely inspired book it is not false or mistaken. Over the years as a Bible teacher, I have enjoyed studying those passages that critics have cited as examples of "errors" in Scripture. And most of those "errors" or "apparent contradictions" have been resolved through careful study.[1] Others await resolution as a result of future archaeological discovery and biblical research. The term *infallible* refers to the reliability of the Scriptures as a guide. God's love letter to humanity will not deceive us or lead us astray. If we follow its teaching, we will walk with God and be welcomed by Christ at heaven's gate.

Fourth, the Bible is a *living* book. The author of Hebrews wrote, "The word of God is living and active. Sharper than any double-edged sword, it penetrates even to dividing soul and spirit, joints and marrow; it judges the thoughts and attitudes of the heart" (Heb. 4:12). Although more than two thousand years old, God's Word contains no "dead" utterance of the past. The Bible contains "living words" (Acts 7:38). It is the "living and enduring word of God" (1 Pet. 1:23) because when planted in human hearts, it yields eternal life! It is *active* in that it fulfills the purpose for which it has been uttered (Isa. 55:11). God's prophecies are always realized. His words never fail.

Fifth, God's Word is *sufficient*. After describing the Bible as "God-breathed," Paul stated that it was "useful for teaching, rebuking, for correcting and training in righteousness, so that the man of God may be thoroughly equipped [literally, 'proficient' and 'fully outfitted'] for every good work" (2 Tim. 3:16–17). When carefully applied, God's Word makes us proficient for life and equips us for ministry. The Bible reveals all we need for knowing God and living the Christian life. In the past God revealed Himself "at many times and in various ways" (Heb. 1:1). But in contrast to the former revelation, which was piecemeal and bit by bit, "in these last days he has spoken to us by his Son" (1:2). God's full and final revelation is through His Son, Jesus Christ, as recorded on the pages of the New Testament.

Although the Bible remains a bestseller among religious books, it is often the one on the shelf that gathers the most dust. But for those who want to know God better, it is a book that is cherished and loved. It is a book that is read and studied, because it is God's personal message telling us what He wants us to know and do.

COMMUNICATION WHICH IS NOT FROM GOD

I have two areas of concern regarding the subject of God's communication. First, I am concerned about those who say, "God told me this" or "God told me to do that," when these "revelations" are not found in the Bible. I read the testimony of a prominent pastor who wrote that God had told him that a great spiritual revival would take place in America, and that he was to conduct one-night meetings across the country to start this revival. God even told him the specific name to be used for this campaign. Now I believe that this man is sincere and has good intentions. But how do I know that he didn't just imagine these things or wish them to be true?

Church history is full of illustrations of people who claimed that God told them certain things. In 1981 Bill Maupin, founder of a fundamentalist Christian group, became convinced that God had revealed to him that the rapture of the church would take place on Sunday June 28, 1981.[2] Bill and his small band of disciples sold their belongings, quit their jobs, said good-bye to their friends, and gathered together to wait for God to take them up to heaven. I don't know what has happened to Bill and his followers since June 28, 1981, but Christ's church is still waiting to be raptured. Obviously, God didn't say what Bill thought He said.

A similar event occurred in Portland, Oregon, several years ago. John Gunter, a professing Christian and church member, came to believe that a disastrous earthquake would hit Portland on May 3, 1993. According to his own testimony, God had given him a "sign" that this earthquake was coming.[3] Convinced that he should warn others, John wrote a letter predicting a "catastrophic and disastrous earthquake" that would completely topple all of downtown Portland. But May 3 came and went without so much as a tremor in the city of Portland.

False prophets abounded among the ancient Israelites, professing to speak for God. Many well-meaning and sincere people were deceived and led into error by the vain imaginations of false prophets. God's people today must beware as well. If someone says, "God told me" this or that, I ask, "Where do you find that in His Word?"

A second area of concern is about those who use the Bible as a magic book for receiving personalized revelations or directions from God. This often results from a misapplication of the stories and principles of Scripture. Recently I read the testimony of a Christian leader whose daughter was sick with cancer. While anguishing over this difficult situation, he read Jesus' words in John 11:4, "This sickness will not end in death. No, it is for God's glory." On the basis of this verse, he concluded that God would heal his daughter of cancer.[4] Of course, a brief examination of John 11 reveals that Jesus was referring in verse 4 to Lazarus who died, but for whom death was not the ultimate outcome of his illness. This verse applies to a very specific historical situation. It is a grave misuse of Scripture to apply such a verse to an individual case of illness today. While all Scripture is for us, it is not all addressed to us in terms of direct application or promise. The principle of John 11:4, which applies across time to every situation, is that a trial, like sickness, can bring glory to God as we respond with faith, trusting God with the difficulties in our lives.

GOD'S PEOPLE RESPOND THROUGH PRAYER

One of the greatest privileges God has given His people is the opportunity to communicate with Him through prayer. While you need an appointment to speak with an important person, like the city mayor or the United States president, God has an open-door policy. No matter what your position or social status, you may approach the Creator of the universe through prayer at any moment, without waiting and without an intermediary. You will never get a busy signal or an answering machine informing you that "God is out for the evening; please leave a message." And the message you send will never get delayed or lost.

What is prayer? The best answer is one I learned in college through the ministry of Campus Crusade for Christ. New believers were instructed by Crusade staff members that prayer is simply "talking to God." This helpful definition suggests that prayer doesn't have to be stiff or formal. We don't need to use the "Thee's" and "Thou's" of King James English. We don't need special books or written prayers. Cameron V. Thompson, formerly the director of the Pan American Testament League, wrote, "Prayer is the spreading out of our helplessness and that of others in the name of the Lord Jesus Christ before the loving eyes of a Father who knows and understands and cares and answers."[5]

Through prayer and the Word, God's people have the privilege of entering into a "conversation with God." But conversation involves two-way communication. Have you ever observed a conversation in which two people were talking at each other but not really listening or responding to what the other person was saying? The wife says, "Honey, I am concerned about your mother." The husband responds, "That's nice. What did the stock market do today?" Parents write to their son, a college freshman, asking if he has met any Christians and how he is doing spiritually. The collegian writes back that he has joined a fraternity and needs more money. Something is wrong here. These people are not really communicating.

Unfortunately, this is often the case with Christians in their communication with God. Through the Scriptures God communicates His deep concern about our spiritual lives. We respond by praying, "Help Aunt Mabel to get over her gout; don't let it rain this Saturday at the church picnic; and please help me work out a deal to buy that new car." How much improved our communication with the Lord would be if we let Him lead the conversation and responded to the issues raised in His Word.

The Prelude for Daniel's Prayer

A good example of this pattern for prayer can be found in the Book of Daniel. The historical situation was that of the Babylonian Captivity. In 605 B.C. Daniel and a number of young men of the royal family had been taken captive by Nebuchadnezzar, king of Babylon. Eight years later ten thousand Jews had been deported. Finally, in 586 B.C., Jerusalem was destroyed and most of the Judeans were exiled to Babylon.

The exile of the Jews was no accident in God's program for His people. This judgment was God chastisement for Israel's disobedience to the Mosaic Covenant. In Deuteronomy 28:41 God had warned the nation that disobedience would result in captivity—dispersion from the land. Yet with that promise of judgment came a promise of restoration. God promised to respond to the people's repentance by restoring the nation from captivity and regathering them to the land of Israel (Deut. 30:1–4).

Jeremiah, a prophet in Judah contemporary with Daniel, had prophesied God's judgment on Judah and announced that the people would remain in Babylon for seventy years (Jer. 25:11). Then after the seventy years, Babylon would be destroyed and the Judeans returned to their land (29:10).

As Daniel was reading the writings of Jeremiah, he noted that God had said the Judean captivity would last "seventy years" (Dan. 9:2). Daniel realized that the period of captivity was nearly complete; the time was approaching for the exiles to return! Daniel undoubtedly wondered about the details of God's future program for His people. How would God bring about the restoration and what would follow?

Daniel was a man of prayer. He had already demonstrated that he would rather spend a night with lions than miss a day of prayer! He knew that God would bring about the return of his people, but he recognized the necessity of faith and prayer in response to God's revealed program. The point here is that the Word of God led Daniel to pray and gave him the very topic to pray about. The study of the Word was the prelude for Daniel's prayer. Daniel prepared for prayer by studying God's Word. Then he prayed in light of what God had written. He prayed about the fulfillment of God's plan.

The study of God's Word before you pray helps you respond to Him and helps you know what to pray about. If you are a beginner in the discipline of prayer, studying God's Word beforehand will help you know what to talk to God about.

In his prayer Daniel didn't ask for better conditions for the exiles in Babylon. He didn't ask God to protect the Jewish children from the pagan influences of Babylon. He didn't ask God to do away with the lions' dens. Daniel prayed about what God had revealed through his reading of God's Word. He let God set the topic of conversation and then stuck to the subject.

The Pattern of Daniel's Prayer

Daniel's prayer is one of the classic prayers of the Bible. We can learn much about communicating with God from the pattern of prayer exemplified by Daniel.

- *Adoration (Dan. 9:4).* Knowing that he was speaking with the Almighty God, the Creator of the universe, Daniel appropriately began his prayer with adoration. He said, "O Lord, the great and awesome God, who keeps his covenant of love with all who love him and obey his commands" (9:4). Daniel recognized with the psalmist, "Great is the LORD, and most worthy of praise" (Ps. 48:1). He recognized that God is awesome, inspiring reverence and obedience among those who truly know Him (Eccles. 12:13). Daniel also acknowledged that God is loyal or faithful. He keeps His covenant and remains faithful to those who know and love Him. His promises can be relied on. His Word is sure.

Daniel began his prayer by praising God's greatness and goodness. What a splendid example for us to follow. How often we break into prayer with hardly a thought about the awesome One whom we are addressing. I have never met anyone of great political stature or of international prominence. But if I ever did, I know I would address that person with respect and no doubt express something of my admiration. Why do we treat God with less respect and honor when we pray? Our prayers don't have to be formal or stilted as we express our heartfelt gratitude and appreciation to our wonderful, awesome Lord.

- *Confession (Dan. 9:5–15)*. After acknowledging the greatness and goodness of God, Daniel immediately entered into an extensive confession of sin. This may be surprising, because Daniel was a man of high integrity and is not known for any blatant personal sin. Yet here he identified with his people as he confessed the nation's sin. Daniel said, "We have sinned," not "They have sinned." He recognized that a sincere confession of sin was the first step toward the nation's broken fellowship being renewed and the people being restored to their land.

Daniel began, "We have sinned and done wrong. We have been wicked and have rebelled; we have turned away from your commands and laws" (9:5). Here we see a growing intensity as Daniel used increasingly stronger expressions to refer to sin. Daniel then recalled how the Judeans disregarded the prophets whom God had sent to rebuke the people and turn them back to Himself (9:6). He elaborated on the shame of sin and its result in the lives of God's people (9:7–15). For Daniel, confession of sin was not a minor issue.

Acknowledging one's sin is an absolute necessity when encountering the living, holy God. When Isaiah received his vision of the holy God seated in glorious splendor on His throne, the prophet could not help but acknowledge his sins. He said, "Woe to me! . . . I am ruined! For I am a man of unclean lips, and I live among a people of unclean lips, and my eyes have seen the King, the LORD Almighty" (Isa. 6:5). Confession of sin is an important part of Christian prayer. "If we confess our sins, he is faithful and just and will forgive us our sins and purify us from all unrighteousness" (1 John 1:9).

- *Supplication (Dan. 9:16–19).* The final part of Daniel's prayer was his supplication or request. By contrast this is where most of our prayers *begin.* "Dear God, please bless us and help this to be a good day." While there is nothing inherently wrong in a brief cry for help (see Matt. 14:30), Daniel's prayer provides a good pattern for us.

As we study Daniel's supplication, we discover an important truth. Daniel based each request on an attribute of God. He prayed to God in light of what God had revealed about Himself. Daniel's first request was based on God's righteousness. He said, "O Lord, in keeping with all your righteous acts [literally, righteousness], turn away your anger and your wrath from Jerusalem, your city" (Dan. 9:16). Daniel knew that God is righteous, that He always does what is right and just. In the light of this attribute Daniel prayed that God would turn His wrath from Jerusalem, restoring the people and their temple.

Daniel's second request was based on God's compassion. "Give ear, O God, and hear; open your eyes and see the desolation of the city that bears your Name. We do not make requests of you because we are righteous, but because of your great mercy" (9:18). God is compassionate. This is the first thing that God said about Himself in His grand self-revelation to Moses (Exod. 34:6). The word *compassion* is derived from the word for womb and signifies a mother's feelings and tender concerns for her child. On the basis of God's compassion, Daniel prayed that God would answer his prayer and meet his need. Richard C. Trench, late archbishop of Dublin, said, "Prayer is not overcoming God's reluctance, but laying hold of his willingness." In his prayer Daniel was laying hold of God's willingness, based on His attribute of compassion.

Daniel's third supplication was based on God's reputation. He said, "O Lord, listen! O Lord, forgive! O Lord, hear and act! For your sake, O my God, do not delay, because your city and your people bear your Name" (Dan. 9:19). In biblical times a person was often named or renamed on the basis of some noticeable character trait. A person's name signified his or her reputation. The "name" of God is the revelation of His being, His character, His reputation. God had a great reputation among the Israelites and even among the gentile nations. Daniel prayed that God would extend His loyal love to His people and take action on their behalf on the basis of His glorious reputation.

We should not be surprised that God answered Daniel's prayer. God sent Gabriel, an angelic emissary, to respond to Daniel's request (9:20–22). Gabriel explained that the Jews would be restored from the Babylonian Captivity, but He also told Daniel about God's prophetic program for Israel (9:24–27). God not only answered Daniel's prayer; He gave him even more than he asked for!

Daniel's prayer provides us with an excellent pattern for communication with God—adoration, confession, supplication. As God speaks to us through His Word, we are encouraged to respond to Him in prayer and to thank Him in advance for what He's doing. As Paul wrote, "Do not be anxious about anything, but in everything, by prayer and petition, with thanksgiving, present your requests to God" (Phil. 4:6).

PRINCIPLES OF PRAYER

In addition to the principles exemplified in Daniel's prayer, I would like to suggest some guidelines that have helped me in developing my communication with God.

Pray in Jesus' Name

Jesus told His disciples, "I will do whatever you ask in my name, so that the Son may bring glory to the Father. You may ask me anything in my name, and I will do it" (John 14:13–14). What does it mean to pray in Jesus' name? This is not a magic formula, and it is more than a way to conclude our prayers. To pray in Jesus' name is to pray a prayer that He would be pleased to pray on our behalf. It is like signing Jesus' name to our prayer, saying in effect, "I think this is what Jesus would want."

Pray Persistently

Jesus said, "Ask and it will be given to you; seek and you will find; knock and the door will be opened to you" (Matt. 7:7). The imperatives in this verse are in the present tense, indicating continuous activity. "Keep on asking; keep on seeking; keep on knocking." Persistence in prayer is not a means of forcing God's hand: instead it demonstrates the seriousness of our requests. And being persistent in prayer differs from being insistent. We shouldn't demand that God answer in our way and our time, but we should continue to let Him know our requests.

Pray with Genuine Piety

Jesus rebuked the Pharisees who were using prayer as a means of gaining attention and parading their piety. They prayed in the synagogues and on the street corners "to be seen by men" (Matt. 6:5).

Pray with Sincerity

Jesus pointed out the error of the Gentiles who thought length made their prayers more effective (Matt. 6:7). They were guilty of meaningless repetition. Our prayers should be the expressions of a sincere heart, not mindless recitation by rote memory.

Pray with Faith

Jesus promised, "If you believe, you will receive whatever you ask for in prayer" (Matt. 21:22). God is honored when we make requests believing He is able to respond and answer.

Pray with a Pure Heart

The Bible teaches that sin in our lives is a hindrance to prayer. Isaiah warned, "But your iniquities have separated you from your God; your sins have hidden his face from you, so that he will not hear" (Isa. 59:2). The psalmist wrote, "If I had cherished sin in my heart, the Lord would not have listened" (Ps. 66:18). Similarly, Peter instructed husbands to honor their wives, treating them respectfully, "so that nothing will hinder your prayers" (1 Pet. 3:7). David wrote that to enter God's presence our hearts must be pure (Ps. 24:3–4).

Pray about Whatever Is on Your Heart

There is no subject which is not a worthy matter for prayer. Paul wrote, "Present your requests to God" (Phil. 4:6). If it is on your heart, it is a legitimate matter for prayer. Bring all your concerns before the God who loves you, who cares, who hears, and who answers. "Cast all your anxiety on him because he cares for you" (1 Pet. 5:7).

IMPROVING COMMUNICATION

Communication is one of the greatest challenges in life. I want to be a better communicator. I want to improve my communication with my wife, my children, my colleagues, my students. But most of all, I want to improve my communication with God. I long to experience something of what Moses encountered when God spoke to Moses "face to face, as a man speaks with his friend" (Exod. 33:11). Since communication is a key to developing and improving relationships, every believer should seek to improve his communication with God.

For Further Study

Carson, D. A., ed. *Teach Us to Pray*. Grand Rapids: Baker Book House, 1990.

Cedar, Paul. *A Life of Prayer*. Swindoll Leadership Library. Nashville: Word Publishing, 1998.

Houston, James M. *The Transforming Power of Prayer: Deepening Your Friendship with God*. Colorado Springs: NavPress, 1989.

Hunter, W. Bingham. *The God Who Hears*. Downers Grove, Ill.: InterVarsity Press, 1986.

20

Answers to Tough
Questions about God

*But in your hearts set apart Christ as Lord. Always be prepared
to give an answer to everyone who asks you to give the reason for
the hope that you have. But do this with gentleness and respect.*

—1 Peter 3:15

As a seminary professor I am asked many questions about
the Bible, theology, and the Christian life.[1] But the questions I find most
challenging and stimulating are the questions people ask about God.
The challenge lies in the fact that finite human creatures are seeking to
understand the mysteries of the infinite Creator. The stimulation comes
in trying to express clearly what the Bible has revealed without modify-
ing the truth.

It is presumptuous to think we can completely understand the nature
of the Almighty. But God has revealed certain things about Himself that
we can embrace, affirm, and declare. This chapter is designed to provide
brief answers to some of the most frequently asked questions about God.[2]
While some of these answers summarize material given in earlier chapters, they all seek to give succinct answers to frequently asked questions.

*How can I believe in God? If there is a God, why did He allow so many
people to be killed in the Vietnam War?*

This question was raised by an atheist who had planned to become a
Baptist minister until he served as a medical lab technician during the
Vietnam War. The issue of God's goodness and justice in a cruel and

unfair world is one of many of the objections raised against the existence of God. "If God exists, why does He allow human tragedy?" The implication of this sort of question is that if all the objections about God's existence were answered, then people would most certainly believe in Him. But no matter how many objections are answered, there are always more that can be raised (1 Cor. 1:18). In the end, believing in God requires a step of faith.

Christian evidences, apologetics, and philosophy can provide reassurance for those considering the claims of Christianity. But this is like a sky diver checking how well he has packed his parachute as he is standing in the doorway of the airplane. No matter how many times he checks his parachute, he will still need to exercise faith as he jumps out. And so it is in making a decision to believe in God and trust Christ. It requires a step of faith. Only then, after we have taken that first step, do we begin to understand something of the nature of God and why He might allow such tragedies as the Vietnam War.

In Hebrews 11:6 we read, "Without faith it is impossible to please God, because anyone who comes to him must believe that he exists and that he rewards those who earnestly seek him." Belief in God comes through a recognition of His existence as demonstrated through creation and revealed through His Word. Belief is not something a person can come to on the basis of logic and reason alone. God has to do a work in the heart of the individual to draw the person to Himself. Jesus said, "No one can come to me unless the Father who sent me draws him, and I will raise him up at the last day" (John 6:44; see also Matt. 11:27). Many people take this first step of faith like the man with the demonized son who cried out, "I do believe; help me overcome my unbelief" (Mark 9:24). But God honors that tentative step of faith and encourages it to grow like the tiny mustard seed into a faith that is strong and steadfast.

Only then from a position of faith can we begin to understand something of the complexities of God's nature and accept the truth that God's Word reveals (Heb. 11:3). (For further study, see the books listed at the end of chapter 1, "Does God Exist?")

If God is good, why did He allow evil to enter the world?

This question is related to the question about God's existence and the presence of evil. For those who have affirmed their faith in God, there remains the question of why He would allow the evils of war, starvation, and mass murder to be perpetrated here on planet earth. Chapter 12 addresses this problem in depth, but I'll provide a summary here.

First, the Bible makes it absolutely clear that God is good (Nah. 1:7) and that He is opposed to evil (Jer. 44:4; Zech. 8:17; James 1:13). Evil came into the world as a result of Adam's sin and fall (Rom. 5:12). Murder, drug abuse, and pornography exist because people have turned away from God and have pursued selfish pleasures instead of the blessings offered through faith in Christ. We should blame these things not on God but on ourselves and on fallen humanity (Rom. 3:10–18).

And yet God is sovereign over evil just as He is sovereign over good. God could intervene to prevent human tragedies. Many times He does. We can all think of circumstances which may have resulted in death if God had not providentially and graciously delivered us. But when He chooses to allow us to encounter evil rather than good, He is not to be blamed. God should never be credited with evil. Even in God's sovereign plan, which may include sinful activity, people are accountable for their sin (Acts 2:23; James 1:13). (For more on this issue, see the books listed at the end of chapter 12, "God and the Presence of Evil.")

If God could prevent suffering, why does He allow it?

The Bible teaches that "in all things God works for the good of those who love him, who have been called according to his purpose" (Rom. 8:28). It is reassuring to know that when God allows suffering, He is accomplishing something good. These good things include building endurance and perseverance into our lives (5:3; James 1:3), helping us grow in Christian maturity (1:4), proving our godly character (Rom. 5:4), developing Christlikeness (8:28–29), helping us grow in personal holiness (Heb. 12:10), and giving us the assurance that we are His children (12:7–8). We may not see the good that God is accomplishing, but we can be confident that His eternal purposes are being fulfilled through our trials. Sometimes the dark threads are as needful as the threads of gold and silver in the pattern God has planned. But someday He will unroll the tapestry of our lives, and we will see the beautiful work God has accomplished, partly through suffering. It is important to keep an eternal perspective when going through suffering. Paul wrote, "For our light and momentary troubles are achieving for us an eternal glory that far outweighs them all. So we fix our eyes not on what is seen, but on what is unseen. For what is seen is temporary, but what is unseen is eternal" (2 Cor. 4:17–18).

God recognizes that sometimes greater glory will come to His name by permitting evil rather than disallowing it altogether. It is hard to understand from a human and earthly perspective why God sometimes allows human suffering for the purpose of bringing greater glory to Himself. But if the purpose of our lives is to glorify God (1 Cor. 10:31), then we will accept suffering gladly in order to exhibit more adequately the greatness of our God. (Also see chapters 19 and 22 in Terry L. Miethe and Gary R. Habermas, *Why Believe? God Exists!* [Joplin, Mo.: College Press, 1993].)

If God has no physical body, what did He mean when He said, "Let us make man in our image, in our likeness" (Gen. 1:26)?

Although Genesis teaches that humans are made in the "image" of God, nowhere in Scripture is this precisely explained. Hence there is a lot of debate on the subject. Theologians agree that this resemblance to God makes mankind unique among God's creatures. No animal is said to be made in God's image. Theologians also agree that this resemblance to God is not physical, since "God is spirit" (John 4:24) and has no material body.

Usually the "image of God" is explained in terms of the immaterial aspects we share with God—our intellect, emotions, and will. Others suggest that this "image" refers more specifically to the spiritual qualities shared by God and humanity. Another view is that being created in the image of God means that human beings are to fill, subdue, and rule the earth (Gen. 1:28). Humankind was created to exercise lordship and dominion over creation as God's visible image and representative.[3] David declared in Psalm 8:5–6 that this is a noble and honorable calling. Although our capacity to fill, subdue, and rule has been disturbed by the entrance of sin into the world, Scripture indicates that mankind retains the divine image (9:6; 1 Cor. 11:7). (For further study see Robert A. Pyne, *Humanity and Sin,* Swindoll Leadership Library [Nashville: Word, 1999].)

Is God a "He"?

During Holy Week, the week before Easter, a crucifixion statue representing Christ as a woman was displayed behind the altar at an Episcopal cathedral in New York. The bronze work, created by sculptor Edwina Sandys, was referred to as "Christa."[4] I once heard a female pastor begin her prayer, "Dear God, our Father and Mother." This raises an interesting question for a gender-conscious generation. Is God male or female? Or is He gender neutral?

It is quite clear from Scripture that Jesus Christ was a male. The angel Gabriel announced that Mary would "bear a son" (Luke 1:31, NASB). Luke recorded that Mary "gave birth to her first-born son" (2:7, NASB). The idea of a female Christ is indefensible biblically and historically. In His incarnation, Jesus Christ, the second person of the Triunity, is clearly male.

But how about the first person of the Trinity? Speaking of God's work among the Israelites, Moses said, "Is he not your Father, your Creator?" (Deut. 32:6). The prophets frequently referred to God as "Father" (Isa. 63:16; 64:8; Jer. 3:4, 19; 31:9; Mal. 1:6; 2:10). Jesus consistently referred to God as His "Father" (Matt. 5:16, 45; 6:1, 4, 6, 8). He taught His disciples to pray to their "Father" in heaven (6:9). Paul affirmed that there is "one God, the Father" (1 Cor. 8:6), and he prayed to God "the Father" (Eph. 3:14). In the Bible we discover that the language that is used to describe God is predominately masculine.

Certainly some caution is in order here. First, we must recognize that "God is spirit" (John 4:24), and so the masculine language cannot refer to God's physical being. God does not have a male body. Second, the fact that the Bible depicts God as masculine does not preclude a feminine aspect of His nature. Indeed, the first thing God says about Himself in His self-revelation to Moses is that He is "compassionate," a word based on the Hebrew root for "womb." God's love and compassion for us is like that which a mother has for her child. God has a mother's kind of love for His own.

It is clear that the living God transcends sexuality so that the categories of male and female do not properly apply to Him. God is presented in the Bible as a "he," but this word does not demand precisely the same thing it does when used of human beings. Some have suggested we ought to change the biblical references to God as Father from masculine to a designation that is nongender specific. But I believe this would be wrong. God has chosen to reveal Himself in the Bible predominately as masculine. Yet in view of God's spiritual nature, we must be careful not to interpret the masculine terminology as reflective of His divine essence. (For further study see Donald G. Bloesch, *Is the Bible Sexist?* [Westchester, Ill.: Crossway, 1982], 61–82; and *The Battle for the Trinity* [Ann Arbor, Mich.: Servant, 1985], 29–41.)

Is one of God's attributes more prominent than others?

Theologians debate whether God's love or His holiness is His greatest or most prominent attribute. For the most part, I see the attributes of God like the facets of a precious diamond. Each facet reflects and displays the light radiating from the gem. The diamond needs each of the facets to display the brilliance of the stone fully. Both God's love and His holiness are fundamental attributes of God, and it would be wrong to emphasize one over the other.

There is, however, one attribute that is first in the list of things God said about Himself in His self-revelation to Moses (Exod. 34:6–7). The first thing someone says about himself or herself is usually rather important. This may be the case with God. I believe it is significant that the first attribute God mentioned to Moses was His compassion. "And he passed in front of Moses, proclaiming, 'The LORD, the LORD, the compassionate and gracious God, slow to anger, abounding in love and faithfulness'" (34:6). Since it is mentioned first in God's self-revelation, "compassion" may be God's preeminent personal attribute. As noted earlier, the word "compassion" is based on the Hebrew word for "womb." Like a loving mother, God has a compassionate concern for His people.

On the other hand, when Moses and the Israelites sang a song commemorating their victory over the Egyptians, they said God is "majestic in power" and "majestic in holiness" (15:6, 11). Is it possible, then, that one of these attributes is most prominent? Tozer believes holiness is a key attribute of God. He writes, "Because He is holy, all His attributes are holy; that is, whatever we think of as belonging to God must be thought of as holy."[5] Whether God's love is more important than His other attributes could be debated. But it is prominent in God's description of Himself and it seems to be foundational for our relationship with Him. (For further study, see chapter 5, "God's Self-Revelation.")

Is it wrong for God to seek a greater display of His own glory through human suffering?

When Jesus learned that Lazarus was sick and dying, He explained to His disciples, "This sickness will not end in death. No, it is for God's glory so that God's Son may be glorified through it" (John 11:4). Some have wondered if it is prideful and wrong for God to seek to increase His own reputation through human pain. But how can it be right for God to glorify Himself when Scripture discourages self-glorification as a form of pride (Ps. 115:1; 1 Cor. 1:27–29; 10:31; 1 Thess. 2:6)?

The glory of God refers in Scripture to His reputation as made known and displayed through His attributes. God is glorified when His reputation is enhanced in the sight of others through the actions of obedient and submissive people. Jesus Christ glorified God the Father through His obedient life and completed ministry (John 17:4). Believers, too, can display God's greatness and grace (1 Cor. 10:31).

As Creator of the physical universe and all it contains, it is entirely appropriate for God to seek to display His glorious reputation (Pss. 29:1; 96:8). As God, He is worthy of this display. In seeking to glorify Himself, God is seeking what is rightfully His and belongs to no other. He said, "I am the LORD; that is my name! I will not give my glory to another or my praise to idols" (Isa. 42:8).

On the other hand, glorifying ourselves is a form of pride that detracts from God's glorification. This is selfish and prideful, because there is nothing we have or accomplish that has not come as a gift of God's grace (1 Cor. 1:4; 4:7; 2 Cor. 9:11; Eph. 1:3).

What does the Bible mean when it says, "God changed His mind"
(Exod. 32:14, NASB)?

When the Israelites turned aside to worship the golden calf at Mount Sinai, God warned Moses, "Now leave me alone so that my anger may burn against them and that I may destroy them" (Exod. 32:10). But Moses interceded on behalf of the people and prayed, "Turn from your fierce anger; relent and do not bring disaster on your people" (32:12). Then God responded positively and "changed His mind about the harm which He said He would do to His people" (32:14, NASB). How is this statement consistent with the biblical teaching on God's immutability? The prophet Malachi spoke for God saying, "I the LORD do not change" (Mal. 3:6). James wrote that God "does not change like shifting shadows" (James 1:17; see also 1 Sam. 15:29; Ps. 110:4). Does God change or not?

The immutability of God means that there is no quantitative or qualitative change in His character or attributes. "The nature of God does not undergo modification. Therefore God does not change his mind, plans, or actions, for these rest upon his nature, which remains unchanged."[6] It is encouraging to know that God is dependable. He will be the same tomorrow as He is today.

When it comes to God's nature, His promises, or His specific decrees, God does not change. However, God can and often does retract announcements based on human repentance or change in behavior. Jonah's announcement of judgment on Nineveh served as a call for the people to repent. When the Ninevites repented, "God relented concerning the calamity which He had declared He would bring upon them" (Jon. 3:10, NASB). In his probing article, "Does God 'Change His Mind'?" Robert Chisholm concluded, "If God has not decreed a course of action, then He may very well retract an announcement of blessing or judgment."[7] In this situation, it is not God who has changed, but people who have changed.

Announcements of judgment are conditioned on repentance. If the people repent, God will withhold judgment because He is unchanging in

His compassion and grace, "not wanting anyone to perish, but everyone to come to repentance" (2 Pet. 3:9). (For further study, see Erickson, *Introducing Christian Doctrine*, 86–87, and Chisholm, "Does God 'Change His Mind'?")

Why has God elected some for salvation and passed over others? Is this fair?

The biblical doctrine of election may be defined as God's act of choosing those who, through personal faith, will be saved. This truth was expressed by Paul in Ephesians 1:4, "For he chose us in him before the creation of the world to be holy and blameless in his sight." The Greek word translated "chose" *(eklegō)* means "to pick out or select." The verbal form in this verse means "to choose someone for oneself." It is important to remember that God's choosing never cancels out or eliminates the necessity of personal faith. Although God elects people for salvation, they are not saved apart from believing (trusting) in Jesus.

One might wonder, "If God loves the world, why has He chosen only some people for salvation?" It might seem that the doctrine of election is in conflict with God's universal love. We know, of course, that God has an immense love for sinners and desires to bring them to Himself. And the only reason that anyone is chosen for salvation is because of His great love and mercy (1 John 4:8–10). But why didn't God decree a universal election along with a universal offer of salvation? Because this would have undermined human freedom. Also, knowing that God chose us (totally apart from any merit of ours) gives us a greater appreciation of God's sovereign grace.

Is this doctrine of election in conflict with God's justice? Paul responded in Romans 9:14–29 to the charge that election is unjust. He demonstrated from God's dealings with Esau and Jacob that divine election is neither arbitrary nor unjust.

First, Paul appealed to history (9:15–18), reminding his readers of Israel's experience with Pharaoh. As an exercise of His sovereignty, God granted mercy according to His will and hardened Pharaoh according to His will. Second, Paul appealed to logic (9:19–24). He argued that as the potter has sovereignty over his clay, so God has sovereign authority over His creatures.

Third, Paul appealed to the Old Testament prophets (9:25–29). He cited several passages from the prophets (Hos. 2:23; 1:10; Isa. 10:22–23) to demonstrate that election is consistent with the Old Testament.

Paul's main point in Romans 9:14–29 was that no one should complain that God's elective purposes are unjust. Election is consistent with God's work in history, with His sovereignty, and with the teaching of the Old Testament. From a limited human perspective election may seem to be unjust. But when we have questions about the justice of God, we must remember that God is holy, righteous, and just. He will do nothing contrary to these basic attributes.

Did God predestine some people to eternal judgment in the same way He predestined some people for salvation?

As already noted, the Bible teaches that as an exercise of His sovereignty God chose certain individuals to believe and be saved. In choosing some to believe, did He predestine others to disbelieve and be condemned? This seems unfair and contrary to the mercy of God. The ultimate question for students of Scripture is whether this doctrine is biblical.

As a potter over his clay, so God has sovereign authority over His creatures (Rom. 9:19–24). From the same lump of clay He has the right to make "some pottery for noble purposes" and some "for common use." Some are "objects of his wrath—prepared for destruction," and others are "objects of his mercy, whom he prepared in advance for glory" (9:21–23). The Greek verbal form rendered "prepared" (in 9:22) could be translated "prepared themselves," indicating permanent involvement and accountability. Or, taken another way, the verb could be understood as referring to God's act of preparing certain people for destruction. In Paul's analogy with the potter, these people did not determine their own destiny.

Several Bible passages seem to support the latter view: Exodus 4:21; Proverbs 16:4; Isaiah 6:9–10; 1 Peter 2:8; and Jude 4. But we must be careful here. While God stands behind the destiny of both the elect and the nonelect, He may not do so in exactly the same way. When Paul used *katartizō* ("prepared") in Romans 9:22 to speak of the nonelect, he did not specifically refer to God as the subject as he did when he wrote of the elect's destiny in 9:23. The difference is subtle but significant. While God is sovereign over the destinies of both the elect and nonelect, He is not behind the destiny of the nonelect in the same way He is behind the destiny of the elect. The problem with "double predestination" is that it gives the idea that the two predestinations are of equal character, when actually they are not. This crucial difference is supported in Romans 6:23 where punishment is considered as "wages" earned while eternal life is considered as a "free gift." God chooses some to be saved (the elect), but He bypasses others, who, because of their sin, must pay the wages of sin and thus are "prepared for destruction."

If God has chosen the elect to be saved, why is it necessary to preach the gospel?

The key in answering this question is to understand that God's sovereignty over salvation does not cancel out the human responsibility of a faith response to the gospel. And that response cannot happen if the good news is not preached. As Paul wrote, "How, then, can they call on the one they have not believed in? And how can they believe in the one of whom they have not heard? And how can they hear without someone preaching to them?" (Rom. 10:14).

While our salvation is decreed and assured by our election, some aspects of God's decree are carried out by people, as Paul Enns has pointed out.[8] God's decree involves the means as well as the end. Paul affirmed the doctrine of election (Rom. 1:1; 8:30; 9:11), but with equal fervency he emphasized the necessity of preaching the gospel so that people will be saved (Acts 16:31; Rom. 10:14–15; 1 Cor. 9:16).

Rather than discouraging evangelism, the doctrine of election should serve as a great impetus to evangelism. It is encouraging to know that there are elect people in the world who have not yet heard the message of salvation. They are chosen sheep who have not yet heard the voice of the Good Shepherd. But when they hear His voice through the preaching of the gospel, they will respond positively to the message (John 10:16). As we present the gospel to the unregenerate world, the doctrine of election assures us that those whom God has chosen will believe!

Why would a good God condemn ignorant, unbelieving people to an eternity in hell? Wouldn't such punishment contradict any reasonable standard of justice and mercy?

Every soul will spend eternity somewhere—either with Christ in heaven (John 14:3) or with the devil in the lake of fire (Rev. 20:10, 15). Yet there are some who have questioned the traditional view that those who have rejected Christ will suffer the pains of an everlasting, fiery hell.

Two biblical texts provide convincing evidence that hell involves everlasting punishment. Jesus summed up the judgment on the sheep and goats with the words, "Then they will go away to eternal punishment, but the righteous to eternal life" (Matt. 25:46). Significantly the same word *aiōnion* ("eternal") is used to describe the punishment of the wicked and the blessing of the righteous. Since the "life" granted to believers is everlasting (John 10:28), so the punishment for unbelievers must be eternal. In a second text, Revelation 20:10, John described those in the "lake of fire" as being "tormented day and night forever and ever." Then at the end of his discussion of the Great White Throne judgment, John wrote, "If anyone's name was not found written in the book of life, he was thrown into the lake of fire" (20:15).

The thought of someone suffering everlasting torment in a fiery hell is terrible to consider. I could not wish that on the worst of criminals. Much less would I wish such a fate on good friends and relatives who have lived decent lives but have not accepted Christ. How can God, who is infinitely loving and compassionate, commit decent, moral, benevolent people to a fiery eternity simply because they have refused His offer of salvation in Christ? Perhaps some even died without ever hearing a clear presentation of the gospel.

I share concern over this troubling issue. Yet I am unwilling to allow personal compassion for those in judgment or wishful thinking regarding the lost to deter my acceptance of a thoroughly biblical doctrine. I seek to balance the truth of eternal punishment with the truths of God's mercy, justice, and holiness. God does not want to send anyone to hell. What He desires is for sinners to repent and be saved (2 Pet. 3:9). All creation testifies to the existence of a God who loves and cares for fallen humanity (Ps. 19:1–6; Rom. 1:18–21). Those who respond to this witness are given sufficient light to respond to the truth of Christ (Heb. 11:6). And those who trust in Him will be saved (John 5:24; 6:37).

Because God is holy and just, He must judge those who have allied themselves with Satan in rebelling against their Creator. Yet He takes no pleasure in passing a sentence of eternal judgment on any wicked sinner. Through the prophet Isaiah, God said, "All day long I have held out my hands to an obstinate people, who walk in ways not good, pursuing their own imaginations—a people who continually provoke me to my very face" (Isa. 65:2–3; see also Rom. 10:21). God is very patient with sinners, appealing for them to repent and be saved. But in choosing life without God they also determine their sad destiny. If anything grieves God, I believe it is the sobering reality that persistently rebellious and disbelieving sinners will be confined in hell for eternity.

How do we reconcile the justice of God's judgment with His love?

This question is closely related to the previous question on eternal punishment. Here the question is whether God's attributes cancel out each other. We know that God is holy (Lev. 11:44–45; 1 Pet. 1:16), and this attribute requires that He respond with wrathful judgment when confronted with sin and disobedience. The judgment He executes in responding to sin is just and right. It is never based on merely outward actions or superficialities, but on the inward condition and attitude of the heart (Isa. 11:3; John 8:15–16).

But in addition to being a God of infinite holiness, who must pour out His wrath on sin and disobedience, He also possesses infinite mercy and love (Lam. 3:22; John 4:8–9). His love for even the most wicked and sinful people is illustrated by the tragic story of the prophet Hosea and his wife Gomer. In spite of her unfaithfulness and adulteries, Hosea still loved her "as the Lord loves the Israelites, though they turn to other gods" (Hos. 3:1). Because of God's love, He does not want anyone to perish (2 Pet. 3:9).

So how can the justice of God be reconciled with His love? How can God maintain proper justice and still be merciful toward sinners? Paul answered these questions in Romans 3:23–26. All people have fallen short of God's standard of righteousness and are subjects of His wrathful judgment. God's wrath on sinners is serious and well deserved. If we fail to understand God's justice, we will never fully appreciate the depth of His love. When people trust in Christ for salvation, God declares them righteous. They are "justified freely by his grace through the redemption that came by Christ Jesus" (3:24). The judgment they had coming to them was assigned instead to Jesus, who stood in the place of sinners by receiving the divine wrath they deserved (3:25). God was faithful to His standards of justice in that His holy demands were satisfied. But He is also faithful to His attribute of love by providing a Substitute for our sins, the Lamb of God. In this way God demonstrated that He could be both "just and the one who justifies those who have faith in Jesus" (3:26). And so in the wonderful plan of redemption, neither God's holiness nor His love are compromised.

Does God have a sense of humor? Does He enjoy a good joke?

The answer to this question depends on what is meant by "a sense of humor." If this means does God likes jokes or should He be the object of a jokes, the answer is no. God is too holy and awesome to be trivialized as a cosmic Joker or the subject for joking. Jokes about God are disrespectful and in poor taste.

On the other hand, there is biblical evidence that God takes delight in surprising His creatures with the extraordinary and unexpected. And this lies at the core of humor. Jokes are funny because of the unexpected ending or surprise twist. I find a good deal of this in Scripture. That a donkey spoke to Balaam is unusual. But the fact that Balaam spoke back without so much as the blink of an eye is humorous (Num. 22:29)! And the fact that the donkey saw the angel blocking the path (22:27) while the "seer" didn't adds another touch of humor to the story.

The story of Jonah has many great theological lessons. But these are presented through the medium of a humorous story. We are surprised by the fact that the fish was more obedient than the prophet, for when God commanded Jonah, he fled. But when God commanded the fish, it obeyed! There is also humor in the fact that the pagan sailors had more respect for human life than Jonah. He wanted to be thrown into the sea, but they refused and tried to save the ship (Jon. 1:12–13). Also Jonah's death plea over the demise of the little plant—"It would be better for me to die than to live" (4:8)—is intended to elicit a chuckle.

If you find puns or wordplays humorous, don't miss Micah 1:10–15. Here Micah employed a number of puns in mourning a number of towns to be attacked by the Babylonians. He wrote things like, "Hightown will be laid low," and "Cannon Falls will fall by the cannon." Shaphir ("Beauty town") will be made ugly and shameful as a result of the Babylonian destruction, and Beth-ezel ("House of removal") will be removed to captivity.

I find humor in the fact that Paul could not seem to recall how many people at Corinth he had baptized and he kept on correcting himself to make sure that he was not in error (1 Cor. 1:14–17). Even the most sober soul smiles when reading Paul's comment that those advocating circumcision should emasculate themselves (Gal. 5:12).[9]

While God seems to have a sense of humor in that He enjoys surprising us with something unanticipated, He Himself cannot be amused. This is because God is never surprised. He knows the end from the beginning. He knows the punch line before a story is even told.

To what degree is God involved in our daily experiences as Christians?

Most Christians would agree that God is involved in our lives to some degree or other. Some see God as rather remote. They believe God created the world and then, besides occasional visitations and revelations, He allows it to run on its own. What happens in our lives, these people say, depends on us. Others see God more actively involved, providentially leading people along the path of life He has sovereignly determined.

The Bible affirms that God is actively involved in our lives, accomplishing His purposes through the exercise of His sovereignty. Paul wrote, "In him we were chosen, having been predestined according to the plan of him who works out everything in conformity with the purpose of his will" (Eph. 1:11) The word predestined means God has "marked out the boundaries" of our lives. The words "all things" indicate that God providentially determines all that takes place in our lives. Nothing is left to chance and circumstance. God is the "hand in the glove" of history, working through natural, human means to accomplish His purposes.

God's involvement in human lives is evident in the words of Ecclesiastes 3:1: "There is a time for everything, and a season for every activity under heaven." Verses 2–8 point out that there is a divinely ordained time for all of life's events. Paul wrote, "And we know that in all things God works for the good of those who love him, who have been called according to his purpose" (Rom. 8:28). Once again, note the words "all things." To what degree is God involved in our experiences? The biblical answer is that God is fully involved. There is nothing in our lives that has not been determined by God's sovereign decree.

This doctrinal affirmation raises another question: If God is absolutely sovereign over us, shouldn't He take responsibility for our sins and mistakes? No, because the sovereignty of God never abrogates the responsibility people bear for their actions. A good example of this is seen in the crucifixion of Christ. Peter said that Jesus was betrayed and crucified by "God's set purpose" (Acts 2:23; see also Luke 22:22; Acts 4:28). But he also rebuked the godless people by whose actions He was sent to the cross. "The God of Abraham . . . has glorified his servant Jesus. You handed him over to be killed, and you disowned him before Pilate, though he had decided to let him go. You disowned the Holy and Righteous One and asked that a murderer be released to you" (3:13–14).

The biblical teachings of God's sovereignty and human responsibility must be kept in careful balance. In His absolute sovereignty God has predetermined all that takes place. But the sovereignty of God does not eliminate human responsibility for our actions. Sin and mistakes take place in our lives because of our own choosing. God, who is perfect and holy, is not to blame. (For further study see chapter 11, "The Decree of God.")

If God is all powerful and unrelenting in His love, why doesn't He answer my prayers?

Some people see belief in God as a way to get things, manipulate people, avoid unpleasant consequences, and maintain a certain level of happiness. And when God does not seem to provide these desired outcomes, they are disappointed and disillusioned. The main problem here is that such people have an inadequate view of prayer. Prayer is a means of communicating with God, expressing our love through adoration, confession, and thanksgiving. Yes, petition has its place in prayer. But the great prayers in the Bible focus more on the development of spiritual qualities than on personal, material gain.

Yet God can and does answer prayer. During my life as a Christian, I have seen God answer many of my petitions in ways that evidence His supernatural intervention. Several years ago I lost my wedding ring during a mountain-climbing trip. When I discovered that it was missing, I thoroughly searched my friend's car and my clothing and equipment, praying that this little item would appear. It was nowhere to be found. After several days, I called Timberline Lodge, where we parked at Mount Hood, to see if someone might have found my ring. To my astonishment, they had a ring and it matched the description I gave! When the ring came in the mail, several days later I thanked God for answering my prayer!

But if God is able to answer all our prayers, why doesn't He do so? The following are five reasons why our prayers sometimes seem to fail.

First, sometimes God does not answer our prayers because our faith is small. When the disciples asked why they were unable to deliver a boy from demonic bondage, Jesus explained that it was because they had so little faith. "I tell you the truth, if you have faith as small as a mustard seed, you can say to this mountain, 'Move from here to there,' and it will move. Nothing will be impossible for you" (Matt. 17:20).

Second, sometimes God does not answer our prayers because of sin in our lives. The psalmist wrote, "If I had cherished sin in my heart, the Lord would not have listened" (Ps. 66:18). There is no point in seeking God's help if we are unwilling to acknowledge known sin.

Third, God may not answer our prayers because of irreconciled relationships. Peter instructed Christian men to live with their wives in an understanding way, granting them honor as fellow-heirs of the grace of life "so that your prayers" will hinder nothing (1 Pet. 3:7, NASB).

Fourth, God sometimes delays His answer for a more appropriate time.

In some cases it is not that God won't answer our prayer, but that the answer will be given later, in accord with His timing.

Fifth, God's greater purposes are sometimes accomplished through unanswered prayer. Paul prayed three times that God would deliver him from "a thorn in my flesh" (2 Cor. 12:7–8). But God didn't answer Paul's prayer. Instead, God taught him an important lesson: "My grace is sufficient for you, for my power is made perfect in weakness" (2 Cor. 12:9). Unanswered prayer may help us learn of Christ's sufficiency in a troubling situation.

Sometimes there is no apparent reason for God's not answering our prayer. Yet, when an answer is not forthcoming, we have opportunity to demonstrate patience, persistence, and persevering faith—to the glory of God. (For further study see chapter 19, "Communicating with God.")

Appendix
Classic Texts about God

Oh, the depth of the riches of the wisdom and knowledge of God!
How unsearchable his judgments, and his paths beyond tracing
out!

—Romans 11:33

Some years ago the Coca Cola Company made a disastrous blunder. After years of serving up the same soft drink, one which had gained worldwide favor, the Coke company changed the traditional formula and introduced the "New Coke." The new drink still tasted like Coke, but was sweeter and milder in flavor. Market research indicated that the "New Coke" would be well received by thirsty pop-drinkers.

However, Coke company officials were shocked by the negative reaction to the new product by Coca Cola fans around the world. They complained about the new product. They wrote letters to the company president. They bought up the "old Coke" which was still on grocery-store shelves and hoarded it in anticipation of a Coke-less future.

Quick to respond to the concerns of loyal Coke drinkers, the company decided to keep producing the original formula and to call it "Coke Classic." The "New Coke" remained on the store shelves for a year or so but has long since disappeared. Now Coke fans drink "Coke Classic," and they love it!

Everyone appreciates a classic—whether it is a Coke, a car, or a fine piece of furniture. This is true of biblical texts as well. While fully recognizing that "all Scripture is God-breathed" (2 Tim. 3:16), I also appreciate the fact that there are some "classic" biblical texts that reveal with particular power and clarity the greatness and goodness of God. These are texts which you may want to consider for devotional reading, memorization, or further study.

OLD TESTAMENT

Genesis 1:1–3
Genesis 22:1–14
Exodus 3:13–15
Exodus 6:2–8
Exodus 15:1–18
Exodus 34:6–8
Leviticus 11:44–45
Deuteronomy 6:4–5
1 Samuel 2:1–10
2 Samuel 22:2–51
Nehemiah 9:5–8
Job 38:1–39:30
Job 40:1–41:34
Psalm 2
Psalm 18
Psalm 22
Psalm 23
Psalm 24
Psalm 91
Psalm 96
Psalm 99
.Psalm 100
Psalm 103
Psalm 110
Psalm 139
Ecclesiastes 7:13–14
Isaiah 6:1–13
Isaiah 9:1–7
Isaiah 40:12–26

Isaiah 52:12–53:12
Jeremiah 9:23–24
Lamentations 3:22–25
Ezekiel 1:4–28
Daniel 7:9–14
Joel 2:12–13
Jonah 4:2
Micah 7:18–20
Zephaniah 3:15–17

NEW TESTAMENT

Matthew 1:18–23
John 1:1–18
Acts 2:22–36
Romans 8:28–39
Romans 11:33–36
Ephesians 1:3–14
Philippians 2:5–11
Colossians 1:15–20
1 Timothy 1:17
1 Timothy 3:16
2 Timothy 2:11–13
Hebrews 1:1–3
Hebrews 12:5–11
James 1:17–18
2 Peter 3:3–9
1 John 4:8–16
Revelation 1:10–20
Revelation 4:1–11
Revelation 5:8–14
Revelation 19:11–16

Endnotes

CHAPTER 1—DOES GOD EXIST?

1. M. D. Gibson, *Horae Semiticae x* (Cambridge, 1913), quoted in F. F. Bruce, *The Book of Acts* (Grand Rapids: Eerdmans, 1954), 359.
2. Ibid.
3. Paul P. Enns, *The Moody Handbook of Theology* (Chicago: Moody, 1989), 185.

CHAPTER 2—FAULTY VIEWS OF GOD

1. Judith Weinraub, "Paganism Attracts More and More Women," *Oregonian*, 11 May 1991, C10.
2. Ibid.
3. Paul D. Feinberg, "Agnosticism," in *Evangelical Dictionary of Theology*, ed. Walter A. Elwell (Grand Rapids: Baker, 1984), 25.
4. Blaise Pascal, *Pensées*, trans. A. J. Krailsheimer (New York: Penguin, 1966), 149–54.
5. D. B. Fletcher, "Polytheism," in *Evangelical Dictionary of Theology*, 862.
6. Shirley MacLaine, *Dancing in the Light* (New York: Bantam, 1986), 358 (italics hers).

7. M. H. Macdonald, "Deism," in *Evangelical Dictionary of Theology*, 305.

8. For a discussion of the consequences of parental action on their children, see Walter C. Kaiser Jr., *Toward Old Testament Ethics* (Grand Rapids: Zondervan, 1983), 87.

9. Millard Erickson, *The Evangelical Left* (Grand Rapids: Baker, 1997), 87.

10. Ibid., 89.

11. John C. Cobb and David Ray Griffin, *Process Theology: An Introductory Exposition* (Philadelphia: Westminster, 1976), 8-10.

12. Clark H. Pinnock, "Between Classical and Process Theism," in *Process Theology*, ed. Ronald Nash (Grand Rapids: Baker, 1987), 313–14.

13. Clark Pinnock et al., *The Openness of God* (Downers Grove, Ill.: InterVarsity, 1994), 118.

14. Ibid., 117.

15. Ibid., 124.

16. Ibid., 122.

17. Glenn D. Kreider, "Review of *The Openness of God*, by Clark Pinnock et al.," in *Bibliotheca Sacra* 152 (October–December 1995): 489.

18. Erickson, *The Evangelical Left*, 92.

CHAPTER 3–THE NAME OF GOD

1. Dale Carnegie, *How to Win Friends and Influence People* (New York: Simon & Schuster, 1936), 84.

2. Jerry W. Lee, "The Power of a Name," *Biblical Illustrator* (Fall 1996): 27.

3. The imperfect of *yārad*, "go down," is used here to describe God's future action, "I will go down."

4. Ronald B. Allen, "What Is in a Name?" in *God: What Is He Like?* ed. W. F. Kerr (Wheaton, Ill.: Tyndale House, 1977), 122. I am indebted to Ronald Allen, my teacher and friend, for his insights into the meaning and significance of God's name.

5. Walter Eichrodt, *Theology of the Old Testament* (Philadelphia: Westminster, 1961), 1:190.

6. Alfred Edersheim, *The Temple: Its Ministry and Services* (Grand Rapids: Eerdmans, 1958), 310–11.

7. Leon Morris, *The Gospel According to John* (Grand Rapids: Eerdmans, 1971), 473, n. 116 (capital letters his).

8. For a full presentation of the deity of Christ see John A. Witmer, *Immanuel: Jesus Christ, Cornerstone of Our Faith*, Swindoll Leadership Library (Nashville: Word, 1998).

CHAPTER 4–DESIGNATIONS OF DEITY

1. W. F. Albright, *From the Stone Age to Christianity*, 2d ed. (Garden City, N.Y.: Doubleday, 1957), 213.

2. "Great and mighty God" in the NASB translates the Hebrew, "the great El, the mighty Yahweh."

3. T. E. McComiskey, "God, Names of," in *Evangelical Dictionary of Theology*, 466.

4. For a discussion of the more than one hundred names and titles of Jesus in the Scriptures, see Witmer, *Immanuel: Jesus Christ, Cornerstone of Our Faith*, chapter 4.

5. L. Berkhof, *Systematic Theology*, 4th ed. (Grand Rapids: Eerdmans, 1939), 50.

6. O. Hofius, "Father," in *New International Dictionary of New Testament Theology*, ed. Colin Brown (Grand Rapids: Zondervan, 1975), 1:614.

7. Mary Foxwell Loeks, *The Glorious Names of God* (Grand Rapids: Baker, 1986), 136–38.

CHAPTER 5—GOD'S SELF-REVELATION

1. This was not the tabernacle, for the tabernacle was not yet constructed (see Exod. 40).

2. Scholars differ as to whether the pronoun "he" in Exodus 34:5 refers to Yahweh or to Moses. Either Moses "called on the name of Yahweh" or God "proclaimed his name [Yahweh]." Within the context the latter interpretation seems more likely. This view is supported by

Exodus 33:19 where God promised, "I will cause all my goodness to pass in front of you, and I will proclaim my name, the LORD, in your presence."

3. Leonard J. Coppes, "*raham*," in *Theological Wordbook of the Old Testament*, ed. R. Laird Harris, Gleason L. Archer Jr., and Bruce K. Waltke (Chicago: Moody, 1980), 2:841.

4. Charles C. Ryrie, *The Grace of God* (Chicago: Moody, 1963), 9.

5. Exodus 34:6; Numbers 14:18; Nehemiah 9:17; Psalms 86:15; 103:8; 145:8; Joel 2:13; Jonah 4:2; Nahum 1:3.

6. R. Laird Harris, "*ḥesed*," in *Theological Wordbook of the Old Testament*, 1:305–67.

7. Nelson Glueck, *Ḥesed in the Bible*, trans. Alfred Gottschalk, ed. Eleas L. Epstein (Cincinnati: Hebrew Union College, 1967).

CHAPTER 6—WHAT THE PENTATEUCH TEACHES ABOUT GOD

1. A. W. Pink, *The Attributes of God* (Swengel, Pa.: Reiner, 1975), 75.

2. Leon Morris, "The Wrath of God," *Expository Times* 63 (1951–52): 145.

3. S. Erlandsson, "The Wrath of YHWH," *Tyndale Bulletin* 23 (1972): 116.

4. J. I. Packer, *Knowing God* (Downers Grove, Ill.: InterVarsity, 1973), 151.

5. Matthew 3:7; John 3:36; Romans 1:18; 2:5, 8; 5:9; 9:22; 12:19; Ephesians 2:3; 5:6; Colossians 3:6; 1 Thessalonians 1:10; 2:16; 5:9; Hebrews 10:31; 12:29; Revelation 6:16–17; 11:18; 14:10, 19; 15:1, 7; 16:19; 19:15.

6. William L. Moran, "The Ancient Near Eastern Background of the Love of God in Deuteronomy," *Catholic Biblical Quarterly* 25 (1963): 77–87.

7. Zossima, quoted in G. Walter Hansen, "Paul's Conversion and His Ethic of Freedom in Galatians," in *The Road from Damascus*, ed. Richard N. Longenecker (Grand Rapids: Eerdmans, 1997), 236.

CHAPTER 7—THE GREATNESS OF GOD

1. A. H. Strong, *Systematic Theology* (Valley Forge, Pa.: Judson, 1907), 244.

2. For a helpful chart showing the various ways to group God's attributes see Enns, *The Moody Handbook of Theology*, 189–91.

3. For example, Millard J. Erickson, *Introducing Christian Doctrine* (Grand Rapids: Baker, 1992), 80.

CHAPTER 8—THE GOODNESS OF GOD

1. F. B. Meyer, source unknown.

2. Lee Siegel, "With Lungs Fine, Woman Discharged," *Oregonian*, 6 March 1993.

3. For a philosophical presentation on the subject of objective truth, see Peter Kreeft and Ronald K. Tacelli, *Handbook of Christian Apologetics* (Downers Grove, Ill.: InterVarsity, 1994), 362–83.

4. James M. Reese, "Christ as Wisdom Incarnate: Wiser than Solomon, Loftier than Lady Wisdom," *Biblical Theology Bulletin* 11 (April 1984): 44–47.

5. W. E. Vine, *An Expository Dictionary of New Testament Words* (Old Tappan, N.J.: Revell, 1940), 3:60.

CHAPTER 9—IMAGES OF GOD

1. C. S. Lewis, *Mere Christianity* (New York: Macmillan, 1943), 69.

2. See, for example, Psalms 18:2; 19:14; 61:2; 62:2, 6; 71:3; 78:35; 94:22; 95:1.

3. Millard C. Lind, *Yahweh Is a Warrior* (Scottdale, Pa.: Herald, 1980).

4. Suetonius, *The Twelve Caesars* 12.2.

5. R. Laird Harris, "*gā'al*," in *Theological Wordbook of the Old Testament*, 1:144.

6. Leo G. Perdue, "The Household, Old Theology, and Contemporary Hermeneutics," in *Families in Ancient Israel* (Louisville: Westminster Knox, 1997), 230.

CHAPTER 10—THE TRIUNITY OF GOD

1. Charles C. Ryrie, *A Survey of Bible Doctrine* (Chicago: Moody, 1972), 31.

2. J. H. Hertz, ed., *The Pentateuch and Haftorahs* (London: Soncino, 1981), 770.

3. Peter C. Craigie, *The Book of Deuteronomy* (Grand Rapids: Eerdmans, 1976), 168–69.

4. Herbert Wolf, "'*eḥad*," in *Theological Wordbook of the Old Testament*, 1:30.

5. For more on the identity of "the Angel of the LORD" as the preincarnate Christ, see Witmer, *Immanuel: Jesus Christ, Cornerstone of Our Faith*, 13–22, and Robert P. Lightner, *Angels, Satan, and Demons*, Swindoll Leadership Library (Nashville: Word, 1998), 60–63.

6. I omit any appeal to 1 John 5:7–8, which appears in the Textus Receptus on which the King James Version is based. The questionable text reads: ". . . in heaven: the Father, the Word, and the Holy Ghost: and these three are one. And there are three that bear witness in earth." This reading is absent from all but four very late Greek manuscripts, and it does not appear in any of the ancient versions. Nor is it quoted by any of the Greek church fathers, who certainly would have appealed to it in the Trinitarian controversies had it been available to them in the biblical manuscripts. For further discussion, see Bruce M. Metzger, *A Textual Commentary on the Greek New Testament* (London: United Bible Societies, 1971), 716–18.

7. Ryrie, *A Survey of Bible Doctrine*, 33.

8. G. H. Bromiley, "Trinity," in *Evangelical Dictionary of Theology*, 1113.

9. For further study see Johannes Schneider, "God," in *New International Dictionary of New Testament Theology*, 2:75–76; and J. V. Dahms, "The Johannine Use of *Monogenē* Reconsidered," *New Testament Studies* 29 (April 1983): 222–32.

CHAPTER 11—THE DECREE OF GOD

1. *The Westminster Shorter Catechism*, Question 7.

2. Erickson, *Introducing Christian Doctrine*, 109.
3. T. K. Abbott, quoted in Fritz Rienecker, *A Linguistic Key to the Greek New Testament*, ed. Cleon L. Rogers Jr. (Grand Rapids: Zondervan, 1976), 521.
4. F. H. Klooster, "Decrees of God," in *Evangelical Dictionary of Theology*, 303.
5. For further study see B. B. Warfield, "Predestination," in *Biblical and Theological Studies*, ed. Samuel G. Craig (Philadelphia: Presbyterian and Reformed, 1952), 329–33.
6. I am grateful to Bard Pillette for helping me see these distinctions.
7. Klooster, "Decrees of God," 304.
8. Over one hundred years ago theologian William G. T. Shedd made this helpful distinction between God's decree making our actions certain but not forcing or compelling those voluntary actions (*Dogmatic Theology* [1888; reprint, Grand Rapids: Zondervan, n.d.], 1:413).
9. Klooster, "Decrees of God," 303.

CHAPTER 12—GOD AND THE PRESENCE OF EVIL

1. Erin Hover, "Couple Draw Strength from Adversity," *Oregonian*, 2 July 1997, B1.
2. Steven Amick, "Truck Collision Kills Boy on Bicycle," *Oregonian*, 23 July 1997, C1.
3. Alisa Rivera, David R. Anderson, and Jennifer Bjorhus, "Violence Claims Four in Family," *Oregonian*, 18 July 1997, A1.
4. J. S. Feinberg, "Theodicy," in *Evangelical Dictionary of Theology*, 1083.
5. Millard J. Erickson, *God the Father Almighty* (Grand Rapids: Baker, 1998), 218.
6. Feinberg, "Theodicy," 1083.
7. Harold Kushner, *When Bad Things Happen to Good People* (New York: Avon, 1981).
8. Friedrich W. Nietzsche, *Thus Spoke Zarathustra*, trans. Thomas Common (New York: Modern Library, 1905).

9. Mary Baker Eddy, *Science and Health with Key to the Scriptures* (Boston: Stuart, 1906).

10. For a brief discussion on the woman's "desire," see my book *Answers to Tough Questions* (Grand Rapids: Kregel, 1997), 19–20.

11. The judgment resulting from the Fall was not all bad. Satan, the enemy of mankind, will be defeated. Genesis 3:15 predicts the coming of a promised Seed of woman who would share in humanity and would sacrifice Himself to achieve victory over Satan.

12. D. A. Carson, *How Long, O Lord?* (Grand Rapids: Baker, 1990), 213.

13. Erickson, *Introducing Christian Doctrine*, 140.

14. This paragraph summarizes Carson's very helpful discussion on "Compatibilism" in *How Long, O Lord?* 201–27.

CHAPTER 13—GOD'S PLAN FOR THE AGES

1. Richard Foster, "Getting the Big Picture," *Christianity Today*, 18 April 1986, 12–13.

2. Graeme Goldsworthy, *Gospel and Kingdom* (Exeter, U.K.: Paternoster, 1981), 47.

CHAPTER 14—BEING A FRIEND OF GOD

1. Harold H. Hoehner, *Chronological Aspects of the Life of Christ* (Grand Rapids: Zondervan, 1977), 111. For further study on the phrase see John Crook, *Concilium Principiis* (Cambridge: University Press, 1955), 21–30.

2. Harold H. Hoehner, "Historical Backgrounds of the Gospels" (class lectures, Dallas Theological Seminary, 1976).

3. Hoehner provides an excellent summary of Sejanus's activities, with full documentation from ancient sources (*Chronological Aspects of the Life of Christ*, 105–9).

CHAPTER 15—BELIEVING IN GOD

1. Jack B. Scott, "'āman," in *Theological Wordbook of the Old Testament*, 1:51.
2. Allen P. Ross, *Creation and Blessing* (Grand Rapids: Baker, 1988), 310.
3. J. Carl Laney, *John* (Chicago: Moody, 1992), 87.
4. The imperative and the indicative have the same form in the second person plural. However, the context suggests that Jesus intended the imperative with both words here.
5. Chris Myers, "Chance Encounter Led to a Truly High Time," *Oregonian*, 3 September 1987.
6. Merrill C. Tenney, "Topics from the Gospel of John, Part IV: The Growth of Belief," *Bibliotheca Sacra* 132 (October–December 1975): 357.
7. Ibid., 351.
8. Leon Morris, *The Gospel of John* (Grand Rapids: Eerdmans, 1971), 603.

CHAPTER 16—RESPONDING TO GOD

1. Ronald Allen and Gordon Borror, *Worship: Rediscovering the Missing Jewel* (Portland, Oreg.: Multnomah, 1982), 16.
2. Ibid.
3. Ronald B. Allen, "When the Psalmists Say 'Praise the Lord!'" *Worship Leader* 1 (October/November, 1992): 8.
4. For further study, see my chapter "Worshiping in the Spirit," in *Everything I Know about Success I Learned from the Bible* (Grand Rapids: Kregel, 1996), 111–21.
5. J. W. McKay, "Love for God in Deuteronomy and the Father/Teacher—Son/Pupil Relationship," *Vetus Testamentum* 22 (1972): 431–32.
6. McBride, quoted in W. C. Kaiser, "me'ôd," *Theological Wordbook of the Old Testament*, 1:487.

7. Ronald B. Allen, *The Majesty of Man* (Portland, Oreg.: Multnomah, 1984), 158.

CHAPTER 17—DEALING WITH YOUR DOUBTS

1. Os Guinness, *Doubt* (Tring, U.K.: Lion, 1976), 17.
2. Gary R. Habermas, *Dealing with Doubt* (Chicago: Moody, 1990), 10.
3. Ibid., 25–35.
4. C. S. Lewis, *The Screwtape Letters* (New York: Macmillan, 1961), 126–27.
5. In Habakkuk 1:6 the New American Standard Bible calls these people "Chaldeans." They were originally a Semitic people of southern Babylonia. In Assyrian records they are referred to as *Kaldu.* When Nabopolassar, a native Chaldean governor, ascended to the throne of Babylon in 626 B.C., he inaugurated a dynasty that made the name "Chaldean" famous. The term is used in the Bible as a virtual synonym for "Babylonian," a designation taken from the name of the capital city, "Babylon."
6. Gamaliel Bailey, quoted in *New Dictionary of Thoughts,* ed. Tyron Edwards (Cincinnati: Standard, 1961), 154.
7. Richard Wolff, *How to Live with Doubt* (Wheaton, Ill.: Key, 1971), 67.
8. John Bunyan, *The Pilgrim's Progress in Modern English,* retold by Jean Watson (Grand Rapids: Zondervan, 1978), 95–101.

CHAPTER 18—KNOWING THE WILL OF GOD

1. These principles were first published in my article, "God's Guidelines for 'Grey Areas,'" *Good News Broadcaster* (July/August 1983): 32–34.
2. Bruce K. Waltke, *Finding the Will of God* (Gresham, Oreg.: Vision, 1995), 31.
3. Garry Friesen, *Decision Making and the Will of God* (Portland, Oreg.: Multnomah, 1980), 257–79.

4. Waltke, *Finding the Will of God*, 155.
5. Ibid., 102–14.

CHAPTER 19—COMMUNICATING WITH GOD

1. See my book, *Answers to Tough Questions from Every Book of the Bible*.
2. *Oregonian*, 29 June 1981.
3. Cornerstone Church, letter to Portland, Oregon churches, 5 April 1993.
4. Henry T. Blackaby and Clyde V. King, *Experiencing God* (Nashville: Broadman & Holman, 1994), 119–20. I appreciate many excellent points made by these two authors and I commend their desire to help believers grow in their Christian experience. But I find that their book *Experiencing God* emphasizes experience at the expense of careful exposition of the Scriptures and interpretive principles. Our experience must always be measured by Scripture, and we must distinguish between interpretation and personal application. The best way to experience God is *through* Scripture, which reveals His character and will.
5. Cameron V. Thompson, *The Master Secrets of Prayer* (Lincoln, Nebr.: Good News Broadcasting, 1959), 10–11.

CHAPTER 20—ANSWERS TO
TOUGH QUESTIONS ABOUT GOD

1. See my book, *Answers to Tough Questions from Every Book of the Bible*.
2. I want to express my thanks and appreciation to the following faculty, staff, and students of Western Seminary who responded to my appeal for questions for this chapter: Philip Mathew, Harley Jamieson, Kelley Mata, Gregg Allison, Jay Hadley, John Willsea, and Galen Currah.
3. Eugene H. Merrill, "A Theology of the Pentateuch," in *A Biblical Theology of the Old Testament*, ed. Roy B. Zuck (Chicago: Moody, 1991), 14.

4. Nick Ludington, "'Christa' Statue Gets Praise, Hoots," *Oregonian*, 25 April 1984, A8.

5. Tozer, *The Knowledge of the Holy*, 113.

6. Erickson, *Introducing Christian Doctrine*, 86.

7. Robert B. Chisholm Jr., "Does God 'Change His Mind?'" *Bibliotheca Sacra* 152 (October–December 1995): 387–99.

8. Enns, *The Moody Handbook of Theology*, 206.

9. For numerous examples of humor in Jesus' teachings and Paul's writings see Roy B. Zuck, *Teaching as Jesus Taught* (Grand Rapids: Baker, 1995), 203–6, and *Teaching as Paul Taught* (Grand Rapids: Baker, 1998), 216–17.

Bibliography

Arthur, Kay. *Lord, I Want to Know You.* Sisters, Oreg.: Multnomah Books, 1992.

Blackaby, Henry T., and Claude V. King. *Experiencing God.* Nashville: Broadman & Holman Publishers, 1994.

Chafer, Lewis Sperry. *Systematic Theology.* 8 vols. Dallas: Dallas Seminary Press, 1948. Reprint, 8 vols. in 4, Grand Rapids: Kregel Publications, 1993.

Charnock, Stephen. *Discourses upon the Existence and Attributes of God.* 2 vols. 1853. Reprint, Grand Rapids: Baker Book House, 1979.

Curtis, Brent, and John Eldredge. *The Sacred Romance.* Nashville: Thomas Nelson Publishers, 1997.

Erickson, Millard J. *God the Father Almighty.* Grand Rapids: Baker Book House, 1998.

———. *Introducing Christian Doctrine.* Grand Rapids: Baker Book House, 1992.

McCullough, Donald W. *Trivialization of God.* Colorado Springs: NavPress, 1995.

Miethe, Terry L., and Gary R. Habermas. *Why Believe? God Exists!* Joplin, Mo.: College Press Publishing Co., 1993.

Needham, David. *Close to His Majesty*. Portland: Oreg.: Multnomah Press, 1987.

Packer, J. I. *Knowing God*. Downers Grove, Ill.: InterVarsity Press, 1973.

Pink, Arthur W. *Gleanings in the Godhead*. Chicago: Moody Press, 1975.

———. *The Attributes of God*. Grand Rapids: Baker Book House, 1975.

Piper, John. *Desiring God*. Portland, Oreg.: Multnomah Press, 1986.

Ryrie, Charles C. *Basic Theology*. Wheaton, Ill.: Victor Books, 1986.

Strauss, Richard L. *The Joy of Knowing God*. Neptune, N.J.: Loizeaux Brothers, 1984.

Tozer, A.W. *The Knowledge of the Holy*. New York: Harper & Row, 1961.

Watkins, William D. *The Busy Christian's Guide to Experiencing God*. Ann Arbor, Mich.: Servant Publications, 1997.

Wells, David F. *God in the Wasteland*. Grand Rapids: Wm. B. Eerdmans Publishing Co., 1994.

Willard, Dallas. *The Divine Conspiracy*. New York: HarperSanFrancisco, 1998.

Scripture Index

Subject Index

birth of nation, 63–64
breaking Covenant, 46–48
in Millennium, 163
Iuiguez, Garcia, 174

—J—

Jacob, 50, 251
Jairus, 180
Jefferson, Thomas, 20
Jehovah, 32–33. *See also* Yahweh
Jehovah's Witnesses, 119
Jeroboam, 149
Jerusalem, in Millennium, 163
Jesus Christ, xiv, 9, 50–51, 107, 185–86
    as Bridegroom, 108
    as eternally begotten, 120
    as God incarnate, 8, 18
    as Lamb of God, 61
    as male, 247–48
    as Messiah, 163
    as Righteous One, 89
    as Rock, 99
    as son of David, 161–62
    atonement, 61–62, 159–60
    believers as friends of Jesus, 172–76
    in Triunity of God, 113–17
    incarnation, 119–21
    meaning of his name, 33
    prophesied, 114–15
    resurrection, 9
    sacrifices and, 158–59
    titles in New Testament, 39
    Yahweh and, 33–34.
    See also God; Triunity of God
Jews. *See* Judaism
Job, 141–42
    as righteous sufferer, 144–48
Johannes Askunages, 118
Johannes Philiponus, 118
John the Baptizer, 128, 174, 180
Jonah, 256–57
Joseph, husband of Mary, 33
Joseph, son of Jacob, 61, 130, 223
Josephus, 169–70

Joshua, 179, 198
Josiah, 204
Judaism, 2, 128
    "abba" for father, 42
    on name of God, 31–32
Judas (not Iscariot), xiv
Judgment of God.
    See God, judgment of God
Jupiter, 6

—K—

Kingdom of God, 156, 160–63
    present age, 163
    realized, 162–63
    rejected, 162
Klooster, F.H., 131, 136, 137
Knowing God.
    See God, believer's response
Koran, 184
Krause, Karl C.F., 18–19
Kushner, Harold, 141
Kyrios, 40–41

—L—

Laney, David, 176
Laney, Elisabeth, 176
Laney, John, 176
Laney, Laura, 176
Laney, Nancy, xi, 4, 45–46, 167–68, 193, 230
Lazarus, 182, 249
Leviticus
    revealing God's holiness, 64–66
Lewis, C. S., 97, 203
Lindsey, Duane, 168
Loeks, Mary, 43
Logic, as proof of God's existence, 6–7
Love
    God as love, 90–91
    love for God, 191–93
    love of God for humanity, 52–53, 54, 67–69